# Minorities, Rights and the Law in Malaysia

This book analyses the mobilisation of race, rights and the law in Malaysia. It examines the Indian community in Malaysia, a quiet minority which consists of the former Indian Tamil plantation labour community and the urban Indian middle-class.

The first part of the book explores the role played by British colonial laws and policies during the British colonial period in Malaya, from the 1890s to 1956, in the construction of an Indian "race" in Malaya, the racialization of labour laws and policies and labour-based mobilisation culminated in the 1940s. The second part investigates the mobilisation trends of the Indian community from 1957 (at the onset of Independent Malaya) to 2018. It shows a gradual shift in the Indian community from a "quiet minority" into a mass mobilising collective or social movement, known as the Hindu Rights Action Force (HINDRAF), in 2007. The author shows that activist lawyers and Indian mobilisers played a crucial part in organizing a civil disobedience strategy of framing grievances as political rights and using the law as a site of contention in order to claim legal rights through strategic litigation.

Highly interdisciplinary in nature, this book will be of interest to scholars and researchers examining the role of the law and rights in areas such as sociolegal studies, law and society scholarship, law and the postcolonial, social movement studies, migration and labour studies, Asian law and Southeast Asian Studies.

**Thaatchaayini Kananatu** is a Lecturer in Law at the School of Business, Monash University Malaysia.

# Routledge Contemporary Asia Series

For more information about this series, please visit: https://www.routledge.com/Routledge-Contemporary-Asia-Series/book-series/SE0794

# Minorities, Rights and the Law in Malaysia

Thaatchaayini Kananatu

Routledge
Taylor & Francis Group

LONDON AND NEW YORK

First published 2020
by Routledge
2 Park Square, Milton Park, Abingdon, Oxon OX14 4RN

and by Routledge
605 Third Avenue, New York, NY 10017

First issued in paperback 2022

*Routledge is an imprint of the Taylor & Francis Group, an informa business*

*British Library Cataloguing-in-Publication Data*
A catalogue record for this book is available from the British Library

*Library of Congress Cataloging-in-Publication Data*
A catalog record has been requested for this book

ISBN: 978-1-03-240048-8 (pbk)
ISBN: 978-0-367-86239-8 (hbk)
ISBN: 978-1-003-01921-3 (ebk)

DOI: 10.4324/9781003019213

Typeset in Times New Roman
by codeMantra

# Contents

# Tables

# Abbreviations

| | |
|---|---|
| ABIM | *Angkatan Belia Islam Malaysia* (Muslim Youth Movement of Malaysia) |
| AMCJA | All-Malayan Council for Joint Action |
| BERSIH | Coalition for Clean and Fair Elections |
| BN | *Barisan Nasional* (National Front) |
| CIAM | Central Indian Association of Malaya |
| DAP | Democratic Action Party |
| DHRRA | Development of Human Resources in Rural Asia |
| GCC | Group of Concerned Citizens |
| HINDRAF | Hindu Rights Action Force |
| ISA | Internal Security Act |
| JERIT | *Jawatankuasa Jaringan Rakyat Tertindas* (Oppressed People's Network) |
| LGBTQ | Lesbian Gay Bisexual Transgender Queer |
| MCA | Malaysian Chinese Association |
| MHS | *Malaysia Hindu Sangam* (Malaysian Hindu Association) |
| MIC | Malaysian Indian Congress |
| MP | Member of Parliament |
| NCP | National Cultural Policy |
| NDP | National Development Policy |
| NEM | New Economic Model |
| NEP | New Economic Policy |
| NIAT | National Indian Action Team |
| NUPW | National Union of Plantation Workers |
| NVP | National Vision Policy |
| PAS | Pan-Malaysian Islamic Party |
| PERKASA | *Pribumi Perkasa Negara* (Malay Rights Group) |
| PERNAS | *Perbadanan Nasional* (National Corporation) |
| PKR | *Parti Keadilan Rakyat* (People's Justice Party) |
| PNB | *Permodalan Nasional Berhad* (National Equity Corporation) |
| PRIM | *Parti Reformasi Insan Malaysia* (Malaysian Peoples Reform Party) |

| PSM | *Parti Sosialis Malaysia* (Socialist Party of Malaysia) |
|---|---|
| RM | Ringgit Malaysia (Malaysian currency) |
| SUHAKAM | *Suruhanjaya Hak Asasi Manusia* (Malaysian Human Rights Commission) |
| UMNO | United Malays National Organisation |
| USD | United States Dollar (American currency) |

# Acknowledgements

My utmost gratitude and respect for my two PhD supervisors, Professor Helen Nesadurai at Monash University Malaysia and Dr Vanitha Sundra-Karean at the University of Southern Queensland, Australia, for their intellectual support, precious guidance and relentless encouragement.

This book is dedicated to my father, the late Dr Kananatu Krishnan, who believed in the integrity and significance of academic research.

The two pillars of my strength – my husband Dr Arulnageswaran Aruleswaran and my son Vignaraajaa – for their unconditional love, endless support, motivation and inspiration.

# Introduction – The phenomenon of Indian mobilisation in Malaysia

Towards the end quarter of 2007, three collective mobilisations occurred when activist lawyers, Malaysian civil society groups and opposition political parties organised demonstrations, rallies and marches in Malaysia. In September 2007, the *Lawyers Walk for Justice* campaign spearheaded by the Malaysian Bar Council involved lawyers who marched to Putrajaya, the newly developed centre of government, to appeal for integrity in an increasingly corrupt judicial appointment system.[1] Later in November 2007, the *Bersih* ('Clean') movement or the Coalition for Clean and Fair Elections held a mass demonstration and a march which headed towards the National Palace to petition the King. The Bersih movement called for electoral reform, transparency and accountability in a biased electoral system. The third was the Hindu Rights Action Force (HINDRAF) rally, to be discussed below and which serves as the point of departure for this book. The social climate of civil disobedience and acts of mass resistance against an overbearing executive arm of the government was unprecedented, displaying a clear demand for democratisation and political as well as legal reform in an illiberal political system.[2]

Since the 1970s, the post-colonial nation of Malaysia has often been described by political science scholars as a pseudo-democratic, semi-authoritarian or an illiberal democracy.[3] The illiberal democratic system of governance within a parliamentary system has three main features: first, the legislature is controlled by the executive, unlike a liberal democratic system, which allows for a system of checks and balances between the legislature and the executive, with the independence of the judiciary enshrined within the legal system. Second, the executive's command of the legislature places restrictions on liberal rights and civil liberties, particularly the freedom of speech, association and assembly with an emasculated judiciary standing idle. Third, the government of the day conducts regular elections but places constraints on the opposition parties to effectively channel social grievances.[4] In the case of an illiberal Malaysia, the electoral process with severe restrictions on civil liberties allowed the ruling coalition party, the *Barisan Nasional* (National Front) or the BN, to legitimise its perpetual rule since 1957 and hindered opposition parties from gaining electoral leverage in partisan politics.

In the late 1980s, Prime Minister Mahathir Mohamad had utilised severe draconian laws such as the *Internal Security Act 1960* in order to clamp down on leaders in the opposition parties and activists in civil society groups. However, in 2003, a change in the BN leadership brought minor transformations in the political system, where a more 'moderate' Prime Minister Abdullah Badawi had eased restrictions on civil liberties, which resulted in the proliferation of civil society groups.[5] During the 2000s, activist lawyers and Malaysian civil society were already striving to uphold liberal democratic ideals of justice and fairness. However, two of the collective mobilisations in 2007, *Lawyers Walk for Justice* and *Bersih*, had raised non-communal issues such as a biased judiciary and a tainted electoral roll which undermined the liberal rights and civil liberties of an ethno-culturally diverse Malaysian society.

From the 2000s onwards, another collective mobilisation that was communal or ethno-cultural in nature was taking shape among the aggrieved Indian minority in Malaysia. The gradual mobilisation of Indians had led to the HINDRAF movement in 2007. Two weeks after the *Bersih* demonstration, HINDRAF organised a rally where thousands of Indians marched into Kuala Lumpur city centre to present a petition to the British High Commissioner of Malaysia. The petition was directed to the British monarch, Queen Elizabeth II, with a request for a Queen's Counsel to represent the Indians in Malaysia in an ostensible civil action suit being initiated in the United Kingdom against the British government. The activist lawyers who were vanguards of the HINDRAF cause had galvanised online support from the Indian minority for the alleged legal suit to be filed in the Royal Courts of Justice on behalf of the descendants of Indian indentured labourers in British Malaya.[6] The leaders of the HINDRAF movement had also submitted a letter addressed to the British prime minister describing the grievances of the minority Indian community with allegations of racial prejudice, inequality and unjust treatment of the Indian minority by the Malay component party of the BN ruling coalition known as the United Malays National Organisation (UMNO).[7] Following the petitions and the threat of litigation in the United Kingdom, the HINDRAF rally claimed for 'Indian rights', 'constitutional rights', 'equality' and 'minority rights', details of which are discussed in Chapter 1. A preliminary examination of the HINDRAF civil disobedience strategy described above signalled an extensive use of legal principles such as equality, justice, non-discrimination, fairness and rights. HINDRAF's objectives and claims of grievances were explicitly couched in legal expression and rights-based language. There was also an implicit link between the 2007 HINDRAF rally and the use of the law as well as rights by the movement's key leaders who were all activist lawyers.

Further to the use of legalisms, the HINDRAF activist lawyers and leaders seemed to have mobilised the Indians around a few ethno-religious incidents which had gravely affected particular Indian Hindu individuals and enraged the Indian Hindu community as a whole. As Chapter 5 will

elaborate, by the 2000s, there was an accumulation of ethno-religious grievances relating to the legal status of non-Muslim Indians and the freedom
of religious belief, which included cases of Hindu temple demolitions by
state agencies. The rise in litigation of ethno-religious issues among Indian Hindus also prompted Indian lawyers to offer their *pro bono* or free
legal services in order to represent aggrieved individuals in court. A few of
these Indian lawyers became the key leaders and activists in the HINDRAF
movement. Hence, HINDRAF's overwhelming focus on ethno-religious
rights or 'Hindu rights' and the call for legal protection of the minority Indians in Malaysia indicated a link between the nature of the grievances and
the culmination of the 2007 Indian mobilisation.

Religious issues appeared to cut across prevalent Indian ethno-cultural
cleavages and diverse pockets of Indian sub-groups. As Chapter 1 will elaborate, the Indians are a diverse and heterogeneous ethno-cultural group.
However, does the disunity of the Indians explain the general submissive-
ness of the group before 2007 despite persistent grievances? Since the 1890s
the Indians who were brought into British Malaya for colonial labour purposes were culturally perceived as being stoic and docile.[8] The Indians in
post-colonial Malaysia are often marked as being politically acquiescent,
while a majority of Indians, particularly the Indian Tamil plantation labour who are referred to by the HINDRAF leaders as the descendants
of Indian Tamil indentured labour, are socioeconomically marginalised.[9]
Despite the socioeconomic grievances especially among the underclass of
the Indian community, the Indians as a whole have rarely come together
in order to mobilise *en masse*. As Chapter 3 discusses, the earliest record
of a significant Indian mobilisation was the short-lived 1941 Indian rubber
plantation labour strikes, which witnessed walkouts and work stoppage in
several British-owned rubber estates in Malaya. The acts of mass resistance
of Indian Tamil plantation labour against the British planters hinged on
labour-based grievances such as low wages. However, the 1941 mobilisation
of the Indian Tamil plantation labour differed from the post-colonial 2007
Indian mobilisation, which was oriented around ethno-religious as well as
ethno-class grievances and the claim for rights of the Indians.

These two rare occurrences of Indian mass mobilisation are divided by
a period of more than fifty years between the 1950s and the 2000s that witnessed little or no acts of collective Indian resistance. In May 1969, racial
riots broke out between the Malay and Chinese communities. Although the
racial riots did not directly involve the Indian community, the post-1969
phase witnessed a general acquiescence of the two main minority ethno-
cultural communities, the Chinese and the Indians. This was the start of
the illiberal phase in Malaysia, where the state established repressive laws
and policies to curb the freedom of speech, assembly and association in order to suppress future acts of civil disobedience. During this time, from
the 1970s onwards the BN ruling party had also entrenched preferential
treatment for the Malays and other native groups in Malaysia through an

affirmative action policy. The policy disregarded the socioeconomic problems of non-Malay or non-native groups, which led to an increase in class-based and race-based grievances among the Indians. The Malaysian Indian Congress (MIC) party, which is the Indian component of the ruling BN party, attempted to solve prevailing Indian issues on its own. However, the measures it adopted were largely ineffective due to the weak political clout of the MIC within the BN structure of racial politics and the lack of unity among the Indian leaders. Despite the accumulation of Indian grievances, the Indians did not mobilise *en masse* or make any unified claims. The phenomenon of Indian acquiescence despite serious grievances poses the question of whether legal repression and racial discrimination had hindered any possibility of minority mobilisation.

It was not until the mid-1990s that any sort of minority mobilisation began to take shape. The period from the mid-1990s to 2018 witnessed the expansion of Malaysian civil society, which consisted of numerous non-governmental organisations (NGOs) and grassroots community groups that were actively involved in addressing socioeconomic issues which affected all vulnerable groups in Malaysia. The two groups who were perceived by Malaysian civil society as being socioeconomically marginalised were the native *Orang Asli* or indigenous people in peninsular Malaysia and the former Indian Tamil plantation labour who had become the Indian underclass. The main grievances of these two groups were eviction from traditional homes and the lack of access to land. Private corporations, land developers and landowners had taken legally repressive measures in order to evict the two groups. Furthermore, these legal measures had been authorised by state agencies and state government officials.

Specific issues which affected the Indian underclass revolved around the unfair terms of retrenchment from rubber plantations, the legal eviction of the former plantation workers and their families without adequate compensation, as well as the forced relocation of the Indian underclass to urban squatter settlements. NGO efforts in the 1990s were focussed on providing counselling and advisory services to the aggrieved Indians, as well as assisting in negotiations with state agencies, the federal government, private corporations and landlords. However, the latter actors often resorted to leveraging their bargaining power by using court-based actions such as injunctions to evict without adequate notice and applying for summary judgements in order to bypass a lengthy negotiation process with the plantation labourers. As these powerful actors attempted to utilise municipal law in order to quash the claims made by aggrieved Indians, *pro bono* lawyers and activists stepped in to defend the legal rights of the aggrieved labourers. Hence, Indian issues were being shifted from the negotiation table to the court domain.

By the 2000s, the problems faced by the Indian underclass, which had earlier remained hidden within the confines of the rural rubber plantations, seemed to have become more apparent to the urban Indian middle class.

In 2001, an alleged racial unrest between the Malays and the Indian under-class took place in an urban squatter settlement known as *Kampung Medan* located within the city of Petaling Jaya, in the state of Selangor. The high incidence of deaths and injured among the Indian residents in *Kampung Medan* propelled Malaysian civil society to demand for a police investi-gation and for an inquiry by the Malaysian Human Rights Commission. However, both the federal and state governments, the police as well as the Malaysian Human Rights Commission failed to institute any investigation of the incident. The negative response from the authorities led several hu-man rights NGOs, legal activists and Indian NGOs to reprimand the gov-ernment for the apathetic treatment of minority issues. Indian lawyers and Indian NGOs then worked together to take the issue to the courts. Several of the *pro bono* Indian lawyers involved in the case proceedings were later the key leaders of the HINDRAF rally.

Although a composite of class- and race-based issues had been mobilis-ing the Indians from the 1990s onwards, it was not until the occurrence of ethno-*religious* incidents in the mid-2000s that the HINDRAF movement emerged and adopted a direct action strategy. There were two types of ethno-religious incidents or 'trigger' events which took place: the first in-volved the legal demand made by the Islamic Department of Malaysia at the Islamic *Shariah* court for the body of a deceased Indian Hindu man who had allegedly converted to Islam. The second was a string of legal cases regard-ing the contestation of custodial rights between Indian Hindu women and their husbands who had converted to Islam after marriage over their chil-dren. The courts decided in favour of the Muslim convert husbands and al-lowed the unilateral conversion of the respective couples' children into Islam without the Hindu wives' permission. Both trigger events involved a conflict of legal jurisdiction between the civil and Islamic *Shariah* courts, with the non-Muslim party in the respective cases left with no legal remedy as the civil courts refused to decide cases which involved Islamic issues and non-Muslims have no *locus standi* in the *Shariah* courts. Indian activist lawyers were intensely involved in the cases, and the ethno-religious dimension of the incidents drove the Indian NGOs and Hindu community groups to come together as the HINDRAF in order to defend the rights of Indian Hindus.

When the courts became an unfavourable avenue to fight for the rights of the aggrieved, HINDRAF activists turned to political lobbying and di-rect action strategies. The MIC lacked the political clout to push forward ethno-religious issues, but HINDRAF leaders began to gather support from the urban Indian middle class and Indian leaders in the opposition parties. Despite adverse decisions by the courts, Indian activist lawyers continued to use the courts to seek justice for the aggrieved parties. The law seemed to be utilised hand in hand with acts of civil disobedience which eventually culminated in the 2007 HINDRAF rally. The way the law was used raised the question of whether the law mattered to Indian minority mobilisation and if the law did play a role in mobilising the Indians, *how* did it matter.

## Notes

1 Malaysia is ranked 61/180 on Transparency International's 2018 Corruption Perception Index (<http://www.transparency.org/country/MYS/>), while neighbouring authoritarian Singapore ranks 3. The higher the ranking, the more corrupt the country.

2 See Lilian Miles and Richard Croucher, 'Gramsci, Counter-Hegemony and Labour Union-Civil Society Organisation Coalitions in Malaysia' (2013) *Journal of Contemporary Asia* 1; Julian Lee et al, 'Elections, Repertoires of Contention and Habitus in Four Civil Society Engagements in Malaysia's 2008 General Elections' (2010) 9(3) *Social Movement Studies* 293; and Kim-Hui Lim and Wai-Mun Har, '"Political Volcano" in 12th Malaysian General Election: *Makkal Sakthi* (People Power) Against Communal Politics, "3C's" and Marginalization of Malaysian Indian (2008) 1(3) *Journal of Politics and Law* 84.

3 Harold Crouch, *Government and Society in Malaysia* (Cornell, 1996) 96; William Case, 'New Uncertainties for an Old Pseudo-Democracy: The Case of Malaysia' (2004) 37(1) *Comparative Politics* 83, 88. See generally William Case, *Elites and Regimes in Malaysia: Revisiting a Consociational Democracy* (Monash Asia Institute, 1996) and William Case, 'Southeast Asia's Hybrid Regimes: When Do Voters Change Them?' (2005) 5 *Journal of East Asian Studies* 215.

4 Case (2004), above n 3, 83–83.

5 James Chin and Wong Chin Huat, 'Malaysia's Electoral Upheaval' (2009) 20(3) *Journal of Democracy* 71, 76.

6 Asha Rathina Pandi, *Blogging and Political Mobilization Among Minority Indians in Malaysia* (PhD Thesis, University of Hawai'i at Manoa, 2011).

7 Ibid.

8 See Kernial S Sandhu, *Indians in Malaya: Immigration and Settlement, 1786–1957* (Cambridge University Press, first published 1969, 2010 ed).

9 See Francis Loh, 'The Marginalization of the Indians in Malaysia', in James T Siegel and Audrey R Kahin (eds), *Southeast Asia over Three Generations: Essays Presented to Benedict R. O'G. Anderson* (Ithaca, NY: Cornell, 2003) 223.

# 1 Indians in Malaysia

## A diverse and 'quiet minority' in an illiberal polity

### 1.1 Introduction – the phenomenon of Indian mobilisation

This book is a case study of Indians in Malaysia, a minority that was originally a migrant group from the Indian sub-continent. This chapter narrates a historical overview of the group's origin and explains the ethno-cultural as well as socioeconomic diversity of the group. It then charts the trends of Indian mobilisation and acquiescence from the 1890s to 2018, beginning from the colonial British era in Malaya and proceeding to the post-colonial period in Malaysia, which has been described by scholars as an illiberal period particularly after the May 1969 race riots. Despite the hyper-diversity and generally compliant nature of the Indians, this chapter reveals that there have been two occurrences of mass Indian mobilisation: the 1941 Indian Tamil plantation labour walk-outs (referred to in this book as the 'Klang Strikes')[1] and the 2007 mass demonstration of Indians organised by the Hindu Rights Action Force (known as the 'HINDRAF rally'). The chapter ends with an account of the growing incidents of mobilisation by Indians preceding the HINDRAF rally and the electoral mobilisation of Indians during the 2008 General Elections following the HINDRAF rally, as well as the 2013 and 2018 General Elections. In essence, the chapter sets the stage for the study of the role of the law and rights in the mobilisation of minority Indians in Malaysia.

### 1.2 Origin of Indians in Malaya

The Indian presence in Malaya[2] dates from the first century AD, beginning with the coming of Indian traders, military conquerors and Hindu/ Buddhist cultural influence (or Indianisation) in the northern region of the Malay Peninsula.[3] Archaeological and historical evidence of Hindu/ Buddhist relics and temple ruins showed that the early Malay Kingdom of Kadaram, located in the present-day state of Kedah was subject to eleventh-century conquests from the Chola Dynasty of the Coromandel Coast of Southern India.[4] Despite the Indianisation of early Malay royal culture and local Malay customs, the Indians themselves were passing through to reach other dominions in Southeast Asia. Indian presence was again apparent in the fifteenth-century port of Malacca, which was a trade hub for Indian merchants. Most of the Indian traders were transitory, but a few settled down with local Malays and assimilated into Malay culture forming the hybrid (*peranakan*) Malacca Chitty community.[5] However, early Indians in Malaya were mostly sojourners and are not the forefathers of contemporary Indians in Malaysia.

The modern Indians in Malaysia are mostly descendants of the citizens of British India and British Ceylon who came to Malaya during the nineteenth-century British colonial rule. The late 1800s has been recorded as an intense period of Indian labour migration from British India to her other colonies such as Guyana and Trinidad in the British Caribbean islands, Ceylon (Sri Lanka) and Mauritius in the Indian sub-continent, as well as the Straits Settlements (Malaya) and Burma in Southeast Asia.[6] The colossal movement of Indian labour across the colonies was due to the high demand for cheap labour to work in the agricultural plantations of tea, coffee, sugar cane and rubber. The rapid development of the industrial revolution and production of goods in Britain had propelled a rising need for inexpensive raw materials. At the same time, British humanitarian lobbyists had placed political pressure on the British parliament which led to the termination of the old system of slavery. Hence, the high demands of industry and the search for inexpensive labour required a 'new system of slavery', which was obtained from cheap and compliant labour from British India.[7] The British colonial government in India (also known as the British Raj) set up an Indian labour policy and an immigrant control system with stringent requirements to ensure the transportation of a submissive Indian labour force.[8] India had a large populace which was acclimatised to an orthodox Hindu social system, that is, the hierarchical caste system that created a ready pool of agricultural workers.[9] The living and work conditions were already severe and harsh for India's landless peasants; hence, many were willing and able to migrate to the other colonies in search of better prospects. The concern of British colonial capitalists and planters was not only in obtaining cheap agricultural labour but also in ensuring an obedient and complacent workforce. The British planters who ran the plantations in Malaya found the 'subordinate class' of Indians to be fitting for this role, and the rigid caste system would ensure minimal risk of a peasant revolt which could destabilise the colonial plantation economy.[10]

Suitable plantation labour was specifically chosen from the state of Tamil Nadu ('Tamil land') where the British Madras Presidency held its office in India. In fact, the migration of the Indian Tamil people to Malaya has been historically documented as a crucial component of the colonial rubber economy.[11] The Tamils are an ethno-linguistic people who speak the Tamil language and practice what is known as the *Dravida* (South Indian) Tamil culture. During the British occupation of Tamil Nadu, severe bouts of droughts had rendered many of the landless peasants jobless, in serious debt and in dire need of new economic opportunities. Furthermore, the lower-caste landless peasants were hoping to escape exploitation by upper-caste landlords under the Indian bonded labour system.[12] The British were familiar with Tamil peasant labour who were first brought into British Ceylon in the 1800s to work in the coffee plantations and in the 1900s for tea cultivation.[13] The flow of Indian Tamil landless peasants to Ceylon in the beginning was almost unrestricted, but by the 1830s, the British Raj enacted the *Indian Immigration Ordinances* which began regulating the indentured and contractual terms of labour. The Indian Tamils were a migrant labour group who were kept spatially and socially separate from the native Ceylon Tamils.[14] The separation of these two Tamil sub-groups created a caste/class wedge and proved to be a useful arrangement for the control of Indian Tamil plantation labour and Ceylon Tamil administrative staff under the British Ceylon administration. Hence, the Indian Tamil peasantry provided the right type of wage labour for the development of rubber, while the division of labour in British Ceylon was easily replicated in the rubber plantations of Malaya. The *1884 Indian Immigration Ordinance* shifted the control of Indian labour emigration from the British Raj to the Straits Settlements Government (Malaya), while the *1908 Tamil Immigration Fund Ordinance* (re-enacted as the *1910 Indian Immigration Fund*) was passed in order to sponsor and support the importation of Indian Tamil labour into Malaya.

The British planters in Malaya purportedly found the Indian Tamil labourers to be weak in morale, fearful of authority and in servile gratitude to the British planters.[15] The British planters' preference for Indian Tamil peasants particularly from low-caste groups, which included a small percentage from the Outcastes or Untouchables group, meant that a majority of the Indians who migrated to Malaya from the 1900s to 1945 were Indian Tamils as plantation labour. By the 1920s, 90% of the Indians in Malaya were said to be members of the Indian Tamil ethno-linguistic group.[16] However, a small number of Tamils were also brought from the Jaffna province of British Ceylon, while other non-Tamil South Indians were transported from the Indian states of Kerala and Andhra Pradesh, in order to fulfil the need for clerical and administrative staff in the British Malayan government and rubber plantations.[17] These migrants were chosen for their level of education, ability to speak English and prior work experience as low-ranking administrators under the British Raj. Other Indians who came into Malaya included the Sikhs from the state of Punjab, who were recruited by the British administration as military, police and security personnel.[18] At the same time, a handful of self-sponsored free migrants also came into Malaya on their own accord for purposes of trade and employment. The free migrants were mostly Indian Muslims (including Tamil and Malabar/Kerala Muslims) and North Indians such as the Gujaratis, Sindhis and Bengalis.[19] Another group which came from Tamil Nadu but as self-sponsored migrants were the Tamils of the *Natukottai Chettiar* caste, usually pegged as traders, merchants, moneylenders, bankers and landowners.[20] However, due to caste cleavages, the Indian Tamil *Chettiars* did not mingle or associate with the Indian Tamil plantation labour. The bulk of the Indian free migrants were a crucial component of an emerging urban Indian middle class. In essence, the origin of modern Indians in Malaya shows extreme diversity in terms of their ethno-cultural identity. The only thread that linked these various groups was that they came from the Indian sub-continent and thus were somehow 'Indians'.

## 1.3   Horizontal and vertical cleavages among Indians in Malaya

The sheer diversity of the Indians who came into Malaya resulted in a hyper-diverse group that experienced horizontal (ethnic, linguistic, religious, regional and cultural) and vertical (caste, class and socioeconomic status) cleavages. Despite the diversity of Indians, the British colonial administration attempted to racialise the group in order to differentiate the Indians from other ethno-cultural groups such as the Chinese and the Malays.

### *1.3.1   Horizontal ethno-cultural diversity of Indians*

In the latest population census of 2010, Indians comprised 7.3% of the Malaysian population, while the main ethno-linguistic sub-group were the Tamils, accounting for 80% of the Indians in Malaysia.[21] The Indian category in current census data consists of the majority Tamils and pockets of ethno-linguistic and regional sub-minorities such as the Malayalis, Telugus, Punjabis, Bengalis, Gujaratis, Sindhis, Oriya as well as Ceylon Sinhalese and Ceylon Tamils. The 2010 census also found that 6.3% of the Malaysian population were Hindu, although there is no breakdown of the percentage of Hindus among the various Indian sub-groups. However, the 2000 census depicted that 84% of the Indians in Malaysia are adherents of Hinduism,[22] with a sub-minority of Indian Muslims, Punjabi Sikhs (this excludes the sub-minority of Punjabis who are not Sikh), Indian Christians and Sinhala/Ceylon Buddhists. Hence, while the majority of Indians in Malaysia today speak the Tamil language and are adherents of Hinduism, the Indians as a whole are an ethno-culturally hyper-diverse group.

As Section 1.2 on the origins of Indians elaborated, the creation of a Tamil Hindu majority is due to the colonial labour policy in specifically choosing the lower-caste agricultural workers from Tamil Nadu. However, the British planters' selection of different ethno-cultural types of Indians for agricultural and clerical jobs in the colonial economy is not the only reason for the vast diversity of Indians in Malaya. The origin of the cleavages and the fractured ethno-cultural identity of Indians are also due to the deep and complex ethno-regional, caste and tribal divisions in pre-British India itself. Although the British colonials brought the Indian princely states together to form a single political unit known as British India,[23] the Indians remained divided by language, religion, cultures and caste divisions.

The Hindu orthodox caste system which was in place in ancient Indian society became a useful colonial tool to legitimise the categorisation of Indians according to their labour-specific role.[24] The idea behind this was to relate racial/ethnic/tribal characteristics to social class, disposition, conduct and aptitude. For example, the Indian Tamil peasantry who were discriminated by upper-caste groups as low caste or in some instances as the Untouchables became classified by the British Raj as coolies, a term which generally referred to unskilled day labour. The colonial control of India oversaw a massive social engineering project, whereby British colonial perceptions of race and social theories like social Darwinism had provided the ideological basis to classify the Indians according to labour needs. Hence, colonial taxonomy and administrative classification of Indian sub-groups based on social Darwinist theory,[25] as well as the orthodox Hindu caste system, ran in parallel to the unification of the Indian provinces into a single colonial territory.

The movement of Indian labour from British India to her other colonies created more complexities in terms of what constituted an Indian person. Outside of British India, there was a necessity to 'racialise' Indian identity in order to differentiate the migrant groups from the British planters and the natives of the land.[26] In Malaya, the colonial division of labour of the Malays, Chinese and Indians force-fitted the otherwise diverse ethnocultural groups into three racialised categories. These racial categories served to physically and culturally separate the three ethno-cultural groups in order to maintain colonial control of labour in Malaya and ensure the smooth running of the colonial economy.[27] The Malay peasantry were kept in the paddy/rice fields and in fishing villages, while Malay rulers from the aristocratic class were given land benefits for restricted agricultural purposes.[28] Chinese indentured labour was brought into Malaya for the single purpose of exploiting the tin mining industry. The Chinese *Kapitan*, who was usually one of the Chinese secret society leaders, was put in charge of the Chinese workers. The Indians, specifically the Indian Tamil peasantry, were used in rubber plantations as indentured labour but were later brought in under a hierarchical *Kangany* system. The Indian *Kangany* (Headman) was in charge of recruiting, transporting and maintaining strict control of Indian Tamil plantation labour. Hence, even though the colonial construction of race in Malaya attempted to unify diverse ethno-cultural groups into broad racial categories such as Malay, Chinese and Indians, an intra-group hierarchical structure was also put in place in order to micromanage the three racial/labour groups. Chapter 3 analyses the role of colonial laws and labour policy in engineering a hierarchical race/class-based structure of labour in Malaya. The colonial 'divide and rule' strategy set the stage for both racial as well as class-oriented grievances to arise.

### *1.3.2  Vertical socioeconomic and political hierarchy among Indians in Malaysia*

The colonial labour system had created the foundation for class cleavages among Indians in Malaya and the socioeconomic exclusion of the Indian Tamil plantation labour. The early system of indentured Indian Tamil labour which was in place between the 1840s and the 1920s created debt bondages between the labour and British planters.[29] The contract between the labourer and the planter was deemed to be an inequitable agreement, where the labourer was compelled to concede his personal liberty as 'legal consideration' in exchange for employment in the Malayan plantation.[30] In the 1880s, British planters began to shift to the less-regulated *Kangany* system, which became instrumental in sowing the seeds of class/caste cleavages among Indians in the Malayan landscape. As discussed in Section 1.2, the British planters chose a particular type of labour for plantation work, that is, the Indian Tamil peasantry who were mostly from the lower castes. The British administration also ensured that only non-Tamil Indians (from Bengal or Kerala) and Ceylon Tamils were brought in as administrative staff.[31] The *Kangany* himself was an Indian Tamil migrant who acted as an intermediary between the plantation manager and the labour, as well as a foreman who was contracted to bring 'coolies' from Tamil Nadu.[32] Hence, the division of migrant labour from the Indian sub-continent (plantation workers, *kanganies* and management) within the plantation system created a complex ethno-cultural and socioeconomic inequality.

Studies contend that there were two strategies imposed by British planters in order to maintain control of the Indian Tamil plantation labour: the first consisted of maintaining an Indian underclass by impeding social mobility and ignoring educational facilities for the children of plantation labour, and second, by deepening existing caste/class cleavages between Indian Tamil plantation labour and Indian management.[33] In terms of social mobility, the children of Indian Tamil plantation labourers were provided with a substandard Tamil education, while the children of the Indian and Ceylon Tamil management attended English schools run by Christian missionary associations. The drastically different education paths of the management and Indian Tamil plantation labour was a major factor in the gradual formation of both a more 'Westernised Malayan elite culture' among the Indian upper class and middle class, as well as a poverty trap for the Indian Tamil plantation labour.[34] The grievances of Indian Tamil plantation labour were drastically different from the Indian estate foremen, clerks and managers. The capitalist structure of the rubber industry meant that the problems of the Indian Tamil plantation labour were oriented around low wages, poor housing conditions, marginal health and educational facilities.[35] The Indian estate foremen, clerks and managers on the other hand did not suffer the same problems as the plantation labour but instead were under pressure by British planters to exert severe discipline and harsh treatment on the Indian

Tamil plantation workers. The laws were also one-sided. For instance, the 1923 *Labour Code* had severe punishments for industrial offences such as vagrancy and desertion, where the Indian Tamil plantation labourer was treated as a criminal. The differential treatment of the Indian Tamil plantation labour and the Indian as well as Ceylon Tamil administrative staff/ management created a class cleavage between the two Indian sub-groups.

After the 1938 abolition of the *Kangany* labour system,[36] the migration scheme shifted towards a 'free market' system, which witnessed the coming of Indians who were highly skilled professionals, merchants, traders and working-class migrants.[37] These Indian free migrants went directly into the urban sectors of Malaya. The urban class-based segmentation of Indians included the elites or professionals and high government officials; the upper middle-class English-educated government servants; the lower middle-class Tamil-educated merchants; and school teachers, journalists and small holders, while the most vulnerable class consisted of labourers in government service and in private plantations.[38] In essence, there was a multiplicity of Indian social classes especially in the urban areas during the colonial era. However, the emergence of the urban Indian middle class during the 1930s to 1940s was crucial in terms of the anti-imperialist and anti-caste ideologies that they introduced to the Indian Tamil plantation labour. While socioeconomic and class cleavages were prominent between an emerging Indian political elite and the Indian Tamil plantation labour from the 1940s to the 1950s, few studies have examined the temporal unity that was also seen between the urban Indian middle class and the Indian Tamil plantation labour during that period.

From 1957 onwards, race was becoming more pronounced as a major division between the Malays, Chinese and Indians through post-colonial identity politics and national policies as well as the practice of Malay preferential treatment. Within this racialised setting, the 1971 New Economic Policy (NEP) and the Second Malaysia Plan (1971–1975) introduced measures to eliminate poverty among Malaysians regardless of race. However, the benefits did not extend to the socioeconomically deprived class of Indians in the plantations. In 1970, income distribution statistics showed that 75.4% of Indians were employed as low-wage labourers in both rural plantations and urban centres.[39] A 1975 study on the Indian Tamil plantation labour found that there were '238,070 plantation workers in Malaysia of whom 188,772 with their dependents of 347,974 totalling more than half a million people, work, live, and die, within a fetid, unending plantation environment, effectively removed from the wider society'.[40] The Indian Tamil plantation labour clearly experienced deep poverty and comprised a large segment of the Indian poor in the 1970s. While the percentage of low-wage Indian labour had not reduced significantly between the 1970s and the 1990s, a majority of the Indian low-wage earners were simply shifted from the rural plantations to the urban centres due to the fragmentation of rubber estates and rural development programmes. In 1995, it was reported that 70.5% of Indians were employed as low-waged labour in agricultural, manufacturing and in-dustrial jobs.[41] The forced urbanisation had exacerbated urban poverty and created a new Indian urban underclass.

The 1971 NEP was criticised in the 1970s by the Malaysian Indian Con-gress (MIC) and from the 1990s onwards by Indian civil society groups for failing to eradicate poverty among Indians. However, the MIC did not have sufficient political clout in the Alliance Party (which was renamed the BN or National Front in 1973) to push forth an agenda to reduce poverty among Indians. Loh points out that the Indian cooptation into the politi-cally dominant Alliance party did not provide any benefit to the socioec-onomically deprived Indians and the Indian community as a whole.[42] In 1974, the MIC with a team of Indian civil servants, economists and public intellectuals produced the MIC Blueprint, a document that encompassed an assessment of the socioeconomic status of Indians, particularly the Indian Tamil plantation labour in relation to the NEP.[43] The biggest criticism of the NEP's poverty reduction strategy was its implicit disregard of the com-mercial plantation sector including the private rubber plantation companies which employed the Indian Tamil plantation labour group. The Blueprint contained significant proposals to ease poverty among the rubber plantation workers, decrease the high unemployment rates among Indians, discussed the principle of proportionate budgetary allocations for Indians and made recommendations on land settlement schemes and university admissions.[44] However, none of the recommendations in the Blueprint were implemented and the reasons for this remain unclear. The Blueprint was gradually forgot-ten until it came into political focus again after the 2007 Indian mobilisation.

The failure of the NEP in removing poverty in the plantations was ac-knowledged in the Third Malaysia Plan (1976–1980) and proposals were made to extend the poverty reduction scheme to all racial groups. However, government officials continued to disqualify the low-waged Indian Tamil plantation labour in financial assistance programmes. Jomo Sundaram argues that although from the 1960s to the 1980s the production rates of the rubber industry had shot up 225%, while the industry's profit margins had reached about 100%, the wages of the plantation labour had remained stagnant.[45] By the 1980s, the rubber plantation industry was owned signif-icantly by government-linked trust agencies and companies, which again failed to increase wages. Hence, the poverty linked problems of the Indian Tamil plantation labour were neglected by the government as well as the private plantation employers. Further to this, due to the national restriction on trade unions, the National Union of Plantation Workers (NUPW) did not have sufficient bargaining power to seek solutions to the poverty related issues of the Indian Tamil plantation labour. In the 1980s, the MIC put forth a second set of proposals for the Fourth Malaysia Plan (1981–1985) which incorporated the problems of the Indian Tamil plantation labour and also proposed measures to increase Indian equity in the corporate sector from 1% to 6%.[46] The proposals were not implemented.

However, in comparison to the statistics on employment of Indians, the official poverty reports generally show a low incidence of 'overall poverty' for Indians.[47] This low number has been contested on the grounds that the government's 'income-based approach' grossly undervalues the incidence of poverty.[48] An MIC think-tank established in 1997 found that the official poverty rate did not include 'quality of life indicators' such as the level of social problems and 'social exclusion' experienced by Indians.[49] Recent studies have also emphasised the high Indian poverty rates and social problems arising from inferior education, criminal activities, low employment, family breakdowns and rising urban poverty.[50] In 2005, the MIC leadership acknowledged that more than 80% of Indians were concentrated in urban living areas, which included what was termed as the 'bottom 30 to 40%' of Indians who were the former Indian Tamil plantation labour.[51] Hence, with a rising number of low-waged Indians in the urban setting especially in urban squatter settlements, Indian civil society groups and the MIC have argued that the government does not acknowledge the extent of poverty among Indians.

While the above socioeconomic statistics and studies show that the percentage of low-waged Indians has remained high, the urban Indian middle class has been generally neglected in these studies. In comparison to the high numbers of Indians in low-waged labour, the number of Indians in professional occupations such as doctors, lawyers and accountants has steadily decreased from 1970 to 1997.[52] For instance, the number of Indian doctors dropped from 40.2% in 1970 to 26.8% in 1997. Studies have also neglected to screen the effect of the NEP and the Malay affirmative action policy on the urban Indian middle class. The affirmative action policy was enacted in favour of the majority Malays as a rights-bearing class; hence, the effects on the urban Indian middle class as a non-rights bearing class have largely centred on the racial quotas in higher education/university admissions and employment opportunities in the public sector. Another major issue which has been neglected in these studies is the socioeconomic divide between the urban Indian middle class and the rural Indian Tamil plantation labour since the 1970s. The most significant symptom of this divide is that economic, educational and job opportunities as well as resources were more accessible to the urban Indian middle class. For example, educational scholarships, study loans and public university seats allocated for Indians under the NEP benefitted the urban Indian middle class and Indian upper class who went through mainstream national education in comparison to the Indian Tamil plantation labour/Indian underclass who had limited vernacular education in Tamil schools and a high dropout rate.[53]

Brennan argues that the urban middle-class Malays and the Chinese merchant class generally disregarded class-based politics and supported the race-based policy of the ruling BN due to the system of political patronage.[54] One of the aims of the NEP/affirmative action policy was the creation of a Malay capitalist class that was linked to the political elites in the United Malays

National Organisation or UMNO. Historically, the main support of UMNO came from the Malay landowning class, while the Malay peasantry supported the class-based religious politics of the Pan-Islamic Party (*Parti Islam Se-Malaysia*, PAS).[55] The Chinese community was characterised by horizontal divisions in terms of different dialects and clans, but there was a vertical allegiance to the Chinese merchants who were able to obtain favours from the political elites in the Malayan Chinese Association (MCA).[56] However, Brennan's argument does not extend to the political inclinations of the fragmented Indian community. The MIC since 1955 has held its political power through the Indian Tamil plantation labour, who had historically viewed the MIC leadership as the political patrons of Indians in Malaysia. This resulted in the creation of an Indian political elite, which not only gained political patronage but garnered support from the Indian Tamil plantation labour and/or Indian underclass who were a larger vote bank than the urban Indian middle class. In contrast, the urban Indian middle class/professionals have gradually veered away from MIC and race-based politics especially since the 1980s and resorted to joining civil society groups and non-governmental organisations. Although the MIC was seen by the *Barisan Nasional* (BN) government as the representatives of the Indians, it was unable to pressure the government to enact an affirmative action policy for the Indian Tamil plantation labour in order to quell class-related poverty issues.

The emergence of an MIC-based Indian political elite supported by the Indian Tamil plantation workers and Indian underclass in urban squatters was also the result of Indian 'self-help' schemes developed in the 1980s. The most notable of these schemes was the 1984 Maika (MIC) Holdings, an Indian investment agency modelled after the Malay-centric *Amanah Saham Nasional* (National Unit Trust) and the Chinese venture, Multipurpose Holdings.[57] The scheme obtained a capital of Malaysian Ringgit (RM) 106 million from mostly 'working class' Indian subscribers but by 2000, the net assets had declined to between RM 30 and 40 million.[58] The failure of the scheme led to allegations of a corrupt management and the loss of trust and confidence especially among the urban Indian middle class, in the political elites of the MIC.[59] The MIC launched other self-help measures such as awareness seminars, research papers and assistance for Indian businesses, but the inability to procure government funding was a strong indicator of MIC's lack of political clout and its weak bargaining position as the sole political representative of the Indians in the BN. Hence, from the 1990s onwards, many of the urban Indian middle class abandoned their support for the MIC and joined opposition parties as well as formed either Indian-centric or class-based non-governmental organisations in order to assist the Indian underclass. Despite the MIC's weak position, the Indian political elites retained substantial support in the plantations and in the urban squatter areas, sometimes through coercive force.[60]

A political shift among all Indian groups was especially evident in the 2008 general election when Indians abandoned the MIC. This led the BN leadership to contend with Indian issues. The federal government in 2010 established a Cabinet Committee (the Special Implementation Task Force for the Indian Community) to investigate and propose plans to eradicate poverty among Indians. The 2010 New Economic Model (NEM) of the Tenth Malaysia Plan (2010–2015), for instance, acknowledged for the first time since Independence the problems of former Indian Tamil plantation labour, which formed the bottom 40% of Malaysian society.[61] The NEM also reported that the poverty among Indians had increased from 1.3% in 1997 to 2.5% in 2007, although the Economic Planning Unit reported that in 2012 Indian poverty had dropped to 1.8%. The approach of the 2010 NEM towards Indians in comparison to the 1970 NEP was radically different, revealing an implicit recognition of the discriminatory effects of the NEP on the Indians. What is important to note is that this change in the government's attitude towards Indian class-based problems is clearly the result of the sudden mobilisation of an otherwise acquiescent and disunited Indian community that did not always mobilise as a single group.

## 1.4  Trends of acquiescence and mobilisation

### 1.4.1  Mobilising amid British colonial repression, Indian nationalism and Tamil cultural ideology

As explained in Section 1.2, the majority of Indians who were brought into Malaya from the 1890s onwards were lower-caste Indian Tamil peasantry, chosen for their docile and obedient nature. The grievances of the Indian Tamil plantation labour mostly centred on the nature of their jobs, that is, low wages, harsh plantation work, long working hours, the inhumane treatment accorded to labourers and the lack of educational as well as medical facilities. Despite the existence of grievances, which will be discussed in more detail in Chapter 3, the Indian Tamil plantation labour did not mobilise from the 1890s to the 1930s. The generally long period of acquiescence can be linked to the nature of the labourers, who due to the cultural practice of the caste system, had generally low morale and were deeply deferential to authority. Furthermore, the indentured labour system and the *Kangany* system that followed were both designed to ensure that labour was severely restricted and heavily controlled in order to impede the formation of any collective interests. The regulatory steps included maintaining a relatively short-term contract of three years to ensure high turnover of labour and meting out severe punishment for breach of contract which included deportation. Although the Parliament of England had enacted the *1871 Trade Union Act*, the British imperial government did not extend this to its colonies like Malaya.[62] Instead, colonial labour codes such as *Sections 229 – 230 Labour Code 1912* hindered both individual and collective bargaining to ensure the continuance of the unequal contractual system of labour.[63] The lack of migrant labour protection applied to both the Indian Tamil plantation labour and the Chinese indentured labour in the tin mines. However, unlike the Indians, the Chinese were protected by groups called the *Kongsi* (Chinese clan halls), which were collective associations that controlled and jointly represented Chinese labour interests.[64] Antagonism between Chinese social classes was buffered by Chinese guilds which represented linguistic and tribal associations rather than class/social status. In the case of the Indians, the lack of cultural affinity and the antagonism between the Indian Tamil plantation labour and the Indian as well as Ceylon Tamil clerks and managers were a major impediment in the formation of any collective interest.

The social climate began to take a turn in the 1930s with the arrival of the Indian middle-class professionals directly into urban Malaya. This group of free migrants from India brought with them ideas for social reform,[65] and were heavily influenced by the *Dravidian* (or anti-caste) ideology. In 1929, Ramasamy Naicker known as *Periyar* (the Elder One), the founder of the Self-Respect Movement visited Malaya and expounded his views on the oppression of the *Dravida* or Tamil people by the Brahmins. The anti-*Brahmin*/caste movement in Tamil Nadu became a source of empowerment with its emphasis on *Dravidian* Tamil culture and language which mobilised the Tamils to unite as a people against the injustices of the *Brahminical* caste system. At the same time, Mahatma Gandhi's anti-imperialist message was spreading throughout the colonies and raising consciousness of an oppressed Indian people.[66] The effect of Gandhi's nationalist ideology was profoundly felt especially among the indentured Indian labourers, particularly those in South Africa.[67] Mahmud suggests that the indentured labour system and anti-imperialist ideologies before Second World War were instrumental in the invention of an Indian collective identity among the Indian Tamil plantation labour in Malaya.[68] While Gandhian ideology was bringing together all 'Indians' in British India as well as in British colonies, the *Dravidian* ideology was forging the identity of Tamils. Hence, both anti-imperialist and Tamil ethno-cultural mobilisation in India were crucial in the creation of a united Indian Tamil identity in Malaya from the 1930s to the 1940s.

While these ideologies were empowering, the emergence of an educated intellectual class of Indians in urban Malaya was a crucial factor in channelling those ideologies to the Indian Tamil plantation labour. The Tamil/*Dravida* connection served to temporarily bring together the Indian Tamil plantation labour and the Indian Tamil urban middle class. The culmination of both these Indian Tamil sub-groups resulted in Tamil cultural associations like the *Adi Dravida Sangam* (Association of the Indigenous *Dravida* People) and the Untouchables Association (which was later renamed the Tamil Reform Association in order to gather wider support from other Tamil caste-based groups). The leaders of these associations were mostly Indian plantation managers, clerks, teachers and newspaper journalists, who wielded a huge amount of influence over the Indian Tamil plantation labour. The associations frequently held conferences that discussed the grievances of Indian Tamil plantation labour and began to make claims on behalf of the Indian

Tamil plantation labourers. These organisations also became a platform for the cooptation of Indian Tamil plantation labour issues by emerging labour unions and politically inclined associations like the Central Indian Association of Malaya (CIAM).[69] The period between 1930 and the 1940s is marked as a Tamil-centric phase of Indian mobilisation in Malaya. Strong cultural affinities even brought together the urban middle-class Ceylon Tamils and Indian Tamils under the Indo-Ceylonese Association. However, the joint venture was short-lived due to political competition between the leaders of the two sub-groups over Indian representation in state and local councils.[70] The CIAM was able to consolidate ethno-cultural sub-groups from the Indian sub-continent under the fervour of Indian nationalism, but this alienated the Ceylon Tamils who perceived themselves as 'Ceylonese' and not 'Indian'. Clearly, the main agenda of CIAM and other Indian Associations was Indian nationalism and not the unification of diverse Indian sub-groups in Malaya.

It is noteworthy that in 1937 and 1941, there were two major plantation labour strikes that occurred in Malaya. However, the 1937 strike was initiated by Chinese plantation labour who sought higher wages and improvements on estate living conditions.[71] The Chinese labour were mostly influenced by the Malayan Communist Party and mobilised to form the Rubber Workers' Union. The climate of labour strikes soon spread to the rest of the plantation labour who were mostly Indian Tamil and led by the Klang Indian Association as well as the Klang District Indian Union.[72] The 'Klang Strikes,' which started on the 8th of April and ended on the 17th of May 1941, involved almost twenty thousand Indian Tamil plantation labourers from various rubber estates mostly in the state of Selangor.[73] The issue that sparked the strike was the introduction of new restrictions regarding wage-fixing during the Second World War. Chapter 3 expounds on the full range of demands made by the strikers but the main grievance was the lowering of wages by the United Planting Association of Malaya or UPAM, an organised lobby of British rubber planters and British shareholders of the rubber industry. The key leaders of the Klang District Indian Union who mobilised the Indian Tamil plantation labour consisted of R.H. Nathan, an assistant editor of an urban-based Tamil newspaper and Y.K. Menon, a rubber plantation clerk.[74] The Klang Indian Association provided support to the labourer's strikes and the president of CIAM, lawyer N. Raghavan lobbied for the introduction of a Trades Union Bill.[75] The colonial response to the strikes was to use military force and repression on the strikers and the deportation of the key leaders who were branded as anti-imperialists. Hence, while it was a plantation labour strike, the organisers were from the urban Indian middle-class group who were empowered by anti-imperialist and socialist ideologies. Nevertheless, the Klang Strikes remain as the most significant mobilisation of Indians in colonial Malaya. While studies on Indian political and social reform organisations in colonial Malaya have charted the trends of Indian leadership, these studies have rarely dwelled into the urban Indian middle-class leadership that championed Indian labour rights.[76] There is a dearth of studies exploring the instrumental role of the urban Indian middle class in Indian labour resistance of the 1940s.

Subsequent to pre-war efforts to mobilise Indians on the basis of Indian nationalism, *Dravidian* ideology and trade unionism, the Japanese invasion of Malaya at the onset of the Second World War in 1941 created a political conundrum among Indian leaders in CIAM. As the Indian National Army in British India had sided with the Japanese, most CIAM members and the leadership were inclined to follow suit. The repercussions were mostly felt by the Indian Tamil plantation labour, many of whom were forced by Indian estate managers and clerks to leave the rubber plantation and work on Japanese railway projects such as the infamous Burma-Siam Railway.[77] During this period, there was severe antagonism between the Indian Tamil plantation labour and the Indian clerks due to the 'tyrannical' manner in which the Indian clerks treated the Indian Tamil plantation labour.[78] The animosity led to many Indian Tamil plantation labourers joining the Indian National Army in order to escape the harsh treatment accorded by Indian clerks and the Japanese. The Japanese Occupation was a significant event in the history of Indians in Malaya, as at the end of the Japanese control of Malaya, many Indian Tamil plantation labourers joined and supported a non-communal resistance movement called the Malayan People's Anti-Japanese Army (MPAJA).[79] Hence, when the war ended in 1945, the Indians were a severely fragmented group but they were now more politically and socially aware of their status in Malaya.

After the Second World War, CIAM had become defunct due to the loss of support from the Indian Tamil plantation labour. There was no single political or social organisation that represented the Indian Tamil plantation labour or the majority of Indians in Malaya. Instead, there were a multiplicity of ethno-linguistic, religious and caste-based associations. As explained in Section 1.3, Indians were already an ethno-culturally and socioeconomically diverse group, hence the various associations reflected the inherent cleavages. The core factor for Indian disunity was the lack of consensus or as Stenson explains, 'the Indians probably had more associations but less co-operation'.[80] After the war, anti-imperialist and Indian nationalist associations disintegrated and were replaced with two broadly defined associations, that is, the Indian 'progressives' and the Indian 'conservatives'.[81] The conservative Indian organisations were a revival of the pre-war Indian Associations but were largely composed of a British-educated Indian upper class. Indians in progressive organisations were more varied and became members of both non-communal associations like the Malayan Democratic Union and the Malayan Labour Party, as well as communal/nationalist associations like the Malayan Indian Congress (MIC). Most of the progressives sought social and political reform, while a few in the radical left became members of the Malayan Communist Party. Arasaratnam noted that Indian leaders were prone to follow two distinct and opposite paths:

politics and trade unionism.[82] The MIC revolved around nationalist politics in India, while the trade unions as well as radical leftists tried to mobilise Indians around non-communal issues like socioeconomic and labour needs. While the politically motivated Indian leadership was well aware of the call for identity politics in Malaya, the trade union leaders rejected the idea of race politics.

During the pre-independence period from 1946 to 1956, the Malayan political landscape was changing rapidly towards decolonisation and self-rule of Malaya. The All-Malayan Council for Joint Action (AMCJA), a non-communal united front, sought to jointly end British colonialism and establish an independent Malaya based on the twin principles of democracy and social justice. The AMCJA had initiated a People's Constitution that proposed to unite the Malays, Chinese and Indians in Malaya, and give equal political rights, citizenship rights and democratic elections, with protective clauses for the Malay language, the Islamic religion, the Malay royal rulers and the economic status of the Malays. The AMCJA had the support of Indians through the Malayan Democratic Union, the MIC and several trade unions. However, the British colonial authority refused to recognise any non-communal coalitions in the negotiations for the independence of Malaya. The colonial authorities suspected non-communal groups and trade unionists as harbouring communist beliefs and hence curtailed the AMCJA through the *Declaration of Emergency in 1948*.[83] The AMCJA was accused of having associations with the Malayan Communist Party, which largely consisted of a Chinese membership. In order to shift Chinese support away from the Malayan Communist Party, the British established the MCA. Hence, the British preferred a race-based coalition in representing the various ethno-cultural groups in order to curb the influence of communism in Malaya.

During this time, the UMNO, an elitist and conservative Malay nationalist party was striving to reinstate the political superiority of the Malays and claim for special status. UMNO supported the colonial divide and rule system and had consistently worked against the idea of true equality and unification of all the ethno-cultural groups in Malaya.[84] Due to the British preference for a race-based solution, the colonial government ultimately sided with the UMNO Malay political elites and the formation of the race-based Alliance Party. In 1952, UMNO and the MCA formed a political alliance in order to stand against the National Party, Malayan Labour Party and the PAS in the 1955 general elections. The Indian political leadership faced discord especially between the 'political elite' and the 'professional elite', which effectively created three types of Indian leaders: the political MIC, the labour and trade union leaders and the 'informal' leaders made up of professionals and public intellectuals.[85] Among these three types of leadership, the MIC became a part of the British-approved coalition of the Alliance Party. The MIC was, in fact, established by Indian nationalists who were involved in the politics of the Indian National Congress in India.

The early leadership of the MIC was branded as an elite group of English-educated North Indians which alienated a large section of the urban Indian middle class and Indian Tamil plantation labour. In fact, many of the urban Indian working class supported opposition parties such as the Malayan Labour Party and the Socialist Front. Hence, from 1946 to 1955, the MIC was not representative of the majority of Indians in Malaya.[86]

In determining whether to be part of the Alliance, the MIC was wary that a race-based political alliance would propagate and maintain the communal or race-based system.[87] However, the MIC decided to be part of the Alliance in order to ensure that Indians were represented in the crucial negotiations for the independence of Malaya. Though the MIC lacked a strong political base, it derived its influence from becoming an accepted partner of the Alliance.[88] Hence, while Indian nationalism, Tamil cultural/social reform, and labour-oriented issues were in the 1930s to 1940s seen as uniting the heterogenic Indian population in colonial Malaya, the 1950s pre-independence identity politics, communal bargaining and the division of the Indian elites and leadership was seen to have created new social and political cleavages among the Indians. The communal politics of the Alliance also set the stage for the creation of an Indian political elite in the MIC in order to control the majority of Indians, that is, the Indian Tamil plantation labour.

### 1.4.2 Acquiescence of the Indian community in an illiberal Malaysian polity

In 1956, the Federation of Malaya Constitutional Commission, known as the Reid Commission, discussed proposals for the *Draft Constitution of the Federation of Malaya* in order to construct a democratic and free Malaya.[89] The most significant event in terms of the political and legal status of Indians in an Independent Malayan polity was the constitutional bargain and the constitution of the *Social Contract* between the three main ethno-cultural groups, that is, the Malays, the Chinese and the Indians. The two main issues pertaining to the Social Contract were the special position of the Malays and the citizenship rights of the Chinese and Indians. In terms of citizenship, the earlier *1948 Federation of Malaya Agreement* had point-blank denied citizenship to many non-Malays, including the Indians. Parmer, in making reference to the colonial divide and rule policy, wrote that '[c]itizenship qualifications discriminated against non-Malays. Chinese and Indians now bitterly charged that the pro-Malay policy had been resumed and that British Imperialism and Malay feudalism were again united.'[90] The 1955 Reid Commission's main contention was the drafting of a constitution that took into account the pluralistic nature of Malayan society at that time. In an attempt to balance the special rights of the Malays, the Commission included a provision to provide citizenship rights to the non-Malays, particularly the Chinese and Indians who were born in Malaya. Hence, *Article 14* of the 1957 *Constitution of the Federation of Malaya* allowed for automatic citizenship by operation of law to all those born in the country on or after *Merdeka* (Independence) Day, on 31st August 1957. The boon of citizenship, of course, came with a price, which was the incorporation of the constitutional clause enshrining Malay rights and privileges.[91] The special position of the Malays along with the group's rights and privileges were enacted under *Article 153* of the Federal Constitution, which states that

> (1) It shall be the responsibility of the *Yang di-Pertuan Agong* ('the King or Ruler') to safeguard the special position of the Malays and natives of any of the States of Sabah and Sarawak and the legitimate interests of other communities in accordance with the provisions of this Article.

The question that was constantly put forth by constitutional law scholars was, as Huang-Thio asked, 'what is the rationale behind the conferment of special privileges ... What is the justification for creating the Orwellian situation that "all persons are equal, but some are more equal than others"?'[92] The British colonial rationale for establishing Malay privileges in the first place was the understanding that the Malays were struggling in terms of economic development in comparison with the non-Malays, particularly the Chinese. The legal privilege was akin to the politico-legal status of the Untouchables/Outcastes in India, who were given legal protection and rights to affirmative action programmes under the British constructed *Indian Constitution 1950*.[93] The colonial British were concerned about the race-based economic inequalities between the Malays and Chinese in Malaya, but they also realised the long-term implications of a race-based legal privilege that would legally discriminate the Chinese and the Indians. During the Reid Commission debates on the Malay rights provision, the Commission made recommendations that after fifteen years Parliament should review the Malay privileges provision and determine whether to diminish or to fully terminate it.[94] However, the provision remained and its discriminatory effects on the Indians became the core of the MIC's political conundrum from the 1970s as the vanguards of Indians in Malaysia.

The enshrined Malay privilege provision posed to be problematic for all non-Malay ethno-cultural groups in terms of the 'positive' racial discrimination and the qualified equality before the law. The most pressing issue was the latent peril if the special privileges were to be exploited by especially race-based political parties and civil society groups.[95] The MIC was in a dilemma in terms of the repercussions of the race-based Malay privileges to the Indians especially those in the lower classes. The provision obviously did not contend with the class-based groups that were lagging behind in terms of educational and economic mobility like the Indian Tamil plantation labour. The MIC held heated debates on the constitutional status of Indians in Malaya and were also concerned with the ethno-cultural rights of Indians in terms of language and education, as well as economic rights such as public service employment and land availability. The MIC President Kundan Lal

Devasar (1951–1955) who was legally trained, made significant claims to safe-guard the legal status and rights of Indians in Malaya. However, Devasar had little support from the Indian Tamil plantation labour and the Indian Tamil middle class, while the MIC itself had no political clout within the Alliance party to push forth Devasar's claims within the Alliance. The subsequent MIC President V.T. Sambanthan (1955–1973) during the Reid Commission proposals had significant grassroots support from a majority of the Indi-ans but pursued a more diplomatic non-confrontational approach with the UMNO leadership through his camaraderie with the Prime Minister Tunku Abdul Rahman (1957–1970).[96] Hence, despite the deep concerns, there was no Indian mobilisation or assertive claims made from 1957 to 1970. The MIC sustained a period of general acquiescence regardless of the serious labour related issues of the Indian Tamil plantation labour and the political status and rights of the Indian community under the *Federal Constitution*.

In any case, *Article 153* was entrenched in the *Federal Constitution* against repeal, as *Article 159(5)* indicated that any amendment to *Article 153* will require a two-thirds majority of the members of Parliament and the consent of the Conference of Rulers. Even if the MIC leadership had attempted to contest the provision, it would have required the support of a substantial number of members of Parliament from the MCA and the UMNO to al-ter or abolish the clause. Further to this, the Malaysian government was beginning to utilise repressive laws relating to detention without trial such as the *Internal Security Act 1960* in order to quell any activism or claims made by opposition politicians, trade union leaders and activists in non-governmental organisations.[97] As described in Section 1.4.1, many of the urban Indian middle class were more inclined towards non-communal trade unions and labour-oriented organisations. Hence, many of the Indian trade unionists were affected by the repressive laws targeted at labour-based or-ganisations that posed a threat to the political hegemony of the Alliance. *Section 8(1)* of the *Internal Security Act 1960* invested the Minister of Home Affairs with the power to call for a preventive detention order of any persons acting in a prejudicial manner for a period of sixty days without the right to legal counsel. The period could be extended up to two years and the two-year period was renewable for an indefinite period, in order to protect the inter-nal security of Malaysia.[98] The provision gave the Minister wide discretion-ary powers, which were outside the ambit of judicial review. The draconian nature of the legislation and the coercive force of the Alliance government was as Scott argued the legal backing of 'everyday repression'.[99] Though the purpose of the Act itself was meant to protect Malaysian citizenry from the threat of communist insurgents, it was utilised by the government to suppress political dissent. Hence, there was no political opportunity for the mobilisation of Indians *en masse* either through the Indian political elites of the MIC or the Indian leadership in non-communal organisations.

The political and sociolegal environment in post-colonial Malaysia changed precipitously after the race riots which occurred on 13th May 1969, referred to here as the May 13 incident.[100] The incident led to the enactment of more repressive laws such as the *Emergency (Public Order and Prevention of Crime) Ordinance 1969* and the utilisation of the British colonial-enacted *Sedition Act 1948*. These new laws restricted the freedom of speech, the freedom of association and assembly, which meant that civil society and social movements were severely curtailed. The Indians were not directly involved in the May 13 incident, but the changes that took place post-1969 accelerated the marginalisation of Indians, especially the Indian Tamil plantation labour. The most pronounced change after the May 13 incident was the 1970 NEP, which was a two-pronged development plan, first to 'reduce and eventually eradicate poverty by raising income levels and increasing employment opportunities for all Malaysians irrespective of race' and second, to accelerate 'the process of restructuring Malaysian society to correct economic imbalance, so as to reduce and eventually eliminate the identification of race with economic function.'[101] The NEP was the primary tool of the affirmative action policy which favoured the distribution of resources to the Malays, and supplemented the Malay special rights in *Article 153* of the *Federal Constitution*.[102] Scholars have commented on the NEP's effects on ethno-cultural minority groups from the 1970s onwards, which was often dubbed the 'Never Ending Policy' for maintaining a perpetual affirmative action programme.[103] The effects of the NEP on the Indians as shown above in Section 1.3.2 was the socioeconomic marginalisation of the Indian Tamil plantation labour. The long-term adverse effects of the NEP on the urban Indian middle class and other minority groups like the Chinese stemmed from, *inter alia*, restrictions on business licences, the race-based quotas that limited non-Malay access to higher education, and restricted employment opportunities in the public service sector.

Another core Indian grievance during the period of 1970 to 2000 was the rise in ethno-cultural as well as ethno-religious issues. After the May 13 incident, a new constitutional amendment had deemed as seditious the questioning of Malay legal privilege. Further to this, the 1971 National Cultural Policy described above was established in order to construct a national culture which stressed the Malay language, culture and the Islamic religion. The policy was implemented in educational institutions and gave prominence to a Malay-oriented education especially in fully government-aided national schools. Chinese and Tamil primary schools which provided education in minority languages were mostly partially aided in terms of government funding and support. Though education in minority languages was tolerated in primary schooling, it was not permitted in secondary and tertiary level institutions. The most crucial case regarding minority language rights was the legal case of *Merdeka University Berhad v. Government of Malaysia*,[104] which concerned a petition to the *Yang Di Pertuan Agong* (King) to operate a wholly Chinese-medium university under the *Universities and University Colleges Act 1971*. The petition was rejected on the grounds that a Chinese-medium university would contravene the National

Education Policy. The courts in judging the matter held that a Chinese-medium university would contravene not only the national education policy but was also against the 'national interest'.[105] The court's decision drove the Chinese education movement to further protect ethno-linguistic rights of minority groups, especially the Chinese.

At the same time, Islamisation was rising among Malay civil society groups and political parties such as the *Angkatan Belia Islam Malaysia* ('Malaysian Islamic Youth Movement') and the opposition PAS. One of the major ethno-religious elements that constituted Indian grievances during this period was the issue of religious hate crimes. From the mid-1970s onwards, a series of attacks on Indian Hindu temples caused deep unease among the Indian Hindu community.[106] The MIC leadership and Indian Hindu civil society groups made several attempts to seek government intervention in order to put a stop to the incidents.

Overall, while the period between 1970 and 1990 witnessed an accumulation of social, economic, cultural and political grievances among the Indians, there was no mobilisation *en masse*. Furthermore, since the May 13 Incident, draconian laws like the *Internal Security Act 1960* were increasingly used as repressive tools of the state. Political scientists contend that from the 1970s onwards, the Malaysian political setting was gradually becoming more 'pseudo-democratic' and 'semi-authoritarian'.[107] A pseudo-democracy or semi-authoritarian government is, in fact, an executive-led administration which restricts civil liberties like the freedom of speech, association and assembly, but unlike the fully authoritarian regime the semi-authoritarian state holds regular elections. Case contends that this practice obstructs the channelling of social grievances through opposition parties and instead diffuses those grievances by holding 'mildly competitive' elections.[108] Hence, the electoral process legitimises the authoritarian government's perpetual rule unlike the democratic process of allowing for a change in government. The repercussion of the restrictions on civil liberties in terms of minority group dissent was exhibited in the Chinese-education movement known as the *Dong Jiao Zong*. In 1987, the movement had rallied against the government's decision to appoint non-Chinese educated school principals and deputy principals in government funded Chinese vernacular schools which was seen as a measure to nationalise Chinese education. The *Dong Jiao Zong* movement was joined by several Chinese-oriented political parties including the MCA, a component of the BN (National Front). In response, the UMNO leaders and pro-Malay groups created a backlash movement which resulted in racial hate speeches by UMNO politicians against the Chinese community in Malaysia.

While there was no mobilisation of the Indian community during the period of increasing authoritarianism in Malaysia, religious issues began to arise again from the 2000s onwards that led Indians to begin to act on these grievances. In 2000, political speeches and calls were made by both the ruling BN as well as the opposition PAS to make Malaysia an Islamic state.

Relatively minor debates originated from the opposition PAS, but after the 1999 General Election, when PAS won considerable seats in the northern Malay states of Kelantan and Terengganu, the discussion on the *Syariah* (Islamic laws) and the Islamic state became more prominent.[109] Perhaps in retaliation to the political control of Islam by PAS, the leader of the UMNO party, Prime Minister Mahathir Mohamad, made several statements in 2001 declaring that Malaysia was already an Islamic state. One such statement made at a political conference stated that

> UMNO wishes to state loudly that Malaysia is an Islamic country. This is based on the opinion of *ulamaks* (religious scholars) who had clarified what constituted an Islamic country ... If UMNO says that Malaysia is an Islamic country, it is because in an Islamic country non-Muslims have specific rights ... There is no compulsion in Islam. And Islam does not like chaos that may come about if Islamic laws are enforced on non-Muslims[110]

The prime minister's statement initiated criticisms from the opposition political parties and civil society, particularly from PAS, the conservative Islamic party; the Democratic Action Party (DAP), the Chinese-dominated party known as the liberal vanguard of non-Malay interests; and liberal constitutionalists consisting of lawyers in civil society. The opposition maintained that Malaysia was not an Islamic state but a secular one, but this view had two different arguments: first, the liberal constitutional argument that was based on the Social Contract and the constitutional bargaining that took place before 1957; second, the Islamic conservative argument that Malaysia was never an Islamic state due to its non-adherence to the *Quran* (holy book of Islam) and the *Hadith* (the teachings of Prophet Muhammad).[111]

Constitutional lawyer Tommy Thomas contends that the prime minister's statement was not legitimate nor legally justified on the grounds of the *Federal Constitution* or the law, and that it was made purely for political purposes.[112] The status of the Islamic religion in Malaysia is indicated in *Article 3* of the *Federal Constitution*, which states that 'Islam is the religion of the Federation; but other religions may be practised in peace and harmony in any part of the Federation'. Freedom of religion is enacted under *Article 11*, which states that 'Every person has the right to profess and practise his religion and, subject to Clause (4), to propagate it.' However, *Article 11(4)* also controls and restricts proselytisation of religions other than Islam to persons who profess the religion of Islam. These provisions stand as they had been agreed on during the pre-1957 constitutional bargain and Social Contract between the Malays and the other ethno-cultural minority groups. Hence, it was understood that Islam would be given official recognition, on accord that other religious minorities were free to practice and within certain restrictions propagate their beliefs. However, a constitutional crisis in 1988[113] that had paved the way for an executive-controlled judiciary had effectively created uncertainty in the court system on these matters. While the constitutional/legal argument of freedom of belief derails the prime minister's political statement, the statement itself reflects an Islamic political agenda led by the authoritative executive arm of the state.

The government-initiated programme of establishing an Islamic state and a few high-profile cases concerning apostasy from Islam led to strong resistance from the non-Muslims in Malaysia. Several civil society groups with the support of the Malaysian Bar Council and lawyers who were involved in the apostasy cases formed the Article 11 Movement (named after *Article 11* of the *Federal Constitution* which provides for the freedom of religion). The Article 11 Movement was instrumental in the legal mobilisation of aggrieved Muslims who wished to convert out of Islam, as well as aggrieved non-Muslims.[114] The legal cases under the purview of the movement related to the absence of legal remedy in the face of jurisdictional clashes between the Civil and *Syariah* courts and the legal rights of non-Muslims.[115] A large number of the legal cases concerned the lack of jurisdiction to decide custodial issues of children born to Indian Hindu parents, but where the fathers had later converted to Islam and intended to unilaterally convert the children as well. These legal cases became a major source of the grievances that mobilised the HINDRAF movement in 2007. Other sociolegal issues which have arisen indirectly from what became known as the creeping Islamisation programme included the legal ban on the use of the word 'Allah' in Malay language bibles and Christian publications,[116] the demolitions of non-Muslim places of worship, and incidents of religious vilification by Muslims of other religions. Chapter 5 will discuss in detail the effect of the political Islamisation on the Indian Hindu community, which led to the sudden mobilisation of Indians in 2007.

### *1.4.3 The 2007 mobilisation of Indians in Malaysia*

On 25th November 2007, an Indian demonstration erupted in the city-centre of Kuala Lumpur, which witnessed between 20,000 and 50,000 Indians protesting against *inter alia* injustice and racism of the Malaysian government and sought compensation from the British government for the treatment accorded to the Indian Tamil plantation labour during the colonial period. Although the movement called itself the Hindu Rights Action Force or HINDRAF, the demonstrators were largely made up of a coalition of forty-eight Indian non-governmental organisations which included Indian cultural and Tamil language associations, Hindu societies, human rights organisations and lawyers. The protestors carried placards with pictures of Mahatma Gandhi, the Indian anti-imperialist movement leader and Queen Elizabeth II, the sovereign of the United Kingdom, as well as banners that read 'The Queen of England- the symbol of justice, we still have hope on you'.[117] The demonstration began as a peaceful march to the British High Commission, where leaders of the HINDRAF movement proposed to pass a petition and memorandum of claims to the British High Commissioner. The Malaysian police had warned the leader that the rally required a police permit for assemblies under *Section 27* of the *Police Act 1967* and had taken a 'rare' court restraining order under *Section 98* of the *Criminal Procedure Code* for urgent 'nuisance'.[118] Despite repeated warnings by the Malaysian police force not to hold the rally, the demonstration went on. The crux of the demonstration was the petition meant for Queen Elizabeth II, which held a request by HINDRAF leaders and 100,000 Indian petitioners, to appoint a Queen's Counsel for a class-action suit that the leaders were planning to initiate in the Royal Courts of Justice, United Kingdom. The HINDRAF leaders claimed that they had filed a legal suit to claim US\$4 trillion from the British government for the exploitation of indentured Indian Tamil plantation labour in colonial Malaya.[119] Three days before the demonstration, the political secretary of the British High Commission, Dawn Houghton, was reported to have been 'ready' to receive the petition, but the Malaysian Home Minister had issued orders for arrest of three HINDRAF leaders for uttering seditious words under *Section 4(1) Sedition Act*.[120] The audaciousness of HINDRAF's legal claims and the arrest of its key leaders attracted both local and international publicity.

Several incidents before the demonstration acted as trigger factors in mobilising a large number of Indians. Two incidents sparked the movement: the first incident was the case of 'Everest' Moorthy, which involved the legal claims made by the Islamic authorities over Moorthy's body for an Islamic burial.[121] Moorthy who was born as an Indian Hindu had allegedly converted to Islam, but this was unknown to his wife and family who claimed he was a practicing Hindu. The forcible removal of Moorthy's body by the Islamic authorities was dubbed by media as a 'body-snatching' case, which rallied several Hindu organisations and the Indian Hindu community to support Moorthy's widow and family.[122] The second incident that propelled the HINDRAF movement was the demolition of a Hindu temple on the eve of a Hindu festival in November 2007, which was part of a series of temple demolitions that had taken place since 2006. Hence, the trigger factors of the HINDRAF rally were ethno-religious in nature which clearly affected the Indian Hindu community as a whole. However, the bulk of the HINDRAF movement's grievances and claims was ethno-racial, spanning from the exploitation of Indian Tamil plantation labour to the discriminatory treatment accorded to the Indian community by the UMNO-led government.

The 2007 HINDRAF rally was an unprecedented event, as the last mobilisation of Indians *en masse* was the 1941 Klang Strikes during the colonial period. A key difference in the two Indian social movements was the utility of legal rhetoric and rights-based lobbying by the leaders of the HINDRAF movement, who were all lawyers. Prior to the HINDRAF rally itself, the courts had been used extensively by Indian civil society groups and Indian activist lawyers in defending aggrieved Indians on ethno-religious matters concerning the religious rights of Indian Hindu plaintiffs as well as matters of civil liberties pertaining to the high number of deaths in police custody (these cases are analysed in Chapter 5). Another main difference between the 1941 Klang Strikes and the HINDRAF rally is the electoral mobilisation that took place during the 2008 General Elections following the HINDRAF rally. The MIC was decimated and the BN lost a large number of seats due to *inter alia* a huge shift in Indian votes towards the opposition.[123] However, in both cases, movements were disbanded after legal repression by the government of protestors and leaders. The labour-oriented Klang Strike leaders were deported, and several HINDRAF leaders were arrested under the *Internal Security Act*, while one HINDRAF leader had sought political asylum in the United Kingdom. There has also been no reported follow-up on the HINDRAF claim filed in the British courts. Nevertheless, the HINDRAF movement had created an impact in terms of publicising Indian minority grievances and embarrassing the pseudo-democratic style of BN's governance.

## 1.5  Conclusion

This chapter sets the stage for the analysis of how law matters in minority group mobilisation. The case of the Indians in Malaysia shows that despite the existence of social grievances, there has been very little resistance, especially in terms of a unified Indian mobilisation. During both the colonial and post-colonial periods, the law was a repressive tool of the state. While the British colonial administration had utilised the law to control an ethno-culturally diverse Indian labour, the Malaysian government used draconian laws to restrict civil liberties and suppress resistance efforts. Despite the legal repression, the Indian case shows instances where Indian civil society, political leaders and activist lawyers have used the law in order to resist the authoritarianism of the government. The sporadic use of rights lobbying in direct action tactics and the use of strategic litigation from the late 1990s onwards indicate an understated legal mobilisation of Indians that has yet to be analysed in the scholarly literature on Indian politics in Malaysia and in legal studies of Indian minority mobilisation. In order to further the analysis of how the law matters in the post-2000 mobilisation of Indians in Malaysia, the next chapter will develop a theoretical framework to understand minority mobilisation using the law in an illiberal polity.

## Notes

1  The plantation labour walk-outs originated from the rubber estates in Klang, situated in the state of Selangor in Malaysia.

2  The term Malaya refers to the Malay Peninsula which was recognised as the Federation of Malay States in 1948. The term Malaysia was utilised after 1963, when Singapore (until 1965), British North Borneo and Sarawak joined the post-independent Malaysian Federation. In this book the use of Malaya refers to the colonial period, whereas Malaysia signifies the post-colonial period.

3 Muzaffar D Tate, *The Malaysian Indians: History, Problems and Future* (Strategic Institute of Research and Development, 2008) 7; Kernial S Sandhu, *Indians in Malaya: Immigration and Settlement, 1786–1957* (Cambridge University Press, first published 1969, 2010 ed) 21.

4 Jane Allen, 'History, Archaeology, and the Question of Foreign Control in Early Historic-Period Peninsular Malaysia' (1998) 2(4) *International Journal of Historical Archaeology* 261, 266. See also Richard Olof Winstedt, 'History of Kedah' (1920) 81 *Journal of the Straits Branch of the Royal Asiatic Society* 29, 30.

5 See Ravec Raghavan, 'Ethno-Racial Marginality in West Malaysia: The Case of the Peranakan Hindu Meleka or Malaccan Chitty Community' (1977) 133(4) *Bijdragen tot de Taal-, Land- en Volkenkunde* 438.

6 Timothy N Thomas, *Indians Overseas: A Guide to Source Materials in the India Office Records for the Study of Indian Emigration 1830–1950* (London: British Library, 1985).

7 Hugh Tinker, *A New System of Slavery: The Export of Indian Labour Overseas, 1830–1920* (Oxford University Press, 1974).

8 Sandhu (1969), above n 3, 45–46; See also Ravi Ahuja, 'The Origins of Colonial Labour Policy in Late Eighteenth-Century Madras' (1999) 44 *International Review of Social History* 159 (British colonial labour policy was based on a coercive and paternalistic social theory).

9 The caste system (known as the *Jati* system) consisted of four distinct occupational groups ordered in a hierarchical structure (*Brahmins* were priests; *Kshatriyas* were rulers/warriors; the third group consisted of agricultural landlords, merchants and traders; and the fourth lowest caste group were mostly landless peasants). There was a group outside the caste structure known as the Outcastes who worked as the latrine cleaners and cemetery workers/gravediggers. The outcaste group was also known as the Untouchables, a name which came from the "unclean" nature of their occupation and the *Brahmin* priesthood's strict requirements of cleanliness and purity in Hindu rituals. (See generally Ramesh Chandra, *Identity and Genesis of Caste System in India* (Kalpaz Publications, 2005); Ekta Singh, *Caste System in India: A Historical Perspective* (Kalpaz Publications, 2009).)

10 Sandhu (1969), above n 3, 45–46.

11 Sunil S Amrith, 'Indians Overseas? Governing Tamil Migration to Malaya 1870–1941' (2010) 208 *Past and Present* 231, 232.

12 Bonded labour in India was only abolished in 1976 by *The Bonded Labour System (Abolition) Act 1976*.

13 Peebles quoted in Roland Wenzlhuemer, 'Indian Labour Immigration and British Labour Policy in Nineteenth-Century Ceylon' (2007) 41(3) *Modern Asian Studies* 575, 579.

14 The Indian Tamil labour in Ceylon are known as the Hill-Country or Up-Country Tamils due to the location of tea plantations in hill stations, while the native Ceylon Tamils are known as the Jaffna Tamils due to their location in the northern province of Jaffna in Ceylon. The Jaffna Tamils typically looked down on the lower-caste Hill-Country Tamils. See generally Valli Kanapathipillai, *Citizenship and Statelessness in Sri Lanka: The Case of the Tamil Estate Workers* (Wimbledon Publishing: Anthem Press, 2009), 149.

15 Prakash C Jain, 'Exploitation and Reproduction of Migrant Indian Labour in Colonial Guyana and Malaysia' (1988) 18(2) *Journal of Contemporary Asia* 189, 197.

16 Sinnappah Arasaratnam, *Indians in Malaysia and Singapore* (Oxford University Press, 1970).

17 See generally Dawn Morais, 'Malaysia: The Writing of Lives and the Constructing of Nation' (2010) 33 *Biography* 84 (the Malayali clerics from Kerala who came into Malaya); R Rajakrishnan, 'Social Change and Group Identity

among the Sri Lankan Tamils' in Kernial S Sandhu and A Mani (eds), *Indian Communities in Southeast Asia* (Institute of Southeast Asian Studies, 1993) 541.

18  Kernial S Sandhu, 'Sikhs in Malaysia: A Society in Transition' in Kernial S Sandhu and A Mani (eds), *Indian Communities in Southeast Asia* (Institute of Southeast Asian Studies, 1993) 558.

19  Judith Nagata, 'Religion and Ethnicity Among the Indian Muslims of Malaysia' in Kernial S Sandhu and A Mani (eds), *Indian Communities in Southeast Asia* (Institute of Southeast Asian Studies, 1993) 513; Tate, above n 3, 33.

20  Paul M Kratoska, *The Chettiar and the Yeoman. British Cultural Categories and Rural Indebtness in Malaya* (Institute of Southeast Asian Studies, 1975).

21  Malaysian Population Census 2010 (Department of Statistics, Malaysia).

22  Graham K Brown, 'Legible Pluralism: The Politics of Ethnic and Religious Identification in Malaysia' (2010) 9(1) *Ethnopolitics* 31, 33.

23  Hermann Kulke and Dietmar Rothermund, *History of India* (London: Routledge, 1997) 256.

24  See Nicholas B Dirks, 'The Invention of Caste' (1989) 25 *Social Analysis* 45; Susan Bayly, *Caste, Society and Politics in India from the 18th Century to the Modern Age* (Cambridge: Cambridge University Press, 1999).

25  Jan Breman, *Imperial Monkey Business: Racial Supremacy in Social Darwinist Theory and Colonial Practice* (Amsterdam: VU University Press, 1990).

26  Tayyab Mahmud, 'Colonialism and Modern Constructions of Race: A Preliminary Inquiry' (1999) 53 *University of Miami Law Review* 1219, 1241.

27  Charles Hirschman, 'The Making of Race in Colonial Malaya: Political Economy and Racial Ideology' (1986) 1 *Sociological Forum* 330, 351.

28  The *1913 Malay Reservation Enactment* established restrictions on Malay agriculture in terms of planting paddy (rice), to ensure that Malays did not encroach into the British-dominated cultivation of rubber. The *Malay Special Rights Programme* was enacted to protect the Malays who were perceived by British colonials as being economically inferior compared to the migrant groups.

29  The indenture or contract usually lasted three to five years, during which the indentured labourer was unable to break the debt bondage. The labourer was bound by stipulated conditions which were most often unfair contractual terms such as fixed low wages. See generally Jain (1988), above n 15, 190.

30  Richard Baxtrom, 'Governmentality, Bio-Power, and the Emergence of the Malayan-Tamil Subject on the Plantations of Colonial Malaya'(2000) 14(2) *Crossroads: An Interdisciplinary Journal of Southeast Asian Studies* 49, 59.

31  Mavis Puthucheary, 'Indians in the Public Sector in Malaysia' in Kernial Singh Sandhu and A Mani (eds), *Indian Communities in Southeast Asia* (Institute of Southeast Asian Studies, 1993) 334.

32  Jain (1988), above n 15, 190.

33  Ibid., 199.

34  Sinappah Arasaratnam, 'Malaysian Indians: the Formation of Incipient Society' in Kernial Singh Sandhu and A Mani (eds), *Indian Communities in Southeast Asia* (Institute of Southeast Asian Studies, 1993) 190, 201.

35  Jain (1988), above n 15, 196; Arasaratnam (1993), above n 34, 195–202.

36  In the 1930s, the Great Depression caused extreme poverty to low-waged Indian Tamil labourers, and the British Indian government (the British Raj) intervened to abolish the *Kangany* labour system, which affected plantation labour in Malaya.

37  Minutes of the Standing Emigration Committee (13 February 1939) quoted in Amrith, above n 11, 258.

38  See Rajeswary Ampalavanar Brown, *Class, Caste and Ethnicism Among Urban Indians in Malaysia, 1920–1941* (Kuala Lumpur: Nusantara 2, 1972) 209.

39  D Jeyakumar, 'The Indian Poor in Malaysia: Problems and Solutions' in Kernial S Sandhu and A Mani (eds), *Indian Communities in Southeast Asia* (Institute of Southeast Asian Studies, 1993) 405, 406.

40 Gordon quoted in N J Colletta, 'Malaysia's Forgotten People: Education, Cultural Identity and Socio-Economic Mobility Among South Indian Plantation Workers' (1975) 7 *Contributions to Asian Studies* 87, 89.

41 Denison Jayasooria, *National Development Plans and Indians in Malaysia: A Need for Comprehensive Policies and Effective Delivery* (JJ Resources, 2011) 11–12.

42 Francis Loh, 'The Marginalization of the Indians in Malaysia', in James T Siegel and Audrey R Kahin (eds), *Southeast Asia over Three Generations: Essays Presented to Benedict R. O'G. Anderson* (Ithaca, NY: Cornell, 2003) 223, 232.

43 First Malaysian Indian Economic Seminar on 'The New Economic Policy, the Second Malaysia Plan, and the Mid-Term Review, and the Role of the MIC' (Kuala Lumpur, 11–12 May 1974) [hereinafter referred to as the 'MIC Blueprint'].

44 Robert Stephen Milne, 'The Politics of Malaysia's New Economic Policy' (1976) 49(2) *Pacific Affairs* 235, 253.

45 Edward Terence Gomez and Jomo Kwame Sundaram, *Malaysia's Political Economy: Politics, Patronage and Profits* (Cambridge University Press, 1999) 13; See generally Jomo K Sundaram and Ishak Shari, *Development Policies and Income Inequality in Peninsular Malaysia* (Kuala Lumpur: Institute for Social Analysis, 1986).

46 Working Paper of the Second Malaysian Indian Economic Seminar (Kuala Lumpur, 13 July 1980); K Anbalakan, 'The New Economic Policy and Further Marginalisation of Indians' (2003) XXI(1–2) *Kajian Malaysia (Malaysian Research Journal)* 379, 389.

47 2.9% in 2004 (Department of Statistics, Malaysia, 2004).

48 Centre for Public Policy Studies, 'Ensuring Effective Targeting of Ethnic Minorities: The Case of Low Income Malaysian Indians' in *Proposals for the Ninth Malaysia Plan* (Asian Strategy and Leadership Institute, 2006) 15.

49 Jayasooria, above n 41, 149, 205.

50 See Jayasooria, above n 41, 149; Centre for Public Policy Studies (2006), above n 48; Jeyakumar (1993), above n 39.

51 Jayasooria, above n 41, 110.

52 Ibid., 36.

53 See Marimuthu Thangavelu, 'The Plantation School as an Agent of Social Reproduction' Kernial S Sandhu and A Mani (eds), *Indian Communities in Southeast Asia* (Institute of Southeast Asian Studies, 1993) 489; N J Colletta, above n 40.

54 Martin Brennan, 'Class, Politics and Race in Modern Malaysia' (1982) 12(2) *Journal of Contemporary Asia* 188, 199. See Gomez and Sundaram, above n 45, 25–27.

55 See James C Scott, *Weapons of the Weak: Everyday Forms of Resistance* (Yale University Press, 1985) 57–58.

56 Brennan, above n 54, 199.

57 K Anbalakan, 'Chapter 23: Socio-economic Self-help Among Indians in Malaysia' in Kesavapany et al (eds), *Rising India and Indian Communities in East Asia* (Institute of Southeast Asian Studies, 2008) 422, 424. Pre-1984 schemes such as the National Land Finance Cooperative Society (NLFCS) in 1960 were more beneficial to the Indian Tamil plantation labour, as it purchased a few small rubber plantations and provided shares to the Indian Tamil plantation labour.

58 Ibid., 427.

59 Thomas Pepinsky, 'Malaysia: Turnover Without Change' (2007) 18(1) *Journal of Democracy* 113, 119.

60 See S Nagarajan, *A Community in Transition: Tamil Displacements in Malaysia* (PhD Thesis, University of Malaya, 2004).

61  Tenth Malaysia Plan (2010–2015), 151, 164.
62  Fransisca Lukose, 'Voluntarism as a Specific Feature of Industrial Relations in an Independent Malaysia: A Critical Analysis' (1991) 4(2) *International Journal of Value-Based Management* 109, 112. See also Jess N Parmer, 'Trade Unions in Malaya' (1957a) 310 *Annals of the American Academy of Political and Social Science* 142.
63  See Amrith, above n 11, 238.
64  Palanisamy Ramasamy, 'Labour Control and Labour Resistance in the Plantations of Colonial Malaya' (1992) 19(3–4) *Journal of Peasant Studies* 87, 95.
65  Social reform was an agenda of the Social Reform Movement and Self-Respect Society, which emerged in Madras, Tamilnadu. Its main aim was to dismantle the caste system from Tamil society.
66  Sinnappah Arasaratnam, 'Indian Society of Malaysia and its Leaders: Trends in Leadership and Ideology among Malaysian Indians, 1945–1960' (1982) 13(2) *Journal of Southeast Asian Studies* 236, 239.
67  Tayyab Mahmud, 'Migration, Identity and the Colonial Encounter' (1997) 76 *Oregon Law Review* 633, 653–655.
68  Ibid.
69  CIAM was formed in 1937, modelled after the Indian National Congress in British India, and sought to elevate the status of Indians in Malaya.
70  Rajakrishnan Ramasamy, 'Social Change and Group Identity Among the Sri Lankan Tamils' in Kernial S Sandhu and A Mani (eds), *Indian Communities in Southeast Asia* (Institute of Southeast Asian Studies, 1993) 541.
71  Ramasamy (1992), above n 64, 95. There existed a minority of Chinese-owned rubber plantations in Malaya. A minority of Chinese labour was recruited through Chinese contractors and not directly by planters (unlike Indian indentured and Kangany systems).
72  Klang is a district in the state of Selangor in Malaya (Malaysia).
73  Ramasamy (1992), above n 64, 103; Harold E Wilson, *The Klang Strikes of 1941: Labour and Capital in Colonial Malaya* (Singapore: Institute of Southeast Asian Studies, 1981) 5.
74  Wilson, above n 73, 6.
75  Correspondent, 'Mr. N. Raghavan's Plea At Annual CIAM Meeting: Advocates Controlled and Regulated Immigration' *The Straits Times* (27 January 1941).
76  See Rajeswary Ampalavanar Brown, *The Indian Minority and Political Change in Malaya, 1945–1957* (Kuala Lumpur: Oxford University Press, 1981).
77  It was reported that at least fifty thousand Indian labourers died working on the Siam-Burma railway project, called the 'Death Railway' (Jain (1988), above n 15, 250). See especially Palanisamy Ramasamy, 'Indian War Memory in Malaysia' in Lim Pui Huen and Diana Wong (eds), *War and Memory in Malaysia and Singapore* (Institute of Southeast Asian Studies, 2000) 90, 93–95.
78  Ramasamy (2000), above n 77, 94 (the Indian clerks were forced to make up Japanese quota for labour recruitment in wartime projects).
79  The MPAJA was linked to the Malayan Communist Party and comprised mostly Chinese, with a minority of Malays and Indians. See Cheah Boon Kheng, *Red Star Over Malaya: Resistance and Social Conflict During and After the Japanese Occupation of Malaya, 1941–1946* (National University of Singapore Press, 2003) 48–49.
80  Michael Stenson, *Class, Race and Colonialism in West Malaysia: The Indian Case* (University of Queensland Press, 1980) 54.
81  Tate, above n 3, 79.
82  Arasaratnam (1982), above n 66, 243.
83  Enacted to ban the Malayan Communist Party due to its militant style anti-colonial activities.

84 Chandra Muzaffar, 'Political Marginalization in Malaysia' in K S Sandhu and A Mani (eds), *Indian Communities in Southeast Asia* (Institute of Southeast Asian Studies, 1993) 211.

85 Arasaratnam (1982), above n 66, 246–247.

86 In 1955, the Malaysian Indian population was 300,000, while the MIC membership was only 20,000 (See Stenson, above n 80).

87 Ampalavanar Brown (1972), above, n 38; Ampalavanar Brown (1981), above n 76.

88 Lian Kwen Fee, 'The Political and Economic Marginalisation of Tamils in Malaysia' (2002) 26(3) *Asian Studies Review* 309, 324.

89 The commission was headed by Lord Reid, and its members consisted of Sri Ivor Jennings from the United Kingdom, Sir William McKell from Australia, B. Malik from India and Justice Abdul Hamid from Pakistan.

90 Jess N Parmer, 'Constitutional Change in Malaya's Plural Society' (1957b) 26(10) *Far Eastern Survey* 145, 146.

91 M Suffian, *An Introduction to the Constitution of Malaysia* (Kuala Lumpur, 1976) 251.

92 S M Huang-Thio, 'Constitutional Discrimination Under the Malaysian Constitution' (1964) 6 *Malaya Law Review* 1, 10.

93 Rajakrishnan Ramasamy, 'Racial Inequality and Social Reconstruction in Malaysia' (1993) 28(3/4) *Journal of Asian and African Studies* 217, 220. Low-caste groups were given preferential treatment and were categorised as Scheduled Castes and Other Backward Castes under the *Indian Constitution 1948* (art 46, 330, 32 and 335).

94 Parmer (1957b), above n 90, 148–149.

95 Huang-Thio, above n 92, 16.

96 Tate, above n 3, 110; Ampalavanar Brown (1981), above n 76, 196.

97 Amnesty International British Section, *Report of an Amnesty International Mission to the Federation of Malaysia 18 November–20 November, 1978* (London, July, 1979) 9.

98 This act was repealed in 2012 after civil society protests called for its abolishment. The act was replaced by the *Security Offences (Special Measures) Act 2012*.

99 Scott, above n 55, 274. Scott's study is in reference to the Malay peasantry in Malaya.

100 The May 13 incident occurred after the 1969 General Elections, where opposition parties, especially the Chinese-dominated DAP, won significant seats in Parliament. What began as a political clash between the DAP and the UMNO escalated into a Chinese and Malay racial conflict. See Kua Kia Soong, 'Racial Conflict in Malaysia: Against the Official History' (2008) 49 *Race & Class* 33.

101 Economic Planning Unit, 'Chapter 1: The New Development Strategy' *Second Malaysia Plan* (1971–1975).

102 Gordon P Means, '"Special Rights" as a Strategy for Development: The Case of Malaysia' (1972) 5 *Comparative Politics* 29.

103 James Chin, 'The Malaysian Chinese Dilemma: The Never Ending Policy' (2009) 3 *Chinese Southern Diaspora Studies* 167.

104 [1981] 2 MLJ 356.

105 Joshua Castellino and Elivira Dominquez Redondo, *Minority Rights in Asia: A Comparative Legal Analysis* (Oxford University Press, 2006) 24–25.

106 Elizabeth Fuller Collins and K Ramanathan, 'The Politics of Ritual Performance and Ritual Authority Among Murugan's Malaysian Devotees' in Linda Penkower and Tracy Pintchman (eds), *Ritualizing In, On, and Across the Boundaries of the Indian Subcontinent* (forthcoming) 15.

107 Harold Crouch, *Government and Society in Malaysia* (Cornell, 1996) 96; William Case, 'New Uncertainties for an Old Pseudo-Democracy: The Case of Malaysia' (2004) 37(1) *Comparative Politics* 83, 88. See generally William

Case, *Elites and Regimes in Malaysia: Revisiting a Consociational Democracy* (Monash Asia Institute, 1996).

108 Case (2004), above n 107, 83–83.

109 Andrew Harding, 'The *Keris*, the Crescent and the Blind Goddess: the State, Islam and the Constitution in Malaysia' (2002) 6 *Singapore Journal of International and Comparative Law* 154, 155.

110 Quoted in Tommy Thomas, 'Is Malaysia an Islamic State?' (paper presented at the 13th Biennial Malaysian Law Conference, Kuala Lumpur, 18 November 2005).

111 Julian Lee, *Islamization and Activism in Malaysia* (Institute of Southeast Asian Studies, 2010) 51–61.

112 See Thomas, above n 110.

113 Discussed in Chapter 4. This crisis saw highly respected senior judges being removed from office by the executive for alleged judicial misconduct.

114 Amanda J Whiting, 'Secularism, the Islamic State and the Malaysian Legal Profession' (2010) 5 *Asian Journal of Comparative Law* 1.

115 See *Shamala a/p Sathiyaseelan v. Dr Jeyaganesh a/l C Moganarajah* [2003] 6 MLJ 515; *Subashini a/p Rajasingham v. Saravanan a/l Thangathoray* [2007] 2 MLJ 205; *Kaliammal a/p Sinnasamy v. Majlis Agama Islam Wilayah Persekutuan (JAWI) (Department of Islamic Affairs, Federal Territory)* [2011] 2 CLJ 165, *Indira Gandhi A/P Mutho v. Jabatan Agama Islam Perak (Islamic Department of the State of Perak) & Ors.* [2013] (Judicial Review No. 25-10-2009). See also *Siti Hasnah Vangarama Abdullah v. Tun Dr Mahathir Mohamad (As the President of PERKIM) & Ors* [2012] 7 CLJ 845.

116 *Titular Roman Catholic Archbishop of Kuala Lumpur v. Menteri Dalam Negeri (Minister for Home Affairs)* [2010] 2 MLJ 78.

117 Baradan Kuppusamy, 'Facing Malaysia's Racial Issues' in *The Time* (online), 26 November 2007 <http://content.time.com/time/world/article/0,8599,1687973,00.html>

118 Soon Li Tsin, 'Cops Obtain Rare Court Order Against Hindraf', *Malaysiakini* (online), 23 November 2007, <www.malaysiakini.com/news/75175>

119 Civil Action No. HQ07X02977 (filed on 30th August 2007).

120 Soon, above n 118. Moorthy was one of two Indians who were the first Malaysians to reach the top of Mount Everest.

121 K. Shanmuga, 'Re Everest Moorthy: A Summary of the Case and Related Events of Kaliammal Sinnasamy v. Islamic Religious Affairs Council of the Federal Territory, Director Kuala Lumpur General Hospital & Government of Malaysia' in *The Malaysian Bar News* (29 December 2005).

122 Debra Chong, 'Everest Mountaineer "Body Snatching" Case Decision on August 6' in *The Malaysian Insider* (online), 21 July 2010 <www.themalaysianinsider.com/malaysia/article/everest-mountaineer-body-snatching-case-decision-on-august-6/>.

123 Julian Lee et al, 'Elections, Repertoires of Contention and Habitus in Four Civil Society Engagements in Malaysia's 2008 General Elections' (2010) 9(3) *Social Movement Studies* 293.

# 2 Theorising politico-legal mobilisation of minority groups in illiberal polities

## The role of the law in constituting identities and grievances

### 2.1 Introduction – studying minority mobilisation

The previous chapter described two instances of Indian mobilisation *en masse*, the 1941 plantation labour strike in colonial Malaya and the 2007 Hindu Rights Action Force (HINDRAF) rally in post-colonial Malaysia. The actions of the HINDRAF movement leaders showed that legal rhetoric and rights-based lobbying were part of the movement's strategy. The use of rights talk was observed during the rally itself, while the grievances listed in the memorandum to the prime minister of the United Kingdom were framed in legal language. The proposed class-action suit against the British government with a petition to the Queen of England for Queen's Counsel indicated that the law, courts and rights were important to the movement. However, the threat of litigation for colonial grievances and the claim for Indian rights was targeted against the former colonial government, while accusations of racial discrimination were directed against the Malaysian government.

Studies that have looked at the HINDRAF mobilisation and strategy are media-centric, focussing on the use of the print media as well as new media in social mobilisation. Contemporary studies on Indians focus largely on the socioeconomic grievances of the Indian underclass.[1] These studies have not adequately analysed how the law mattered in Indian mobilisation despite clear indications of the role of various dimensions of the law in the HINDRAF mobilisation, as noted above. Instead, where the law has been considered it has been in terms of the law as the state's tool of repression. These studies have also emphasised how discriminatory legislation and policy (soft law) has adversely impacted on the Indian underclass. These studies have also looked for the law in institutional spaces such as the courts, the Parliament and the government. Hence, they have missed the non-institutional subaltern spaces where a more subtle mobilisation was taking place since the 1990s, through pockets of direct action tactics and political lobbying for rights.[2] However, the direct action strategy and rights lobbying had an innate connection to the law, through activist lawyers who used the courts extensively as a site of contention. This 'legal' dimension of Indian mobilisation has not yet been studied in a theoretically informed way.

This study fills this gap in the study of Indian minority mobilisation through the main research question, which aims to determine how the law and rights mattered in the recent mobilisation of Indians in Malaysia from the 1990s, despite the serious restrictions on civil liberties and the controlled legal system within the illiberal Malaysian setting. In order to answer this question, this chapter reviews the theoretical literature on the law and legal mobilisation, drawing also on the extensive literature on other instances of minority mobilisation in other countries. The aim is to develop a theoretical framework to study the role of the law and rights in ethno-cultural minority mobilisations that occur in illiberal political settings.

## 2.2 Mobilising law and rights in an illiberal democracy

A review of the literature on ethno-cultural minority mobilisation shows that very few studies have examined the utility of the law and rights in illiberal polities. Scholars who have looked into the emergence of ethnic movements in illiberal polities have focussed on ethnic conflicts and the causal effect of international non-governmental organisations (NGOs) which disseminate human rights ideas to nation states worldwide.[3] These studies emphasise the role of international organisational networks and global civil society in empowering ethnic mobilisation but have failed to discern how human rights matter at the grassroots level of ethnic mobilisation. Furthermore, they follow a pattern of studies that explore the inherent tensions between the international human rights model and illiberal authoritarian regimes.

For instance, Goedde's study of transnational human rights mobilisation against the authoritarian North Korean government showed that despite the leveraging of human rights by international bodies and the mobilisation of the democratic South Korean counterpart, human rights discourse did not matter in North Korea.[4] The primary reason behind this was the non-existence of grassroots human rights mobilisation due to the rigorous suppression of personal liberty and freedom of the North Koreans. Similarly, Massoud's study of human rights education in Sudan found that international organisational attempts at mobilising Sudanese victims of civil war with human rights ideas were counterproductive, and even perilous to victims' personal safety.[5] The alliance between international and local civil society not only failed to empower victims but exposed individuals to counter-retaliation by the authoritarian regime. These studies clearly place importance on global and local institutional responses to human rights injuries imposed by authoritarian governments on its citizenry. These scholars also concede that the repressive nature of authoritarian jurisdictions hinders the collection of empirical evidence necessary to analyse the subtle occasions of grassroots mobilisation that do take place.[6] In any case, these studies are useful as they reveal the political play involved in the use of international human rights discourse by international and local advocacy groups, and the authoritarian state's counter-discourse and backlash against rights.

The studies on authoritarian regimes pose a relevant question for this study: does human rights matter in the mobilisation that occurs in semi-authoritarian or partially democratic states? Following Chapter 1's definition of an illiberal democracy, this study finds that very few studies have analysed the role of law and rights in illiberal democracies where governments curtail civil liberties but unlike authoritarian or totalitarian regimes allow for democratic elections to take place. In a study of legal mobilisation (the interdisciplinary study of law and social movements is reviewed in detail in Section 2.5) in semi-authoritarian Hong Kong, Waikeung Tam showed that activists who were lawyers became instrumental in mobilising the law and rights.[7] However, the study is centred on the Court of Final Appeal in Hong Kong which not only operates as an independent judiciary but was receptive to rights-based arguments based on Hong Kong's *Bill of Rights* and *Basic Law*.[8] It is noteworthy that Hong Kong is not an illiberal democracy like Malaysia but termed a constitutional liberal autocracy that upholds a liberal framework of the rule of law and rights.[9] Although Hong Kong as a liberal autocracy curtails its legislative body and supports an authoritarian executive, the autonomy of the bar (legal profession) and the bench (judiciary) played a significant role in the mobilisation of law and liberal rights.

In contrast, Harding and Whiting's study on illiberal democratic Malaysia found that Malaysian lawyers, both as individual legal activists and as a collective through the professional bar association, the Malaysian Bar Council, have mobilised using the law and rights.[10] However, unlike the legal mobilisation of the bar in the constitutional court of Hong Kong, the Malaysian activist lawyers primarily utilised direct action strategies and political lobbying due to the curtailed independence of the Malaysian judiciary. Activist lawyers have frequently formed alliances with populist movements which fight for civil and political liberties as well as pressure the executive controlled state to uphold the rule of law. An example of this is the 2007 Lawyer Walk for Justice, which was propelled by revelations that judicial appointments had been manipulated by members of the executive in Malaysia.[11]

Nevertheless, there have also been instances where the constitutional rights of individuals have been contested through strategic litigation in the courts alongside direct action tactics which were supported by both activist lawyers and local NGOs. For instance, the Article 11 movement supported litigation which sought to uphold *Article 11* of the *Federal Constitution* (on the freedom of religion). Lawyers for Liberty uses both strategic litigation and direct action strategies to campaign for constitutional and human rights, while MyConstitution or *PerlembegaanKu* was set up by activist lawyers to educate the Malaysian public on their constitutional rights pertaining to civil and political liberties.[12]

Both Tam's as well as Harding and Whiting's studies display the crucial requirement of a rights-receptive judiciary and activist lawyers in the mobilisation of liberal rights as well as human rights in the courts. However, in the case of an illiberal Malaysia, the curtailment of the judiciary and constraints on civil liberties has led to the proliferation of rights-based mobilisation in extralegal spaces, such as political lobbying and direct action. At the same time, rights mobilisation has forged a tight-knit complicity between lawyers and non-legal actors such as NGOs, a relationship which remains understudied. In fact, studies of legal mobilisation in semi-authoritarian polities overemphasise the role of the lawyers, courts and the judiciary. This often leads to the labelling of the law as being illiberal and repressive, while grassroots mobilisation of liberal rights remains understated and acknowledged only in passing. Thus, there is a major gap in terms of the theoretical framework and the methodologies used in order to discern whether the law and rights matter in grassroots movements, especially minority mobilisation that frequently occurs in the fringes of restricted institutional spaces.

Lynette Chua's study on gay mobilisation in semi-authoritarian Singapore revealed that official law is repressive in illiberal democracies, but in its 'cultural form' the law emerges as a source of legitimacy and can be tactically utilised through 'pragmatic resistance' or manoeuvres that interchange between obeying the repressive law of the state and covertly challenging the cultural norms.[13] Chua utilises James Scott's theory of pragmatic resistance,[14] which provides a useful framework in understanding covert, non-confrontational, everyday resistance in illiberal settings. However, Scott's theory does not extend to more extroverted direct action strategies which potentially form mobilisation *en masse* such as protests, rallies and demonstrations. This reveals a lacuna in studies which examine the strategic utility of the law's cultural power in more antagonistic direct action tactics which occur not only within but despite the illiberal settings. Moreover, these studies do not examine the legal mobilisation of ethno-cultural minority groups in illiberal democracies. There is a need therefore to first examine the role of law and rights in ethno-cultural minority mobilisation in order to gain insights into how ethno-cultural *identity* relates to law, rights and mobilisation.

## 2.3  Ethno-cultural minority movements, law and rights

Research inquiries on ethno-cultural minority movements, law and rights in illiberal democracies are mostly centred on the indigenous peoples' movement. These studies explore the legal status of indigenous people as a minority group as well as the legal rights and protections accorded to them under international law.[15] Specific case studies of indigenous groups in illiberal polities have focussed on the connection between the grassroots mobilisation of indigenous groups and internationally recognised indigenous group rights,[16] as well as the role of indigenous rights in empowering ethno-cultural minority groups.[17] These studies focus on the international legal framework and global civil society networks that present opportunities for indigenous groups in illiberal polities to galvanise local support and link their cause to regional and global indigenous movements. However, local understandings of indigenous rights to land, resources and citizenship have become entrenched in the international legal definition of indigenous people, which in turn influences particular minority groups to frame their group identity in accordance to the rights claimed. For instance, Yoko's study of the Karen hill-dwellers in Thailand found that in order to seek national land rights from the Thailand government, the Karen hill-dwellers had collectivised and labelled themselves as an indigenous group, which gave them the opportunity to contest for indigenous land rights.[18] While the international legal framework is useful to probe into how indigenous rights movements emerge and function in illiberal polities, the framework also inevitably narrows the analysis to the 'indigenous' identity of the group. Hence, not only does the framework fail to take into account the internal cultural identity of specific indigenous groups, but it also excludes the legal status and rights of non-indigenous ethno-cultural minority groups in illiberal polities, like the Indians in Malaysia.

In comparison, sociolegal studies (or the American 'law and society' scholarship, which is reviewed more fully in Section 2.4.2) on the 1960s Native American Movement, an indigenous people's movement in liberal democratic United States, show that native groups have historically utilised their internal cultural identity as well as treaty-based legal identity in order to mobilise native group rights. To date there are 375 Native American treaties recognised by the U.S. government, all of which are legally binding according to *Article VI Clause 2* of the *U.S. Constitution* which states, 'all treaties made, or which shall be made, under the authority of the United States, shall be the supreme law of the land'.[19] Studies on the Native Americans have shown that group rights accorded by the Native American treaties did not originally intend to protect the cultural life of various tribes, but instead coerced the tribes into accepting the Euro-American state's ideology of tribal identity, property rights and law. Susan Gooding's study of the Colville Confederated Tribes of Washington State found that Native American treaties often provided legal rights such as fishing rights and land rights, but the language used to describe these rights and the litigation that surrounded tribal rights served to racialise Native American identity.[20] Furthermore, the legal recognition of individual tribes under the separate treaties also facilitated the political division of Native Americans into smaller groups, which ensured the American colonial state's bargaining power in the purchase of native land and signing of contracts or treaties.

Although the *Indian Citizenship Act 1924* was enacted to recognise all Native Americans as individualised citizens of the United States and the *Indian Reorganization Act 1934* gave Native Americans a larger degree of self-government, by the 1950s the government began minimising native land reservations. This resulted in the forced relocation of many Native Americans to urban settings where they were assimilated into a Euro-American society.[21] The mandatory removal from tribal lands and coercive

acculturation of Native Americans resulted in a pooling of shared grievances among the different tribal groups in terms of the loss of land, livelihood and culture. Anderson's study of fishing rights of the Salish people in
Washington State found that 'a pan-Indian movement' had emerged in the
1960s, where movement leaders sought both political and legal rights of a
united Native American community as well as a reinforcement of the Salish cultural identity.[22] In 1968, the American Indian Movement was gaining momentum, led by urban Native Americans and heavily influenced by
the American Civil Rights Movement's dual tactics of rights and collective
identity (Section 2.4 discusses the civil rights strategy of the Black minority
group in the United States).

The legal mobilisation of Native Americans from the 1960s was a combination of civil disobedience and court-based strategies but centred on particular treaty-based issues like the fishing rights in the Pacific Northwest.
Tribes held 'fish-ins' or direct action tactics which involved fishing in reservation land against state regulations and later made active legal claims in
court for fishing rights. An example of the legal mobilisation was the 1969
case of *United States v. Oregon*,[23] where the Colville tribe claimed fishing
rights under the *Yakima Treaty 1855*. The legal mobilisation tactics continued to be utilised even until the recent 2004 case of *United States v. Lara*,[24]
which established that tribes had criminal jurisdiction over non-tribal members. Kevin Washburn's study of the Supreme Court decision in the *Lara*
case found that the tribal sovereignty movement was able to successfully
mobilise extensive support for their claims by filing *amicus curiae* briefs,
that is, petitions by non-litigating tribes and Native American organisations.[25] A 2001 joint initiative between the National Congress of American
Indians and the Native American Rights Fund called the Supreme Court
Project led to *amicus curiae* briefings in Supreme Court cases dealing with
tribal sovereignty. This joint strategy, which coordinated independent tribes
to coalesce and file single briefs, with focus on key legal principles and policies, showed that a 'legal forum' like the courts that lies outside the realm of
politics can be utilised as a tool of contentious politics.[26]

The studies of Native American mobilisation show that not only was the
tribal treaty system a source of oppression and division of the Native Americans, but it was used as a site of contestation, where tribes both challenged
their treaty-based legal identity and framed claims based on treaty rights
in order to seek remedies for their grievances. In fact, some studies suggest
that indigenous people have even utilised Euro-centric corporation laws in
order to 'corporatise' their legal identity which became useful to make collective claims against the state.[27] An example of this is the setting up of
development corporations by the Cree and Inuit people in Quebec, Canada,
in order to seek compensation from the federal and provincial governments
over a hydroelectric project on indigenous land.[28] In essence, the corporation laws, which stem from the Euro-American or Euro-Canadian colonial
state, became a site of contestation for native identity and indigenous rights.

A similar pattern of mobilisation is observed in the 1960s Aboriginal Movement in Australia which focussed on maintaining the aboriginal cultural identity along with claims for civil rights like full citizenship, equal pay and land rights.[29] After an unsuccessful legal claim for native land rights by the Yirrkala people in the Australian courts,[30] the Aboriginal movement had turned to utilise direct action and rights-based lobbying to pressure the state. In the 1980s, the Aboriginal Movement, with substantial involvement from both activist lawyers as well as aboriginal rights activists, utilised the courts and successfully won native title rights in the *Mabo case*.[31]

What differentiates the indigenous movement tactics in liberal democratic states is the more extensive use of the courts. Although indigenous movements in illiberal polities have sought to utilise international laws to frame their cultural identity and seek international indigenous rights, what is missing is the opportunity to effectively use non-binding international law, or soft law, in the local courts to claim those rights. This is particularly so in illiberal polities with a curtailed legal system and a judiciary that is not receptive to rights-based claims. In the case of the *Orang Asli* of Malaysia, a collective term which includes numerous tribes of indigenous people in West peninsular Malaysia, an indigenous movement surrounding the rights of the *Orang Asli* had emerged since the 1980s. The movement for many years utilised political lobbying and direct action tactics to seek traditional rights and land rights but from 1998, resorted to using the courts to fight for their rights.[32] In 2002, an unprecedented High Court decision in the case of *Sagong Tasi*,[33] finally recognised the existence of native land titles as common law and based its decision on international indigenous treaties (non-binding soft laws) as well as 'creative' interpretations of the *Federal Constitution* and other legislative measures such as the *1954 Aboriginal Peoples Act*.[34]

Studies that have analysed the legal cases on indigenous rights claims in Malaysia have often disregarded the resistance efforts that took place in the shadows of indigenous group litigation.[35] A purely legal analysis of the native land rights cases in Malaysia fails to scrutinise the mobilisation of the indigenous people through the courts and direct action strategies. On the other hand, studies that have analysed the Malaysian indigenous peoples' movement have focussed on the group's cultural identity and grievances,[36] but failed to discern the utility of rights in the legal and political claims. Aiken and Leigh found that since the late 1980s, indigenous groups in Malaysia with the support of local NGOs and civil society, had utilised both 'passive and active' forms of resistance that included *inter alia* strategic litigation, media publicity campaigns, rights lobbying and protests.[37] While Aiken and Leigh's study makes inroads by analysing both strategic litigation and rights-based activism of indigenous groups in Malaysia, it lacks a theoretical context in which to incorporate both the study of the law (the legal cases and legal rights) and the social movement strategies (resistance and rights lobbying) of indigenous people in Malaysia. At present, there is no appropriate theoretical framework to analyse ethno-cultural minority movements in illiberal settings such as Malaysia.

The preceding discussion first shows that studies on minority movements in illiberal polities have narrowed their focus to analysing indigenous groups as well as the specific body of international legal instruments which identify indigenous group characteristics and rights. While this has limited the degree to which the theoretical insights gained from studies of indigenous groups may be applied to other groups, it has, nevertheless, revealed the significance of cultural identity in coalescing ethno-cultural movements. Although recent studies have attempted to draw both legal and social movement understandings of indigenous mobilisation in illiberal polities like Malaysia, they have not adequately drawn the analytical links between cultural identity and rights in legal mobilisation. The bulk of studies that have sufficiently interrogated these links between a minority group's cultural rights, identity and mobilisation are centred on the Native American movement in a liberal democratic United States. The theoretical framework used in the studies on Native American mobilisation comes from the interdisciplinary sociolegal scholarship and social movement studies. These two streams of scholarship have also been utilised to examine mobilisation of non-indigenous ethno-cultural minority groups, such as the Blacks and the Chicanos in the United States (elaborated further in Section 2.4 and Section 2.5). As there is a lacuna in studies on non-indigenous minority mobilisation in illiberal polities and a gap in terms of an appropriate theoretical framework to analyse the links between ethno-cultural identity, rights and mobilisation, the next section will attempt to draw insights from the two streams that have studied the role of identity, the law and rights in ethno-cultural movements in liberal democratic settings.

## 2.4 Identity, grievance and rights in ethno-cultural mobilisation

The study of ethnic movements has mostly revolved around an array of theories ranging from social movement theories, studies on race or ethnic based 'collective action' (which is more short-term in nature than a sustained social movement) as well as studies on nationalist or secessionist movements seeking autonomy from nation-states.[38] This has produced a highly fragmented range of theoretical frameworks, with no single theory presenting a useful analytical basis to study ethnic movements. Furthermore, there is insufficient attention paid to questions of how the law matters in ethnic mobilisation and especially how identity, rights and law work outside restricted institutional spaces in mobilising such groups. Studies that have examined the links between law, rights and cultural identity have mainly arisen from sociolegal scholarship while the link between collective identity and collective action has been analysed in social movement studies. As these two academic fields are rather diverse in terms of the methodologies used, the following review of both these fields is narrowed down to the relevant theoretical and methodological tools that have been used by scholars to study ethno-cultural movements and minority groups.

### 2.4.1 The social movement perspective on ethno-cultural movements

Studies on social movements have historically taken various analytical pathways, from the psychological and mass behavioural emphasis of collective action tactics like protest,[39] to the current interdisciplinary focus on politics, process and power in movements.[40] The problem with social movement studies is its regional polarisation, which began with the dichotomy between American studies focussed on behavioural psychology and the Continental European studies that took a Marxist approach in analysing social movements. However, most of these theories were unable to explain when, how and why social movements occurred. Studies after the 1970s continued to be divided between the two continents in terms of theoretical approaches to social movements, but this was largely due to the contextual differences in the type of social movements and claims that arose in the two regions. The Americans were confronted with the Black minority group's initiation of the Civil Rights Movement which made claims for racial equality, legal rights and social inclusion of minorities within the liberal democratic state. On the other side of the Atlantic, the Europeans were encountering labour mobilisation and suffrage movements which sought far more radical and socialist changes to the state itself.[41] Hence, American social movement theories rather than the European social movement theories have been utilised more in analysing ethno-cultural minority movements like the Blacks. Nevertheless, the two different approaches are assessed here in terms of how collective identity and identity-based rights factor into mobilisation.

From the 1970s, American social movement scholars developed the resource mobilisation theory, where collective action was attributed to the presence of organisational resources and rational political actors who possessed organisational skill to plan strategic action.[42] Resource mobilisation theorists contend that since collective grievances are somewhat constant and persistent, collective action should be analysed as arising from the availability of capital or 'social resources' to bring together disparate and atomised aggrieved individuals.[43] Hence, resource mobilisation theory shifted academic concern from 'why' mobilisation arises, that is, from collective grievances, to 'how' mobilisation occurs, that is, through organisational support, resources and tactics.[44]

European scholarship did not mirror the American concern for movement mechanics and support structures, but instead developed the new social movement theory in response to the shortfalls of the old Marxist-socialist analyses of collective action.[45] The European concern arose from historical issues such as economic divisions, class and ideology but with a new analytical framework that included collective identity.[46] The European approach aimed to find out 'why' collectives mobilised by examining collective grievances linked to 'new' collective identities of the aggrieved, such as women, students and the Lesbian Gay Bisexual Transgender Queer (LGBTQ) community, as opposed to the 'old' labour-based movements. As ideology was seen to be the primary tool of control by elites in the political and social spheres, social movements were said to construct counter-ideologies. The analysis of new identity-based mobilisation tied in with new ideological beliefs such as feminism, gay rights, environmentalism, peace and animal rights.[47] However, the European new social movement theorists did not seek to utilise the theory to study mobilisation centred on ethno-cultural identities of racial, ethnic, linguistic and religious groups.

Since the 1990s, the Europeans have improvised on the new social movement theory and new social movement theorists have separated their analysis to emphasise two different aspects of mobilisation: the political and the cultural (or social) elements of collective action.[48] New social movement theorists like Alain Touraine contend that the 'political aspects' of new social movements had overridden the 'social aspects' in that the new social movement was prone to be purely political and ideological in nature, like the anti-globalisation movement and the anti-capitalist movement.[49] However, other new social movement theorists like Alberto Melucci found that although new social movements operated in a political sphere, the social construction of the movement's collective identity and shared culture are vital ingredients in the process of collective mobilisation.[50] Despite the move towards the cultural prospects of collective identity, these studies failed to distinguish between ethno-cultural group identity and collective identity associated with social movements. That is to say, there is a gap in the new social movement theory in terms of why and/or how ethno-cultural group identity can transform into the collective identity of an ethno-cultural movement.

As the European debate revolved around the conflict between political ideologies and cultural identity of new social movements, American scholars were moving away from the structure-oriented resource mobilisation theory towards a process-based approach. Doug McAdam in a pioneering study of Black insurgency from the 1930s to 1970s in the United States argued that the American resource mobilisation theory did not accurately pin down the role of political power in the collective utilisation of internal resources such as activists leaders as well as external resources like elite sponsors and public support.[51] McAdam introduced the idea that social movements should generally be analysed as a 'political process' which takes into account three factors: first, the extent to which an aggrieved group is organised; second, whether a collective judgement was made on the prospects of inciting an insurgent revolt; and third, the political position of the aggrieved group within the wider political milieu or in other words, the 'political opportunities' available to the aggrieved group to rouse a rebellion.[52]

The political process theorists recognised that movement activists do not operate in a vacuum in terms of choosing goals, strategies and tactics, and that the outcomes of activists' choices can only be understood by examining the political opportunities available or the 'rules of the games' which determine the choices.[53] However, previous resource mobilisation theorists have warned that social movements need networks and organisational structure to mobilise effectively, without which aggrieved groups are only able to create temporary sparks of protest and riots.[54] McAdam takes this warning into account when he concedes that political opportunity structure in itself is not sufficient to analyse minority mobilisation, as a minority community requires resources to enable the 'insurgents' or activists within the community to take advantage of the political opportunities.[55] In any case, the political process approach failed to take into account the three crucial elements in analysing the legal mobilisation of ethno-cultural minority groups: ethno-cultural collective identity, collective rights and the cultural aspect of the law. Although the law and rights feature substantially in Black grievances, especially in the claims of inequality before the law and the demand for Black rights, McAdam only makes reference to the repressive dimension of the law, which is prevalent in the 'law and order' rhetoric of the state and the dominant role played by 'law enforcement' officials.[56]

In general, most social movement scholars peg the law as a state-controlled mechanism or an institutional form of suppression. Although American social movement studies have taken more convergent approaches using wider social science and political science theories in analysing social movements, the role of the law remained trapped within a top-down analysis and a structural or institutional framework, elaborated in Section 2.5. For instance, a bottom-up grassroots study by John Gaventa on the fluctuating dynamics of collective action by coalminers in the Appalachian Valley found that the coal mining company dominated and manipulated the legal institutional processes in order to defeat coal miners' strikes and intimidate them into quiescence.[57] While the Gaventa study itself was bottom-up, the analysis of the law was top-down. The relatively stagnant role of the law as a mode of repression had led to its general disregard from social movement analysis. In fact, social movement studies were moving further away from analysing the role of the law and moving towards more innovative theoretical approaches to study mobilisation. Dennis Chong for instance takes a game-theoretic approach in deciphering the dynamics of several bouts of direct action tactics by Black activists during the 1960s American Civil Rights Movement.[58] Chong's use of game theory is useful in analysing the complex and dynamic changes of collective action, which traced the occurrences of a united Black mobilisation between intervals of a fragmented Black community during the period of the American Civil Rights Movement.[59]

However, the political process approach remained the dominant theoretical approach to analysing social movements. Key political process theorists such as Doug McAdam, Charles Tilly and Sidney Tarrow amalgamated their studies to produce a single theoretical framework called the 'dynamics of contention'.[60] At this stage, the study of social movements had been slowly absorbed into a wider study of 'contentious politics', which incorporated 'all kinds of collective political struggle'.[61] Contentious politics involves the alliances formed between the common populace and friendly elites with influential power that utilise political opportunities as resource in order to confront adversarial elites or the dominant establishment such as the state.[62] Contentious politics amalgamated political opportunity structure with a new theory that emphasised the cultural and ideological elements of mobilisation: cultural frame processes or frame theory. The frame theory was, in fact, a refined version of resource mobilisation theory and became useful to make sense of rights in mobilisation. For instance, Tarrow's study of contentious politics incorporated a frame analysis on the American Civil Rights Movements and found that constitutional lawyers played the role of friendly elites, while the courts became the primary site of contestation of equal opportunity rights for the Black people.[63] Rights was recognised as the focal point of the American Civil Rights Movement which was not only useful in framing Black grievances but became a strategic tool of the movement.

The cultural frame processes theory is the main theoretical basis used in current social movement scholarship to make sense of the role of rights as well as collective identity. David Snow and Robert Benford explain the theory as 'cultural material' or 'the extant stock of meanings, beliefs, ideologies, practices, values, myths, narratives and the like' which are utilised by movement activists to constitute new 'cultural meanings' or 'frames'.[64] The frame or framework produced becomes a 'schemata of interpretation' that allow actors 'to locate, perceive, identify, and label occurrences within their life space and [the] world at large.[65] The key concept of framing in social movements is not just in the mutual understandings of shared grievances and perceptions of group identity, but in the transference of those understandings into meaningful frames such as rights and collective identity, as well as the utility of those frames in collective action. The whole framing process from which shared grievances are reconstructed into collective action is facilitated largely by social movement activists, the media and elites in society who individually and jointly unscramble, construct and reconstruct particular situations or events.[66]

Snow and Benford divide cultural framing processes into three main tasks: first, the 'diagnostic framing' which identifies and attributes problems, second the 'prognostic framing' which identifies solutions and strategies, and lastly, 'motivational framing', which provides the vocabularies that rationalise collective action.[67] Hence, social movement activists are said to construct particular frames to diagnose social issues or problems, to assign responsibility to persons or circumstances perceived to have caused the problem, and to gather consensus as well as organise concerted action to resolve those problems. For example, the American Civil Rights Movement utilised multiple frames such as equal rights and Black identity in order to diagnose or make sense of Black grievances which arose from racial segregation. The problems connected to racial segregation were depicted as arising from the failure of the state to uphold the constitutional principle of formal equality and the discriminatory treatment accorded to the Blacks by the majority White people. The right to equal treatment and equal opportunity was depicted as the only remedy to the problems associated with inequality and discrimination. This process was not only useful in pinpointing the adversaries but also in producing an integrated civil rights ideology (civil rights include the rights to equality and fundamental liberties) which coalesced, empowered and mobilised the Black people.[68]

While frame theory acknowledges the use of multiple frames by social movements, the links between frames have not been fully explored. Studies on the American Civil Rights Movement contend that 'civil rights' had become a 'master frame' which was utilised not only by other ethno-cultural movements like the Chicano Movement and the Native American Movement but by other identity-based movements such as the women's rights movement.[69] Hence, the two significant frames typically used by identity-based movements are the civil rights frame and the collective identity frame. In fact, the socio-political awakening created by the civil rights and Black identity frames extended even to ethno-cultural movements outside the United States. For example the Dalit Panthers Movement in India, which modelled its movement to mirror the Black Panthers and American Civil Rights Movement in the United States, fought for equal rights of the Dalit community (a self-styled collective identity of the Outcaste people).[70] Despite the obvious connection between the rights and collective identity frames, there have been very few social movement studies which have made substantive inquiries on the linkage between rights and collective identity in mobilisation.

In the social movement studies that focussed on collective identity, theorists have utilised both the political process and resource mobilisation approaches in order to trace the internal and external factors which bring about changes and maintenance of collective identity in social movements.[71] However, collective identity can be complex and problematic if it has not been precisely defined. Polleta and Jasper in an analysis of social movements have defined 'collective identity' as an individual's internal connection or psychological link to an inclusive community, group or association.[72] In other words, collective identity in social movements links individuals to a collective through a self-perceived connection. However, Polleta and Jasper in their study contend that social movement theorists who analysed the American Civil Rights Movement took the connection between Black collective identity and Black grievances for granted and were more concerned on how resources were utilised by civil rights movement activists.[73] Furthermore, the bulk of the literature on collective identity in social movements is focussed on the 'new' collective identities that are formed around particular issues or political ideologies, like the anti-abortionists and animal rights activists. Hence, these studies have disregarded the different processes of collective identity formation that operate in ethno-cultural movements on the one hand and in political or ideological movements on the other hand.

There are a few recent studies that have analysed collective identities of ethno-cultural minority groups and how those identities link to mobilisation. Vermeersch's study on the Roma (Gypsies) ethnic minority in Czech Republic and Slovakia, utilised frame theory to analyse the production of a Romani ethnic identity as a collective identity in the political mobilisation of the group.[74] His study found that the heterogeneous nature of the Romani ethnic group reflected the competing definitions of Roma identity constructed by political activists, movement leaders, the media and the governments although all these diverse definitions of identity helped in the end to mobilise the Roma by utilising ethnic identity as a 'mobilising identity'.[75] A similar study by Garcia-Bedolla on the construction of Latino immigrant identity in Los Angeles found that the Latino racial identity was utilised as a collective identity by activists in the political mobilisation of Latinos.[76] Garcia-Bedolla coins the term 'mobilising identity' as well but does so in reference to (a) a type of identity resource, which exists as a latent form of 'social capital' within an individual's consciousness, and (b) a trigger element when the identity produces a 'positive affective attachment' to a particular racial group that inspires the individual to make demands in the interest of the collective.[77] Hence, the mobilising identity is a type of dormant resource of the ethno-cultural minority group which is strategically sparked off by movement activists or political leaders in a suitable political and social environment. While the concept of a mobilising identity is useful to determine the link between the collective identity of an ethno-cultural minority group and mobilisation, the studies highlighted above failed to discern its connection to rights and the law. Polleta and Jasper concede that identity may be constructed by the law and used by the state as well as later reconceived by movement activists,[78] but this linkage does not adequately explain how rights matter in producing the collective identities of ethno-cultural minority movements. To remedy this gap, it is necessary to examine sociolegal studies, which have contributed substantially to investigations of the link between ethno-cultural group identity and rights.

### 2.4.2 *The sociolegal approach to ethno-cultural minority mobilisation*

Unlike social movement studies, which had a number of divergent strands, sociolegal scholarship has a more concerted academic aim, which is the study of law as a *social* phenomenon. Key sociolegal theorists like Roger Cotterrell found that the law cannot be analysed in isolation from other aspects of society. Cotterrell laid out the philosophical grounds of studying the sociology of law, which is to give paramount importance and preference to the social environment surrounding the law, or the empirical data from the social phenomenon, as opposed to the doctrinal and institutional understanding of the law, or the normative.[79] In contrast, a completely normative or 'black letter' study of the law would focus purely on legal doctrines and disregard the social and political context of legal arguments.[80] The black letter or doctrinal study of the law draws from the philosophy of 'legal positivism' where laws are commands of human beings that are not dependent on morals and are analysed as prescriptive norms as opposed to descriptive facts.[81] In essence, legal positivism is the analysis of legal concepts and can be distinguished from sociological inquiries into the relation of law and other social phenomena.

In studying the relationship between law, rights and ethno-cultural minority movements, a legal positivistic approach would be indifferent to both the ethno-cultural identity of the minority group and the mobilisation which occurs both within and outside the realm of the courts. A doctrinal study would only take into account the aggrieved person's legal identity if relevant to the case and the litigant's standing in court, that is, *locus standi* if it is a public interest litigation on behalf of an aggrieved minority group. The ethno-cultural minority's grievances are only taken into consideration if they are relevant facts to the case and arguments must be based on legislative rules and judicial precedence. A legal positivist analysis of the minority group's litigation will only take into account the legal arguments as well as the judicial decision, and exclude an analysis of the mobilisation strategy of litigation itself. Hence, in an illiberal polity with a curtailed judiciary and restricted civil rights as well as laws on standing, a legal positivist study which centres on purely legal arguments and judicial decisions in the court, is likely to ignore the nuances of law and rights that may arise from minority mobilisation.

In contrast, the sociolegal approach places equal emphasis on the positive law as well as the social and political elements surrounding the law, which are as Vago writes, the 'sources of impetus for law'.[82] This approach provides a more suitable theoretical basis to examine the connection between the law and the social phenomenon of ethno-cultural minority mobilisation. However, very few sociolegal studies have adequately looked into the complex nexus between the law, ethno-cultural group identity, collective rights and mobilisation. Sociolegal scholars who have analysed the law and ethno-cultural minority groups or movements have generally veered into two academic directions. The first range of sociolegal studies views the law as an instrument of social change and investigates the constitutive role of the law and legal rights in constructing group identity. The second strand of sociolegal study investigates the relationship between the law and particular social phenomena, which in this case is the study of law and social movements. This second strand of study is more multidisciplinary in nature as it utilises both sociolegal and social movement theoretical frameworks (reviewed in Section 2.5). The study of law, rights and ethno-cultural movements requires an amalgamation of both these strands of sociolegal studies.

The first strand of sociolegal study that has looked into law as an instrument of social change has generally focussed on the sociolegal construction of identity of particular groups or classes of persons. This type of study is more frequently seen in the American-centric law and society scholarship (which is an epithet for sociolegal scholarship) that draws links between the law and the social or political construction of race. In fact, the study of law and racialisation is significant in the United States, which has since the 1960s become a site of contestation for several ethno-cultural or race-based movements such as the Black American Civil Rights Movement, the Chicano Movement and the Native American Movement. These studies are relevant to the case study of Indians in Malaysia, as race plays a dominant role in Malaysian laws, policies and socio-political landscape, as Chapter 1 has shown. Also, the mobilisation of ethnic minority Indians in 2007 draws on the critical links between law and racial/ethno-cultural identity.

The theoretical basis of the American law and society study of race stems from the 1970s utilisation of critical theory which is a social theory that critiques social order and the elites in society that control society through political ideology.[83] As European sociolegal scholars focussed on the Marxist analysis of class identity and labour divisions, American scholars used critical theory in order to critique the hegemonic role of the law in society. An academic movement of critical legal scholars established that the law is an instrument of ideological control by political elites and dominated by economic elites.[84] There were several deviations from the main movement of critical legal scholars, including those who emphasised the role of power, class and social structure. Gordon, for instance, iterates on the role of law as a repressive power:

> Histories of legal oppressions – of slavery, Indian Removal laws, Black Codes, labor injunctions – are indispensable reminders that there's often nothing subtle about the way the powerful deploy the legal system to keep themselves organized and their victims disorganized and scared.[85]

While Gordon's reminder of the terror of law in the hands of the powerful is placed rightfully in American history, it also disregards the utility of the law by grassroots movements that arose from the legal oppression, such as the American Civil Rights Movement. Furthermore, an off-shoot of the main critical legal studies movement was the critical race theorists who instead of focussing on the physical oppression of law, placed emphasis instead on law's ideological control of race.[86] Laura Gomez, a critical race theorist, expounded that '[r]ace does not exist outside of law; it is constituted by law'.[87] In elaborating on how critical race theorists placed the connection between law and race, it is necessary to analyse the ways in which the law constructs race: first, through legal rules and formalities which categorise racial identities and create racial classifications; second, through legislative measures and judicial decisions which reinforce existing political ideologies of race; and third, as a result of discrimination of particular racial groups and the inequalities of race.

*2.4.2.1 Law and the construction of race*

The first way in which the law constructs race is by imposing legal formalities that require the identification of a person's race or ethnicity. While the theoretical emphasis on legal formalities as a tool of racial categorisation comes from the critical race theorists, there are many cases from outside legal studies especially from the social science and political science studies that emphasise the social and political construction of race, ethnicity and identity. However, the role of the law is understated in these studies, which clearly point to the coercive nature of legal formalities such as census and registration forms which require legal compliance. The legal taxonomy of race in birth registration and census records define and constrain ethnocultural group identity in accordance with the state's political ideology and perception of the group. For example, the Australian Aborigines in the past had been divided through state-imposed legal categorisations in registration and census based on arbitrary linguistic and racial characteristics.[88] Similarly, the Native Americans in the United States and the indigenous people of Canada were historically given Euro-centric patronymic names during the registration of births in an attempt to assimilate the groups under state-approved 'legible identities'.[89]

Post-colonial studies have also drawn connections between the former colonial power's racial ideology and the construction of racial identity. In a study of colonial census records in British Malaya, the classification of 'ethnicity' according to the three main racial categories of Malay, Chinese and Indians was arbitrary and purposeful, as it reflected both the colonial ideology of race and the political economy of that time.[90] The British colonial administration introduced the census and registration formalities in order to both categorise and control the colony's constituents. However, Gorringe found that the British colonial government in India had crystallised existing caste-based cleavages into formal racial categorisations of Indians.[91] Dirk's study supports Gorringe's findings, but Dirk argues that the British colonials indirectly used the caste system by incorporating existing caste categories into institutionalised processes, such as the census as well as legal enactments and legal codes which distinguished groups according to caste.[92] Hence, not only was legal categorisation of groups done in accordance to colonial racial ideology, but at times the law reinforced prevailing social perceptions and existing divisions of identity.

The second way in which the law constructs race is through legal rules in the form of legislation and case-law. Judicial precedence in particular can construct, legitimate and reinforce political ideologies of race. Ian Haney-Lopez, a critical race theorist, discusses the 1923 United States Supreme Court decision of *United States v. Bhagat Singh Thind*.[93] In this case, an Indian-American Sikh man argued for naturalisation rights on the basis of anthropological evidence that Indians were from the 'Aryan race' and therefore should be classified as Caucasian or white.[94] The court's decision that the claimant Thind was not entitled to naturalisation or citizenship in 1920 was based on a 1790 statute which depicted an outdated racial ideology of 'white people' and found that the term 'white people' should be interpreted according to 'common knowledge'.[95] Haney-Lopez explains that race is, in fact, a social phenomenon, which is constructed within the legal sphere, where the law exerts institutional control and operates as a system of coercion in order to suppress and reinforce the formation of race.[96] For instance, repressive laws such as the United States' racial segregation laws of the past have explicitly reinforced the social divisions between the Black and White populace. Even reparative laws like affirmative action laws serve to fortify racial categories through legislative and judicial interpretations of social perceptions of race.[97] This line of reasoning is pertinent to this study, which analyses how race has been constructed in the Malaysian socio-political setting and how the law in the form of the *Federal Constitution*, socioeconomic policies and judicial reasoning have buttressed the socio-political construction of race. Chapter 4 discusses this point in detail.

The third way in which a link between law and racial identity is drawn is through the discriminatory and unequal treatment of specific ethno-cultural groups. Minority groups are particularly affected by discrimination and inequality, especially when these groups do not hold political or economic bargaining power. In liberal democratic settings like the United States, minorities who face the risk of being discriminated against are often protected by anti-discrimination and civil rights legislation. However, Freeman argues that American anti-discrimination laws are limited and narrow, as they merely legitimise prevalent elite conceptions and existing social structures, which reinforce racial identities.[98] In other words, the anti-discrimination laws end up constraining racial identity in order to fit the aggrieved minority person into legal definitions of race and be entitled to legal remedies. An example of this is seen in the anti-caste legislation in liberal democratic India, where Dalits (Outcastes) are legally identified and categorised under a list of Scheduled Castes. Although the legislation is meant to protect the Dalits from the discriminatory practice of untouchability, outlined in Chapter 1, and a special reservation policy was devised to remedy past discrimination, the laws have, in fact, reinforced caste identities and legalised caste divisions.[99] Smitha Narula, from a critical race perspective, iterates that the primary reason for the failure of anti-caste legislation in India is the law enforcement mechanism, which continued to enforce the caste ideology instead of the rule of law.[100] Hence, legal institutions and law enforcement bodies play a crucial role in constraining ethno-cultural identity into racial (or caste) categories and in reinforcing the social construction and political ideologies of race (or caste).

While critical race studies have laid out a useful theoretical basis to study the connection between law and race (or ethno-cultural identity), the studies are American-centric and revolve around the interpretation of the equality clause in the *U.S. Constitution* and other legislative measures within the

American liberal democratic political framework. While a few critical race scholars have explored non-American examples, such as the Dalits in India, the studies are narrow in their focus on protective anti-discriminatory laws and affirmative action or special reservation policy for the aggrieved minority groups. This study on Indian minorities in an illiberal Malaysia shows in Chapters 1 and 4 that racial inequality is legitimised by the constitution itself and socioeconomic as well as cultural policies, which are explicitly discriminatory. In other words, racial discrimination is legal, but minority groups are not under any protective laws nor are they entitled to special rights. In this setting, the mobilisation of law and rights by Indian movement activists and activist lawyers involves a complex nexus between law, rights claims and race or ethno-cultural identity in an illiberal political environment.

### 2.4.2.2 The demand for rights

While the discussion above explains how formal law in its institutional and structural form categorises and designates people into racial groups, it is also important to consider how social cognizance, self-perceptions and socio-political ideologies of ethno-cultural identity can constitute the demand for identity-based rights. In order to unscramble the linkage between race or ethno-cultural identity, rights and the law, it is necessary to first, analyse the 'dialectic process' and 'mutually constitutive' manner in which law constructs race and the way in which race constructs law.[101] In other words, the constitutive manner in which law and ethno-cultural identity mutually relate to each other can be explained through the instrument of rights.

The concept of rights itself has myriad meanings, but in the context of this study, rights has been defined according to the two main theoretical frameworks utilised: the sociolegal group-differentiated rights theory,[102] which explains the correlation between ethno-cultural identity and rights; and the politico-legal rights framework[103] that investigates the political utility of rights. In order to explain how rights factors into the ethno-cultural mobilisation of Indians in Malaysia, three types of rights are identified: first, 'legal rights', which are an actionable form of positive law sourced from legislation (including the constitution) and adjudication (case-law);[104] second, 'political rights', which act as 'political trumps' against the government for fundamental liberties;[105] and third, 'moral rights', which is an abstract category but generally refers to rights which are common to all humanity (human rights) and rights which pre-exist legal rights in an ethical or belief system.[106] While all three forms of rights are crucial to the theoretical framework of this study, and are discussed in more detail in Sections 2.5, the discussion in this section centres on 'legal rights' in order to show the relation between rights and ethno-cultural group identity.

Working within the sociolegal framework, Eric Mitnick's theory on group-differentiated rights makes a substantive connection between legal rights and group identity.[107] Mitnick points out that a constitutive theory of legal rights is useful in deciphering the relational, cultural and social aspect of rights, which connects atomised individuals and forms social groups.[108] Similar to the way legal categorisation occurs through legal formalities such as census codes and registration laws, legal rights contain specific conditions or circumstances which include and/or exclude particular persons. In the case of legal formalities on ethnicity or race, the specific condition is usually a set of cultural markers, for example the adherence to particular customs or traditions. Similarly, certain legal rights also contain an 'investitive criteria' which identifies the characteristics or circumstances of a potential rights-bearer.[109] When an individual rights-claimant succeeds in proving that he/she fits the investitive condition, the individual who qualifies as a rights-bearer becomes a member of a class of rights-bearers who are in identical circumstances. Hence, Mitnick calls such rights as producing 'spheres of membership',[110] where individual rights-bearers can identify and relate to each other by virtue of a common legal condition.

The theoretical framework of group-differentiated rights not only draws a connection between legal rights and the rights-bearer group but also specifies the equally if not more important formation of the non-rights-bearer group or individual rights claimants who were excluded from the ambit of the particular legal right. In comparison to the rights-bearer class, the non-rights-bearer group is said to form a stronger and more intense connection between individuals who were rejected from the ambit of the rights claimed. This is largely due to the deeper social implications and psychological effects on the individual after a claim for legal entitlement is refused by the courts or other administrative bodies. Mitnick explains that '[a] group consciousness has been stirred by the law, and this time, you tell yourself, there shall indeed be a roar.'[111] Although Mitnick concedes that the exclusion of legal rights may constitute collective action by aggrieved groups, he does not elaborate further on why or how this might occur. Hence there is a major gap in the theoretical framework which analyses the link between legal rights and group identity in that the further link to mobilisation is left unexplored.

### 2.4.2.3 Mobilisation is under-theorised

A number of sociolegal studies on ethno-cultural minority groups have attempted to incorporate the analysis of rights as a form of resistance. For instance, Kimberlé Crenshaw in a critical race study argued that the African American Civil Rights Movement's call for legal rights and racial equality was a 'pragmatic strategy' to counter racism, while the assertion of a 'Black collective identity' was a beneficial resource to the movement.[112] Crenshaw submits that although the law legitimised race and reinforced prevailing racial ideology, the repressive nature of the law had propelled the Blacks to collectivise as well as challenge law's legitimacy and ideological force through strategic litigation and rights-based advocacy.[113] This point is supported by Eskridge in his broader study of identity-based social movements and the law, that when law enforcement agencies use legal rules to reinforce existing social stigmas, the aggrieved minority group in turn can utilise the legal repression to collectivise and mobilise.[114] In fact, Eskridge emphasises that the law plays a critical role in the connection between collective identity and collective action, which stems from the way law distinguishes and segregates particular groups. This helps the stigmatised, the discriminated and the marginalised, to identify the law as the source of their grievances and to then challenge it.[115]

However, the legal repression that results from the mass mobilisation of racial or ethno-cultural groups also solidifies the identity of the group. Haney-Lopez uses frame theory as well as critical race theory in his analysis of the 1960s Chicano movement in the United States and draws a link between legal repression, protest and race.[116] Lopez writes that it was legal violence in the form of police brutality and judicial mistreatment (following the unfavourable decision against Chicano activists in the *East LA Thirteen case*)[117] that led to the racialisation of the Mexicans in the United States and sparked off the Chicano movement.[118] The combination of the police brutality experienced by Mexican activists during the East Los Angeles incident and the decision of the legal case substantially contributed to the self-perception of a Mexican group identity as the Chicano. What these studies show is that law as repression, either in its ideological form (in the courts) or in the form of legal enforcement (by legal actors such as the police and judiciary), has the capacity to construct collective identity and provide both resource as well as a site of contestation for aggrieved groups.

The sociolegal studies on identity-based movements or ethno-cultural movements reviewed above have dabbled with social movement theories in order to make a connection between the law and mobilisation. However, apart from the Haney-Lopez study, the others tend to be law-centric and do not provide a comprehensive theoretical framework that sufficiently incorporates insights from social movement theories and methodologies in order to show how ethno-cultural minority movements utilise the law and rights to mobilise. As discussed in Section 2.4.1, social movement studies have, to a large extent, moved away from resource mobilisation and political process approaches but have incorporated insights from them to study cultural framing processes (frame theory) and contentious politics. The resultant interdisciplinary approaches, which integrate frame theory and contentious politics to explore how the law matters in the mobilisation of aggrieved groups, offer relevant theoretical insights for this study.

## 2.5  Mobilising race and rights: the role of the law

As discussed in Section 2.4, social movement studies and sociolegal scholarship have both investigated the emergence and development of ethno-cultural minority movements. However, each type of scholarship has generally veered into different directions in terms of theoretical frameworks, methodologies of analysis and interpretation. There was very little, if any, exchange of ideas, theories and methodologies between the two fields of study. Hence, scholars who attempted to study both law and social movements faced a daunting task. Edward Rubin in reviewing both these scholarships stated,

> Social scientists and legal scholars are ... studying the very same movements ... But the two groups of scholars stand on either side of the courthouse, legislative, or agency door; while they see the same movement, they do not see each other.[119]

While Rubin's study captures the problem to a certain extent, he disregards the role of rights inside and outside the courthouse door, which includes the rights that exist in the subaltern spaces of mobilisation. However, recent law and social movement theorists have begun to identify the interconnections between these two divergent areas of study. For instance, Barclay, Jones and Marshall contend that while law and social movements seem to exist like 'two wheels spinning' and moving along their separate ways, they are, in fact, dynamic, interconnected elements, in continuous conversation with each other.[120] The spinning wheels of law and social movements reveal a paradoxical friction: social movements utilise the law to fight their causes against repressive elements, which are in turn maintained by official laws and legal institutions. Hence, the law is utilised as a tool of institutional repression by dominant groups, but aggrieved groups in turn use the law as a mobilising force against the legal repression. This premise gives an indication of the contemporary methodological directions taken primarily by social science, political science and sociolegal scholars, in determining the role of law in social movements and in theorising legal mobilisation.

Contemporary legal mobilisation theories can be grouped under two camps. The first camp includes theorists who use the structure-based approach and a causal methodology in ascertaining institutional 'legal opportunity structures' and litigation strategies of activists. The second camp of scholars utilise the process-based approach and a constitutive methodology in determining the cultural and political aspects of the law in collective mobilisation. The first camp of legal mobilisation scholars, exemplified by Chris Hilson's work, have amalgamated social movement theories such as resource mobilisation theory and political opportunity structures in order to determine the feasibility of litigation and legal claims by social movement organisations.[121] While this method integrates the analysis of direct action tactics like protest and political lobbying with legal strategy, it also pegs the law as a structural element of mobilisation. The theoretical framework is institutionally biased, as the role of the law is analysed in terms of the causal links between opportunities, resources and court-based action or litigation. For example, legal strategy or litigation is dependent on such variables as the laws on standing (*locus standi*, that is, the claimant's entitlement or status in bringing the case to court) and accessibility to state legal funds (e.g. legal aid to fund the litigation) as well as the conditional aspect of judicial receptivity to policy arguments.[122]

Legal opportunity structure has been utilised by scholars to analyse both new ideological movements such as the environmental movement in the United Kingdom,[123] and the anti-GMO (Genetically Modified Organisms) movement in Europe,[124] as well as new identity-based movements such as the gay rights movement in the United States,[125] and the disability movement in Canada.[126] The institutional basis of the theory has also been useful in investigating groups who mobilise for racial equality in European Union politics,[127] in examining the effect of access to the judiciary on social movement litigation in the constitutional court of Costa Rica,[128] and the study of 'cause-lawyering' (or activist lawyers) in the Court of Final Appeal in Hong Kong (which, as discussed in Section 2.2, is an independent constitutional court which upholds a liberal bill of rights).[129] Although a wide range of studies have utilised legal opportunity structures to examine mobilisation by aggrieved groups, few have done so on social movements that arise in illiberal polities or semi-authoritarian states and none have analysed ethno-cultural minority movements. These gaps in this literature reveal the limitations of an institutional or structural approach in examining cultural or constitutive links between ethno-cultural group identity (collective identity), the collective demand for both civil and cultural rights and mobilisation. Furthermore, the serious restrictions imposed on the laws of standing and the curtailment of the judiciary by an illiberal executive authority suggest that an institutional approach would fail to reveal the nuances of the law that are found in extralegal modes of mobilisation.

A few other studies such as Vanhala's have supplemented the legal opportunity structural framework with culture-oriented social movement theories such as cultural frame alignment processes (frame theory) and collective identity.[130] Others have incorporated cultural resources and movement alliances into the structural analysis.[131] Vanhala's study of the legal opportunities for the disability movement in Canada and the United Kingdom found that a shift in collective identity and grievances of disabled persons from a 'medical model' (where disability is framed as a physical impairment) to a 'civil rights model' or 'social model' (where disability is framed as a social disadvantage or discrimination) gave legitimacy to strategic litigation and raised rights consciousness among the disabled community.[132] Similarly, Andersen's study of gay rights litigation in the United States attempts to incorporate cultural elements into an analysis of the legal opportunity structure while emphasising that 'cultural symbols and discourses shape legal understandings just as legal discourses and symbols shape cultural understandings'.[133] However, mixing both cultural and legal elements in the study of legal opportunity structures has been heavily criticised as leading to an 'analytical eclecticism' whereby scholars are free to pick and choose from diverse cultural variables to integrate into opportunity structures.[134] As culture is a significant element in the mobilisation of ethno-cultural minority groups, like the Indian mobilisation in Malaysia, a study that is focussed exclusively on the institutional dimension of legal mobilisation would be inappropriate to analyse how cultural factors like ethno-cultural identities are implicated in the legal mobilisation of such groups. Furthermore, the legal mobilisation studies reviewed here are litigation-centric, and while they examine the political opportunity of strategic litigation, these studies do not attempt to look for the law in the political and social processes of mobilisation.

The second camp of legal mobilisation scholars have used a process-based theoretical framework, which decentres the institutional aspects of legal mobilisation, and places equal emphasis on the legal, political and cultural aspects of collective action. This extends the analysis into all spaces of contention, from the utility of strategic litigation in the courts to the direct action tactics and political lobbying which takes place outside the court's domain. These legal mobilisation scholars have also unscrambled conventional social movement and sociolegal theories, and have reconstructed an innovative theoretical framework which places emphasis on cultural meanings or the common or grassroots interpretations of law in mobilisation. Hence, these theorists decentred institutional or court-based interpretations of the formal or positive law and derive alternative or 'informal' cultural meanings of the law from the bottom-up. Scholars that have utilised the interpretive approach to study the law have branched into a wide spectrum of studies such as legal consciousness studies, which analyse the 'everyday' interpretations of the law,[135] rights consciousness studies which look at the cultural or common people's perspective on rights,[136] the study of the political utility of rights,[137] and legal mobilisation studies which look at how law matters in social movements.[138]

While sociolegal scholarship has made substantive inquiries on the law in social spaces (see Section 2.4.2) and social movement studies have investigated the role of politics in mobilisation (see Section 2.4.1), legal mobilisation scholars of the constitutive/interpretivist school amalgamated these approaches to make deeper inquiries on how the law matters in political spaces or sites of contention. In this approach, Marc Galanter defines the law as more 'a system of cultural and symbolic meanings' than 'a set of operative controls', it affecting society mainly through 'communication of symbols' such as 'threats, promises, models, persuasion, legitimacy, stigma, and so on.'[139] Legal mobilisation theorists like Michael McCann depart from the institutional or top-down definition of law, which focusses on the coercive power of the state to control and maintain order, and look for the law from the bottom-up. A bottom-up approach would likely reveal that the law exists also in the 'legal discourses, conventions and practices in constructive meaning', which not only include elite discourse and court-centric interpretations of formal law but also the social movement's legal discourse which thrives in the shadows.[140] This second camp of legal mobilisation scholars, the interpretivists, clearly take a more 'fluid, malleable, and constitutive' conception of the law, with less emphasis on law's coercive nature.[141]

This study adopts Galanter's definition of the law as the most relevant to study legal mobilisation of minority groups in an illiberal polity with repressive laws and limited legal opportunities for litigation or legal redress. The next section develops a theoretical framework that employs insights from the interpretivist legal mobilisation approach, in particular, drawing on the works of Michael McCann and Eric Mitnick as well as Ronald Dworkin's conception of rights. The framework also draws on David Snow and Robert Benford's framing theory and Liza Garcia-Bedolla's concept of a mobilising identity.

The constitutive methodology in law has already been introduced by sociolegal scholars[142] and has been utilised in recent sociolegal studies to show the nexus between law, rights and ethno-cultural or racial group identity (see Section 2.4.2). Mitnick, for instance, draws on the constitutive nature of the law and legal rights in constructing groups or classes of similarly situated individuals.[143] Other sociolegal scholars like Gomez and Haney-Lopez have drawn on the constitutive relationship between law and racial identity, as already discussed, in the Chicano mobilisation.[144] Hence, the utility of a constitutive methodology to investigate the role of the law in mobilisation fits the requirements of this study. In order to discern the symbolic and cultural aspect of the law, legal mobilisation theorists have utilised the constitutive methodology, as opposed to the causal methodology preferred by the first camp of legal opportunity structuralists. McCann criticises the causal approach as being too predictive, mechanical and determinate for a study of law and social interactions, and compares the causal method to,

> a bowling ball rolled down an alley [where] the impact is measured by how many pins succumb to the force of the ball; if many fall, the impact is great, but if all or most remain standing, the toss was causally insignificant and the bowling agent ineffective.[145]

In comparison, the constitutive method is more suited to study the dynamic, dialectical and generally unpredictable process of how the law matters in social movement actions, motives and reasons. McCann explains that the constitutive methodology is more inclined towards 'examining research subjects "up close and personal" within densely mapped holistic narratives ("thick descriptions") or analytical accounts of their familiar social settings and interrelationship'.[146] In that sense, the constitutive method looks for how the law relates to the dynamic process of social movement formation, how the law is understood or interpreted by movement activists and the inventive ways in which the law is utilised in political action.

As already noted, this methodology is suited to the study of the law in the mobilisation of minority groups in illiberal polities, where formal legal discourses, conventions and practices are dominated by the state and/or political elites. A constitutive approach would reveal the legal language and legal rhetoric of movement activists, which thrives in the shadows, and provides symbolic and cultural meanings for the minority group to mobilise. In fact, the constitutive perspective of the law is evident in the use of 'rights talk' by social movement activists and activist lawyers. The link between the law and rights in the context of mobilisation can be aptly described though Zeman's quote, that 'the law is ... mobilised when a desire or want is translated into a demand as an assertion of one's rights'.[147] This is affirmed in studies of international human rights law, which found that morally based human rights possesses both power and knowledge, especially in the discourse of human rights which stresses on freedom of the oppressed from domination.[148] While rights can become a bridge between law and mobilisation, the meaning of rights itself differs under the sociolegal, social movement and legal mobilisation perspectives.

Section 2.4.2 laid out that rights in this study refers to first, 'legal rights', which correlate to the construction of ethno-cultural identity, second, 'political rights', which act as trumps against the state, and third, 'moral rights', which mainly refer to human rights. The analysis of rights in the discussion to follow pertains to the political utility of rights by movement activists, or what is referred to here as political rights. The philosophical basis of political rights comes from Ronald Dworkin's theory on rights as trumps:

> Individual rights are political trumps held by individuals. Individuals have rights when, for some reason, a collective goal is not a sufficient justification for denying them what they wish, as individuals, to have or to do, or not a sufficient justification for imposing some loss or injury upon them.[149]

Dworkin's concept of political rights refers to the most fundamental of rights which individuals hold against the 'collective goal' imposed by the government or the state, for example, the 'right to equal concern and respect'.[150] Although the definition of rights specifically refers to individual rights, Dworkin makes a reference to the 'institution of rights' as a representation of the majority's undertaking to respect the 'dignity and equality' of minorities.[151] As such, the right to equality which protects minority groups must act as trumps against all other laws which represent the collective will of the majority and sustained by the executive authority. This premise provides individuals who belong to a minority group the political legitimacy to challenge laws that are not only repressive but are contrary to the right to equality. Using the principle of rights as political trumps, Dworkin explains that acts of civil disobedience, which oppose the law, can be 'morally justified'.[152] The positivist legal scholar's view rests on the assumption that an act of disobedience against the law must be regarded as an illegal act. Dworkin challenges the positivist view and argues that the act of disobedience or the demands of dissent must be treated as 'a man's social duty' to challenge the laws which contradict the moral principles that uphold the political right to equality.[153] Hence, Dworkin's philosophical basis for rights can be extended to support the utility of rights as a political tool – both in civil disobedience as well as political lobbying.

Mitnick's views on legal rights as creating 'spheres of membership' which include excluded groups or non-rights-bearing groups, is also useful to this study in drawing the links between legal rights and an Indian group identity. However, Mitnick's theory does not extend to the illiberal political realm, where fundamental legal rights are qualified by laws and policies that discriminate against minority groups. Dworkin's argument provides the theoretical bridge to connect legal rights to political rights, where an aggrieved minority group's demand for fundamental rights through collective action holds both political and moral legitimacy. In any case, rights contain a political dimension, namely that it possesses symbolic and cultural power that can potentially mobilise the aggrieved group. Stuart Scheingold recognises this latent power, which he termed the 'myth of rights' that not only raises consciousness among activists and movement constituents but also helps aggrieved groups to conceive of and converge their grievances, as well as utilise rights as a political strategy to bring about social change.[154] In essence, the political utility of rights encompasses three types of cultural or symbolic powers: first, the ability to trigger identity consciousness; second, the capacity to bring together individuals who are similarly situated into a united aggrieved group; and third, the power of rights discourse to legitimise collective action both inside and outside the court domain. Furthermore, legal rights can become a site for political resistance and a medium where collectives mediate by decentralising authority and levelling the playing field.[155]

The constitutive legal mobilisation approach can be applied to this study in order to argue that the exclusion of the Indian minority from specific rights, the qualification in Malaysia of equality and the associated legal discrimination led to the development of a consciousness of an Indian identity and brought together aggrieved Indians who were similarly situated. In order to demand for remedies to these grievances, Indian activists utilised legal rights as a site of contention (elaborated in Chapters 3–5). In short, rights has potential constitutive power to construct collective identity and consolidate grievances, and possesses symbolic power, which can mobilise collective action and create opportunities for resistance.

In order to answer the main research question which centres on how the law and rights matter in the Indian mobilisation in an illiberal democratic Malaysia, McCann's constitutive approach to legal mobilisation is suitable in order to examine the cultural and symbolic nuances of the law and rights which thrive in the extralegal spaces of contention – especially in civil disobedience and political lobbying – which lies outside the executive controlled jurisdiction of the courts in Malaysia. In illiberal Malaysia, the independence of the judiciary is curtailed, while the laws on standing are restrictive and the legislature is dominated by the ruling party.

While McCann's constitutive methodology fits well in studying legal mobilisation that occurs in illiberal polities, the theory does not extend to examine elements that are significant to ethno-cultural minority movements, namely collective identity and rights. This is pertinent in answering the first and second research questions which centres on how an ethno-cultural minority group that is diverse and heterogeneous coalesced into an ethno-cultural movement under oppressive and discriminatory conditions. Section 2.4.1 clearly shows that contemporary social movement theorists who theorise on collective identity and cultural frame processes or frame theory have made sufficient linkages between collective identity, rights framing and mobilisation. This framework is useful in examining the utility of the Indian racial identity and rights in mobilising Indians in 2007 by showing that the use of rights frames and identity frames by Indian activists was useful in making sense of grievances and motivating the group to mobilise. However, the linkage between different frames, as well as the role of the law and rights, is missing. This is where the constitutive methodology of sociolegal theorists discussed in Section 2.4.2 can help. These studies have drawn the link between ethno-cultural group identity and the law, specifying the ways in which law constructs racial categories, reinforces racial ideologies and discriminates against racial minorities. This approach becomes pertinent to examining the way in which the Indians were racialised and how racial identity was constructed by the law in Malaysia. Chapters 3 and 4 in particular use the critical race theory/sociolegal framework in order to investigate the role of colonial law and post-colonial laws in creating racial divisions and constructing an Indian racial identity. Chapter 3 focusses on the colonial construction of race utilising the census, labour codes and labour policy. Chapter 4 begins by looking at the pre-independence constitutional bargaining and the subsequent use of census codes and registration laws in post-colonial Malaysia to reinforce the political construction of race. These two chapters demonstrate how the law in its constitutive form constructs ethnic (or racial) identities.

Nevertheless, social movement studies on framing and collective identity (which links rights and identity to mobilisation but separately) and sociolegal scholarship on law and race (which disregards rights) fail to link rights to identity. Mitnick's theory on group-differentiated rights is helpful in this regard, as it can draw the dialectic link between legal rights and social group identity. The most pertinent part of Mitnick's theory to this study is the power of legal rights to exclude individuals from particular rights, creating a non-rights-bearer class. The differentiation or discrimination that results from the conditions imposed by the legal right leads to the coalescence of similarly situated individuals and the creation of a cognitive social identity. Mitnick's theory is helpful in examining the discriminatory effect of majority Malay special rights, the qualified nature of the equality provision of the *Federal Constitution* and the creation of a rights-bearing *Bumiputera* group in policy (soft law) on the Indians in Malaysia (see Chapter 4).

However, there is a gap in Mitnick's theory, which fails to link group identity and rights to mobilisation. In order to make sense of how law matters in ethno-cultural minority *mobilisation*, the three significant elements of law, rights and identity must connect to the mobilisation. There has been no theoretical attempt thus far to analyse this complex nexus. However, this study offers a means to do so by combining Garcia-Bedolla's concept of mobilising identity and Mitnick's concept of cognitive social identity to fuse the links between rights and mobilisation. In doing so, the study differentiates between three forms of group identity: (a) 'legal identity' constructed by legal formalities and legal categories sourced from legal rules, that is, the constitution, legislation, case-law, affirmative action policy and census records; (b) external 'social identity', which is an outsider's social perception or stigmatisation of a group, and internal 'social identity', which is self-constituted in reference to the group's grievances, which may have arisen from legal repression or discriminatory practices; and (c) 'mobilising identity', which is formulated by activists and political leaders in order to both coalesce the group and utilise rights-based claims.

Identity in the above three forms can be used by the group to understand its grievances or circumstances. The process of utilising identity to make sense of grievances is what Snow and Benford call the 'framing process'.[156] These different uses of group identity, or 'identity frames', operate as multiple frames alongside the 'rights frame'. Mitnick has specified the notion of 'legal rights', elaborated in Section 2.4.2, which pertains to rights which arise from legal instruments, but the notion of rights outside the law is problematic. In order to answer the third research question, on how the law matters in the mobilisation of activists and movement leaders who attempt to make rights-based claims on behalf of aggrieved minority groups in illiberal polities, there is a need to integrate theoretically the role of rights. The use of rights by Indian activists and activist lawyers in Malaysia seems misplaced in an illiberal democratic framework where the meaning of legal rights is controlled by the executive authority, and the judiciary is not receptive to rights-based claims especially those pertaining to minorities. In order to address this anomaly or paradox, the study uses Ronald Dworkin's theory of rights which introduces the concept of a 'political right' that operates as a trump on the government. As explained in Section 2.5, the right to equality is the most fundamental of rights, which gives political legitimacy to minorities to disobey laws that contradict the principle of equality.

Not only is the notion of political rights a legitimating tool, but it can also act as a strategic tool in contentious politics and in mobilisation. The discussion on the political utility of rights is crucial as shown in Chapter 5, which discusses the 2007 mobilisation of Indians against discriminatory laws and policies. The use of legal rights, for instance the constitutional right to equality in direct action tactics, is explained as the political utility of rights in mobilisation. McCann's theory on the symbolic and cultural meaning of the law becomes crucial in analysing how legal rights have been interpreted by movement activists and framed as a mobilising tool. Furthermore, the use of human rights principles by Indian activists can be analysed as the political tool of 'moral rights', which ties in with Dworkin's conception of rights as providing moral legitimacy to civil disobedience claims for equal respect and concern. Hence, the amalgamation of sociolegal scholarship and social movement studies provides a more comprehensive theoretical framework to make sense of the fluid and mutual relationship between rights, group identity and mobilisation.

## 2.6 Conclusion

The review of theories in this chapter shows that the study of ethno-cultural movements requires the investigation of relational links between ethno-cultural identity, rights, the law and mobilisation. Drawing on key insights from the theoretical approaches and key scholars' works, outlined in Table 2.1, this chapter proposes an analytical framework that addresses the intricate connections between these variables – identity, rights and mobilisation on the one hand and law on the other. The following empirical chapters use this framework to examine the case of Indian mobilisation in Malaysia. Chapter 3 will analyse the colonial period from the 1890s to 1956, while Chapter 4's inquiry focusses on the post-colonial period, between 1957 and 1989. Chapter 5 examines the phase between 1990 and 2018, which includes the 2007 Indian mobilisation. The division of the analytical discussion into time periods is useful to show the historical culmination of grievances which relates to the construction of identity. The discussions in the following chapters reveals Indian mobilisation as a dynamic process of identity and grievance construction, later progressing to rights formation and shows how, and the extent to which, the law mattered in the mobilisation process.

*Table 2.1* Key Elements of the Theoretical Framework Used in This Study

| Theorist | Theory | Purpose |
| --- | --- | --- |
| Michael McCann | Legal Mobilisation Theory | Overarching approach to study law as *constitutive*, identity and grievance as found outside institutional spaces like the courts. Study mobilisation as a *process*. |
| Eric Mitnick | Group-Differentiated Rights Theory | Links legal rights and its denial to create group identity and grievance as *non-rights bearer group*. |
| Robert Benford and David Snow | Framing Processes | *Framing grievance* as a right or as a strategic resource to identify collective grievances. |
| Liza Garcia-Bedolla | Mobilising Identity | *Mobilising identity* to link rights (and its denial) to mobilisation. |
| Ronald Dworkin | Rights as Political Trumps | How rights can be used as a legitimising and *mobilisation* tool by activists. Thus links identity, grievances and mobilisation. |

# Notes

1 See Introduction.
2 See Chapter 5 for the analysis of legal mobilisation of Indians from 1990 to 2018.
3 Kiyoteru Tsutsui, 'Global Civil Society and Ethnic Social Movements in the Contemporary World' (2004) 19(1) *Sociological Forum* 63, 67.
4 Patricia Goedde, 'Legal Mobilization for Human Rights Protection in North Korea: Furthering Discourse or Discord?' (2010) 32(3) *Human Rights Quarterly* 530, 570.
5 Mark Fathi Massoud, 'Do Victims of War Need International Law? Human Rights Education Programs in Sudan' (2011) 45(1) *Law and Society Review* 1, 23.
6 Goedde, above n 4, 570–571; Massoud, above n 5, 28.
7 Waikeung Tam, 'Political Transition and the Rise of Cause Lawyering: the Case of Hong Kong' (2010) 35(3) *Law and Social Inquiry* 663. See also Waikeung Tam, *Legal Mobilization Under Authoritarianism: The Case of Post-Colonial Hong Kong* (Cambridge University Press, 2013).
8 Tam (2010), above n 7, 664.
9 Fareed Zakaria, 'The Rise of the Illiberal Democracy' (1997) 76 *Foreign Affairs* 22, 29.
10 Andrew Harding and Amanda Whiting, 'Custodians of Civil Liberties and Justice in Malaysia: The Malaysian Bar and the Moderate State' in Terence C Halliday et al (eds), *Fates of Political Liberalism in the British Post-Colony: The Politics of the Legal Complex* (Cambridge University Press, 2012) 247, 261.
11 Ibid., 283–288.
12 See <www.lawyersforliberty.org/> and <www.perlembagaanku.com/>.
13 Lynette J Chua, 'Pragmatic Resistance, Law, and Social Movements in Authoritarian States: The Case of Gay Collective Action in Singapore' (2012) 46(4) *Law and Society Review* 713, 714; See also Lynette J Chua, *How Does Law Matter to Social Movements? A Case Study of Gay Activism in Singapore* (PhD Thesis, University of California, Berkeley, 2011). *ProQuest Dissertations and Theses*, retrieved from http://search.proquest.com/docview/892712857?accountid=12528
14 See James C Scott, *Weapons of the Weak: Everyday Forms of Resistance* (Yale University Press, 1985); James C Scott, *Domination and the Arts of Resistance: Hidden Transcripts* (Yale University Press, 1990).
15 Siegfried Wiessner, 'Rights and Status of Indigenous Peoples: A Global Comparative and International Legal Analysis' (1999) 12 *Harvard Human Rights Journal* 57, 89.
16 Hayami Yoko, 'Negotiating Ethnic Representation Between Self and Other: The Case of Karen and Eco-tourism in Thailand' (2006) 44(3) *Southeast Asian Studies* 385, 407.
17 Jacques Bertrand, '"Indigenous Peoples' Rights" as a Strategy of Ethnic Accommodation: Contrasting Experiences of Cordillerans and Papuans in the Philippines and Indonesia' (2011) 34(5) *Ethnic and Racial Studies* 850, 852–853.
18 Hayami Yoko, 'Introduction: Notes Towards Debating Multiculturalism in Thailand and Beyond' (2006) 44(3) *Southeast Asian Studies* 283, 289.
19 For details see the American Indian Treaties Portal, Oklahoma State University's Library *Indian Affairs: Laws and Treaties* <http://treatiesportal.unl.edu/>.
20 Susan S Gooding, 'Place, Race and Names: Layered Identities in the United States v. Oregon, Confederated Tribes of the Colville Reservation, Plaintiff-Intervenor' (1994) 28(5) *Law and Society Review* 1181, 1187.
21 Roger Chapman (ed), *Culture Wars: An Encyclopaedia of Issues, Viewpoints and Voices* (M.E. Sharpe Inc., 2010) 22–24.

22  Michael R Anderson, 'Law and the Protection of Cultural Communities: the Case of Native American Fishing Rights' (1987) 9 *Law and Policy* 125, 129.

23  D. Oregon No. 68–513 (1969).

24  124 S. Ct. 1628 (2004).

25  Kevin K Washburn, '*Lara, Lawrence*, Supreme Court Litigation and Lessons from Social Movements' (2004–2005) 40 *Tulsa Law Review* 25, 29–30.

26  Ibid, 31. See Section 2.4.1 for further explanation of contentious politics.

27  Martha-Marie Kleinhans, 'Plural Corporate Persons: Displacing Subjects and (Re)forming Identities' (2006) 57 *Northern Ireland Legal Quarterly* 634, 640.

28  Ibid., 647.

29  Verity Burgmann, *Power, Profit and Protest: Australian Social Movements and Globalization* (Allen & Unwin, 2003) 50.

30  See *Milirrpum v. Nabalco* (1970) 17 F.L.R. 141.

31  See *Mabo & another v. The State of Queensland & another* [1988] HCA 69; (1989) 166 CLR 186.

32  Colin Nicholas, *The Orang Asli and the Contest for Resources: Indigenous Politics, Development and Identity in Peninsular Malaysia* (Copenhagen: International Work Group for Indigenous Affairs, 2000) 188.

33  *Sagong Tasi v. Negeri Kerajaan Selangor (Selangor State Government)* (2002) 2 CLJ 543.

34  Cheah Wui Ling, 'Sagong Tasi and Orang Asli Land Rights in Malaysia: Victory, Milestone or False Start?' (2004) 2 *Law, Social Justice and Global Development* <www2.warwick.ac.uk/fac/soc/law/elj/lgd/2004_2> on 30 January 2014.

35  See generally Cheah (2004), above n 34; Garth Nettheim, 'Malaysia's *Mabo* Case' (2000) 4(28) *Indigenous Law Bulletin* 20.

36  See Alice Nah, 'Negotiating Indigenous Identity in Postcolonial Malaysia: Beyond Being "Not Quite/Not Malay"' (2003) 9(4) *Social Identities* 529; Nicholas, above n 32.

37  Robert S Aiken and Colin H Leigh, 'Seeking Redress in the Courts: Indigenous Land Rights and Judicial Decisions in Malaysia' (2011) 45(4) *Modern Asian Studies* 825, 842.

38  Susan Olzak, 'Chapter 28: Ethnic and Nationalist Social Movements' in David A Snow et al (eds), *The Blackwell Companion to Social Movements* (Blackwell Reference Ónline, 2003).

39  See Hadley Cantril, *The Psychology of Social Movements* (Wiley, 1941); Ghanshyam Shah (ed), *Social Movements and the State* (Sage Publications, 2002) 24.

40  Nick Crossley, *Making Sense of Social Movements* (Open University Press, 2002) 11.

41  Graeme Chester and Ian Welsh, *Social Movements: The Key Concepts* (Routledge, 2010) 2.

42  See John D McCarthy and Mayer N Zald, 'Resource Mobilization and Social Movements: A Partial Theory' (1977) 82 *The American Journal of Sociology* 1212.

43  Craig Jenkins and Charles Perrow, 'Insurgency of the Powerless: Farm Worker Movements (1946–1972)' (1977) *American Sociological Review* 249, 266.

44  Chester and Welsh, above n 41, 8.

45  Steven M Buechler, 'New Social Movement Theories' (1995) 36(3) *The Sociological Quarterly* 441.

46  Bert Klandermans, 'New Social Movements and Resource Mobilization: The European and The American Approach' (1986) *International Journal of Mass Emergencies and Disasters* 13.

47  See Crossley, above n 40, 11.

48  Chester and Welsh, above n 41, 16; Buechler, above n 45, 449.

49  Alain Touraine, 'The Importance of Social Movement Studies' (2002) 1 *Social Movement Studies* 89, 93.

50 Alberto Melucci, 'Chapter Three: The Process of Collective Identity' in Hank Johnston and Bert Klandermans (eds), *Social Movements and Culture* (University of Minnesota Press, 1995) 41–43.

51 Doug McAdam, *Political Process and the Development of Black Insurgency, 1930–1970* (University of Chicago Press, 1982) 29.

52 Ibid., 40.

53 David S Meyer, 'Protest and Political Opportunity' (2004) *Annual Review of Sociology* 125, 127–128; See also David D Meyer and Debra C Minkoff, 'Conceptualizing Political Opportunity' (2004) *Social Forces* 1457.

54 Anthony Oberschall, *Social Conflict and Social Movements* (Prentice-Hall, 1973) 119.

55 McAdam, above n 51, 43.

56 Ibid., 194, 247.

57 John Gaventa, *Power and Powerlessness: Quiescence and Rebellion in an Appalachian Valley* (Urbana: University of Illinois Press, 1980) 77–78, 189, 216.

58 Dennis Chong, *Collective Action and the Civil Rights Movement* (University of Chicago Press, 1991). Chong distinguishes between two game theories – the prisoner's dilemma model and the assurance theory, which are beyond the scope of this thesis.

59 Ibid., 141.

60 Doug McAdam, Sidney Tarrow and Charles Tilly, *Dynamics of Contention* (Cambridge University Press, 2001).

61 Doug McAdam et al, 'Dynamics of Contention' (2003) 2(1) *Social Movement Studies: Journal of Social, Cultural and Political Protest* 99, 100.

62 Sidney Tarrow, *Power in Movement: Social Movements and Contentious Politics* (Cambridge University Press, 1998) 31.

63 Ibid., 117.

64 Robert Benford and David Snow, 'Framing Processes and Social Movements' (2000) 26 *Annual Review of Sociology* 611, 629.

65 Ibid., 614; See also David Snow et al, 'Frame Alignment Processes, Micromobilization and Movement Participation' (1986) 51 *American Sociological Review* 464; David A Snow and Robert D Benford, 'Ideology, Frame Resonance and Participant Mobilization' (1988) 1 *International Social Movement Research* 197; Erving Goffman, *Frame Analysis: An Essay on the Organization of Experience* (Northeastern University Press, 1974).

66 Bert Klandermans, *The Social Psychology of Protest* (Wiley-Blackwell, 1997) 44.

67 Benford and Snow (2000), above n 64, 615–617.

68 Stephen M Valocchi, 'The Emergence of the Integrationist Ideology in the Civil Rights Movement' (1996) 43 *Social Problems* 116, 117.

69 Ibid., 120; Tarrow (1998), above n 62, 129.

70 Antonette Jefferson, 'The Rhetoric of Revolution: the Black Consciousness Movement and the Dalit Panther Movement' (2008) 2(5) *Journal of Pan African Studies* 46, 50.

71 Nancy Whittier, 'Political Generations, Micro-Cohorts, and the Transformation of Social Movements' (1997) 62 *American Sociological Review* 760.

72 Fransesca Polleta and James M Jasper, 'Collective Identity and Social Movements' (2001) 27 *Annual Review of Sociology* 283, 285.

73 Ibid., 284.

74 Peter Vermeersch, 'Ethnic Minority Identity and Movement Politics: The Case of the Roma in Czech Republic and Slovakia' (2003) 26(5) *Ethnic and Racial Studies* 879, 885.

75 Ibid., 899.

76 Garcia-Bedolla quoted in David S Meyer and Lindsey Lupo, 'Assessing the Politics of Protest' in Bert Klandermans and Connie Roggeband (eds), *Handbook of Social Movements Across Disciplines* (Springer, 2010) 114, 127.

77  Ibid., 128. See also Liza Garcia-Bedolla, *Fluid Borders: Latino Power, Identity, and Politics in Los Angeles* (University of California Press, 2005) 6.
78  Polleta and Jasper, above n 72, 289.
79  See Roger Cotterrell, *The Sociology of Law* (London: Oxford, 1992); Roger Cotterrell, *The Politics of Jurisprudence: A Critical Introduction to Legal Philosophy* (University of Pennsylvania Press, 1989).
80  Reza Banakar, 'Law Through Sociology's Looking Glass: Conflict and Competition in Sociological Studies of Law' in Ann Denis et al (eds), *The New ISA Handbook in Contemporary International Sociology: Conflict, Competition and Cooperation* (Sage, 2009) 58–73, 61.
81  H L A Hart, 'Positivism and the Separation of Law and Morals' (1957) 71 *Harvard Law Review* 593, 601–602.
82  Steven Vago, *Law and Society* (Pearson Prentice Hall, 2009) 184.
83  Edward L Rubin, 'Passing Through the Door: Social Movement Literature and Legal Scholarship' (2001–2002) 150 *University of Pennsylvania Law Review* 1, 18.
84  See Roberto M Unger, *The Critical Legal Studies Movement* (Harvard University Press, 1983).
85  Robert W Gordon, 'Critical Legal Histories' (1984) 36 *Stanford Law Review* 57, 75.
86  See especially Patricia J Williams, *The Alchemy of Race and Rights* (Harvard University Press, 1991).
87  Laura E Gomez, 'A Tale of Two-Genres: On the Real and Ideal Links Between the Law and Society and Critical Race Theory' in Austin Sarat (ed), *The Blackwell Companion to Law and Society* (Blackwell, 2006) 453.
88  Burgmann, above n 29, 49.
89  James C Scott, John Tehranian and Jeremy Mathias, 'The Production of Legal Identities Proper to States: The Case of the Permanent Family Surname' (2002) 44 *Comparative Studies in Society and History* 4, 18.
90  Charles Hirschman, 'The Meaning and Measurement of Ethnicity in Malaysia: An Analysis of Census Classifications' (1987) 46(3) *The Journal of Asian Studies* 555, 557. See Chapter 3 on the colonial construction of an Indian race in British Malaya.
91  Hugo Gorringe, 'The Embodiment of Caste: Oppression, Protest and Change' (2007) 41 *Sociology* 97, 110.
92  See Nicholas B Dirks, 'The Invention of Caste: Civil Society in Colonial India' (1988) *Comparative Study of Social Transformations* (CSST) Working paper #11, University of Michigan; Nicholas B Dirks, 'The Invention of Caste', (1989) 25 *Social Analysis* 45.
93  261 U.S. 204 (1923).
94  Ian F Haney-Lopez, *White by Law: The Legal Construction of Race* (New York University Press, 1996) 61, 88.
95  Ibid., 61.
96  Ibid., 78.
97  George A Martinez, 'The Legal Construction of Race: Mexican-Americans and Whiteness' (1997) 2 *Harvard Latino Law Review* 321, 325.
98  Alan Freeman, 'Legitimizing Racial Discrimination Through Antidiscrimination Law: A Critical Review of Supreme Court Doctrine' (1978) 62 *Minnesota Law Review* 1049, 1051.
99  See John G Sommer, *Empowering the Oppressed: Grassroots Advocacy Movements in India* (New Delhi: Sage, 2001).
100 Smitha Narula, 'Equality by Law, Unequal by Caste: the "Untouchable" Condition in Critical Race Perspective' (2008) 26 *Wisconsin International Law Journal* 255, 257.
101 Laura E Gomez, 'Understanding Law and Race as Mutually Constitutive: An Invitation to Explore an Emerging Field' (2010) 6 *Annual Review of Law and Social Science* 487.

102 See Eric J Mitnick, *Rights, Groups, and Self-Invention: Group Differentiated Rights in Liberal Theory* (Ashgate, 2006).

103 See Ronald Dworkin, *Taking Rights Seriously* (Harvard University Press, 1977); Stuart A Scheingold, *The Politics of Rights: Lawyers, Public Policy and Political Change* (University of Michigan Press, 2004).

104 Eric J Mitnick, 'Taking Rights Spherically: Formal and Collective Aspects of Legal Rights' (1999) 34 *Wake Forest Law Review* 409, 414.

105 See Dworkin (1977), above n 103.

106 Mitnick (1999), above n 104, 416; Dworkin (1977), above n 103, 235.

107 See Mitnick (2006), above n 102.

108 Eric J Mitnick, 'Constitutive Rights' (2000) 20(2) *Oxford Journal of Legal Studies* 185, 186–188.

109 Ibid., 189.

110 Mitnick (1999), above n 104, 426.

111 Mitnick (2000), above 108, 192–193.

112 Kimberlé Crenshaw, 'Race, Reform and Retrenchment: Transformation and Legitimation in Antidiscrimination Law' (1987) 101 *Harvard Law Review* 1331, 1335–1336.

113 Ibid., 1385.

114 William N Eskridge, 'Channeling: Identity-Based Social Movements and Public Law' (2001) 150 *University of Pennsylvania Law Review* 419, 422.

115 Ibid., 433–436.

116 See Ian F Haney-Lopez, 'Protest, Repression and Race: Legal Violence and the Chicano Movement' (2001–2002) 150 *University of Pennsylvania Law Review* 205. See generally Ian F Haney-Lopez, *Racism on Trial: The Chicano Fight for Justice* (London: Belknap, 2004). See also Edward J Escobar, 'The Dialectics of Repression: The Los Angeles Police Department and the Chicano Movement, 1968–1971' (1993) 79 *Journal of American History* 1483.

117 *People v. Castro*, No. A-2322902 (Cal. Super. Ct. 1968).

118 Haney-Lopez (2001), above n 116, 207.

119 Rubin, above n 83, 51.

120 Scott Barclay, Lynn C Jones and Anna-Maria Marshall, 'Two Spinning Wheels: Studying Law and Social Movements' in Austin Sarat (ed), *Special Issue: Social Movements/Legal Possibilities (Studies in Law, Politics and Society, Volume 54)* (Emerald Group Publishing, 2011) 1.

121 Chris Hilson, 'New Social Movements: The Role of Legal Opportunity' (2002) 9(2) *Journal of European Public Policy* 238, 240; See also Ellen A Andersen, *Out of the Closets and into the Courts: Legal Opportunity Structure and Gay Rights Litigation* (University of Michigan Press, 2005); Lisa Vanhala, 'Legal Opportunity Structures and the Paradox of Legal Mobilization by the Environmental Movement in the UK' (2012) 46(3) *Law and Society Review* 523.

122 Hilson, above n 121, 243.

123 See Hilson, above n 121; Vanhala (2012), above n 121.

124 See Brian Doherty and Graeme Hayes, 'Having Your Day in Court: Judicial Opportunity and Tactical Choice in Anti-GMO Campaigns in France and the United Kingdom' (2014) 47 *Comparative Political Studies* 3, published Online-First 18 April 2012.

125 See Andersen (2005), above n 121.

126 See Lisa Vanhala, 'Disability Rights Activists in the Supreme Court of Canada: Legal Mobilization Theory and Accommodating Social Movements' (2009) 42(4) *Canadian Journal of Political Science* 981.

127 See Rhonda E Case and Terri E Givens, 'Re-engineering Legal Opportunity Structures in the European Union? The Starting Line Group and the Politics of Racial Equality Directive' (2010) 48 *Journal of Common Market Studies* 221.

128 See Bruce M Wilson and Juan C R Cardero 'Legal Opportunity Structures and Social Movements: The Effects of Institutional Change on Costa Rican Politics' (2006) 39(3) *Comparative Political Studies* 325.
129 See Tam (2010), above n 7.
130 See Vanhala (2009), above n 126; Lisa Vanhala, *Making Rights a Reality? Disability Rights Activists and Legal Mobilization* (Cambridge University Press, 2011).
131 Andersen (2005), above n 121, 7–9.
132 Vanhala (2011), above n 130, 50, 203.
133 Ibid., 13–14.
134 Ibid., 18–20.
135 See Susan S Silbey, 'After Legal Consciousness' (2005) 1 *Annual Review of Law and Social Science* 323; David M Engel and Frank W Munger, *Rights of Inclusion: Law and Identity in the Life Stories of Americans with Disabilities* (University of Chicago Press, 2003); Patrick Ewick and Susan S Silbey, *The Common Place of Law: Stories from Everyday Life* (University of Chicago Press, 1998); Alan Hunt, 'Law, Community and Everyday Life: Yngvesson's Virtuous Citizens and Disruptive Subjects' (1996) 21 *Law & Social Inquiry* 173; Austin Sarat and Thomas R Kearns (eds), *Law in Everyday Life* (University of Michigan Press, 1993).
136 See Anna Kirkland, 'Think of the Hippopotamus: Rights Consciousness in the Fat Acceptance Movement' (2008) 42(2) *Law and Society Review* 397; Williams, above n 86; John Brigham, 'Right, Rage, and Remedy: Forms of Law in Political Discourse' (1987) *Studies in American Political Development* 303.
137 See Jonathan Goldberg-Hiller and Neal Milner, 'Rights as Excess: Understanding the Politics of Special Rights' (2003) 28 *Law and Social Inquiry* 1076; Neal Milner and Jonathan Goldberg-Hiller, 'Reimagining Rights: Tunnel, Nations, Spaces' 27 *Law and Social Inquiry* 339; Jonathan Goldberg-Hiller, '"Entitled to be Hostile": Narrating The Political Economy of Civil Rights' (1998) 7 *Social and Legal Studies* 517; Charles R Epp, *The Rights Revolution: Lawyers, Activists, and Supreme Courts in Comparative Perspective* (University of Chicago Press,1998); Scheingold, above n 103.
138 See especially Michael W McCann (ed), *Law and Social Movements* (Ashgate Publishing, 2006a); Austin Sarat (ed), *Special Issue: Social Movements/Legal Possibilities (Studies in Law, Politics and Society, Volume 54)* (Emerald Group Publishing, 2011). See also Michael W McCann, 'Litigation and Legal Mobilization' in Keith E Whittington, et al (eds), *The Oxford Handbook of Law and Politics* (Oxford University Press, 2008); Michael W McCann, 'Law and Social Movements' in Austin Sarat (ed), *The Blackwell Companion to Law and Society* (Blackwell publishers, 2004) 506; Helena Silverstein, *Unleashing Rights: Law, Meaning and the Animal Rights Movement* (University of Michigan Press, 1996); Michael W McCann, *Rights at Work: Pay Equity Reform and the Politics of Legal Mobilization* (University of Chicago, 1994).
139 Galanter quoted in McCann (2004), above n 138, 507.
140 McCann (2006a), above n 138, xii.
141 Lauren B Edelman, Gwendolyn Leachman and Doug McAdam, 'On Law, Organizations and Social Movements' (2010) 6 *Annual Review of Law and Social Science* 653, 654.
142 See Alan Hunt, *Explorations in Law and Society: Towards a Constitutive Theory of Law* (Routledge, 1993); Marc Galanter, 'Why the "Haves" Comes Out Ahead: Speculations on the Limits of Legal Change' (1974) 9(1) *Law and Society Review* 165.
143 See Mitnick (2000), above n 108.

144 See L Gomez (2010), above n 101; Haney-Lopez (1996), above n 94.
145 Michael W McCann, 'Causal versus Constitutive Explanations (or, On the Difficulty of Being so Positive ...) (1996) 21(2) *Law and Social Inquiry* 457, 459; See also Gerald N Rosenberg, 'Positivism, Interpretivism, and the Study of Law' (1996) 21(2) *Law and Social Inquiry* 435.
146 McCann (1996), above n 145, 463.
147 Frances K Zemans, 'Legal Mobilization: The Neglected Role of the Law in the Political System' (1983) 77(3) *The American Political Science Review* 690, 700.
148 Tony Evans, 'International Human Rights Law as Power/Knowledge' (2005) 27 *Human Rights Quarterly* 1046, 1065.
149 Dworkin (1977), above n 103, 6.
150 Ibid., 7.
151 Ibid., 246.
152 Ibid., 249.
153 Ibid., 258–259.
154 Scheingold, above n 103; See also Epp, above n 137.
155 Jonathan Goldberg-Hiller, 'The Boycott of the Law and the Law of the Boycott: Law, Labour, and Politics in British Columbia' (1996) 21 *Law and Social Inquiry* 313, 343.
156 See Benford and Snow (2000), above n 64.

# 3 Race

## Indian identity, grievances and 'rights' in colonial Malaya (1890–1956)

### 3.1 Introduction

This chapter uses the constitutive framework developed in Chapter 2 to analyse how the law and rights shaped the process of Indian mobilisation during the British colonial rule of Malaya. Legal mobilisation of ethno-cultural minorities involves three cr processes: first, the transformation of ethno-cultural identity (which is constituted by legal formalities and social perceptions) into a collective or mobilising identity; second, the pooling of grievances of similarly situated individuals due to the exclusion of the group from legal rights or the differential treatment of the group by state-enforced laws and policies; and third, the strategic use of identity and rights frames by activists in order to unite and mobilise the group. The analysis on minority mobilisation in oppressive conditions also focusses on the formal interpretations of the law (in this case by the colonial power) as a source of political contestation of minority identity, law and rights. The contestation provides the basis from which to analyse the subaltern or alternative meanings of identity, the law and rights used in civil disobedience and political lobbying.

This chapter places emphasis on two significant inquiries: first, the role of the law in constructing ethno-cultural identity from the 1890s to the 1950s, as well as the role of legal repression and rights in the Indian mobilisation that took place in 1941 known as the Klang Strikes. The second inquiry is on the role of the law and rights in the colonial process of racialisation of Indians as well as the construction of historical grievances from the 1890s onwards that laid the grounds for the 2007 Hindu Rights Action Force (HINDRAF) rally. The 2007 HINDRAF mobilisation is analysed in Chapter 5. As one sociolegal scholar noted in a review of law and colonialism, '[e]vents that happened in the past, such as those in the period of colonial conquest and control, can provide insights into processes of domination and resistance in the present.'[1] Hence, this chapter lays the groundwork to answer the second research question: how an ethno-culturally diverse group, which has historically been politically acquiescent, mobilised in the 1990s despite the oppressive environment and intra-group differences?

## 3.2 The racialisation of Indians in colonial Malaya

Indians in Malaysia are a heterogeneous ethno-cultural group with numerous horizontal and vertical cleavages, which were described in Chapter 1. The sheer diversity of various Indian ethno-cultural differences, in terms of the ethnicities, languages, regional origins, cultures and religions, has created deep horizontal cleavages within the group. Furthermore, social and economic factors such as the caste system, social status and class differences have constructed vertical cleavages. The amalgamation of horizontal and vertical cleavages has created a much more complex and multifaceted Indian identity.

### 3.2.1 Colonial categorisation of race

As explained in Chapter 1 (Section 1.3), the British colonial administration had constructed a taxonomy of ethnic/caste/tribal groups in India in order to control its colonised constituents. While the British Raj had reinforced existing caste categories and used colonial ideologies of race such as Social Darwinism to classify the Indians, the British administration also strived to construct a politically unified Indian dominion. The reorganisation of India by the British Raj through the construction of colonial identities had set the stage for the political contestation of Indian identity, especially during the era of Indian nationalism and anti-imperialist movements in the 1930s. Furthermore, the mass movement of Indian labour from British India to other British colonies such as British Ceylon and British Malaya had further complicated the meaning of Indian identity. The British colonial administration found that there was a need to *racialise* Indian identity in order to differentiate and segregate the migrant Indian labour from the 'natives' or the Malays and also other migrant labour groups, such as the Chinese in Malaya, which is discussed further in Section 3.2.2.

While racialisation itself occurred in the socioeconomic environment of colonial rule, the formal process of racial construction occurred through British colonial census classifications and colonial administrative practices. Available scholarly analyses of the historical bases of ethnicity and race in Malaysia show how the British administration constructed race-based categories based on colonial ideologies of race, thus legitimising the paternalistic supremacy of the British over its colonies, which, in turn, enabled the exploitation and control of colonial labour in support of the British planters and industrialists.[2]

In order to categorise the groups that were colonised, the administration relied on external social identities of groups, which was based on peripheral social perceptions of ethno-cultural groups. For instance, in the case of British India, the British Raj based its categorisation of Indians on existing caste-based social identities. However, external social perceptions were fortified by colonial ideologies of race, which became useful to support pre-existing social divisions. This is shown in the way the agricultural peasantry in India were defined as a 'lower caste' labour group by the 'upper caste' landlords, while the British administration legitimised and reinforced the identity of the peasantry as 'coolie' labour. While these neat census categories helped the British colonial administration in its economic management of the colonies, the categories were especially useful in controlling and repressing colonial labour.

Table 3.1 below shows the census categorisation of Indians and the Indian ethno-cultural sub-groups such as the Tamils, from 1871 to 1947. From 1871 to 1891, the census was conducted in the Straits Settlements, while from 1901 to 1911 two separate census exercises were conducted in the Straits Settlements and the Federated Malay States.[3] However, from 1921 onwards, the census was consolidated into a single census report. Table 3.1 also shows the colonial construction of main census categories, which was classified in the early census according to the British understanding of the national origin of the group. For instance, the colonial census from the 1880s onwards shows that the root source of the main category of Indians was not on the basis of any anthropological or sociological theory on ethno-cultural origin but based on colonial official perceptions of *national* origin. However, in later colonial census, the main classification of Indians was *racialised* to reflect an ethnic category.

In contrast to the main categorisation of the Indians, the various Indian ethno-cultural sub-groups, such as the 'Tamils', were categorised in the census classification in accordance to both the British perception of the sub-group as well as the internal or self-perceived ethno-cultural identity of the group. In the first colonial census, known as the *Census of the Straits Settlements* of 1871 (see Table 3.1) the people from the Indian sub-continent were listed under various sub-groupings, for example the 'Parsees', 'Hindoos', 'Klings' and 'Singhalese' under the main grouping of 'Bengalees and Other Natives of India not particularized'. Hirschman suggests that the use of the term 'Bengalees and Other Natives of India not particularized' may have been a case of mistaken identity, as a British reference to Indians from North India in general.[4] The category of 'Hindoos' denotes a religious category rather than an ethnic one. However, after the first colonial census, religious identifications were removed and replaced with racialised categories.[5] It is noteworthy that the phrase 'Other Natives of India not particularized' reveals the categorisation to be based on the national origin of the group from British India, and includes various ethno-cultural groups from the Indian sub-continent. The group listed as 'Klings' is not elaborated, but Nagata suggests the term 'Kling' or *keling* was the Malay reference to the Indian Muslims who were traders in pre-colonial Malaya.[6] During the post-colonial period, the Malay term *keling* was used as a slur to denigrate Indians, which was then taken up by Indian activists as an issue of contention. In any case, the 1871 census clearly shows that the census categories were based on the colonial perception and external identification of various

Indian ethno-cultural sub-groups, which were diverse in terms of ethnic, religious, linguistic and even regional origin.

The *1881 Census of the Straits Settlements* had a slightly modified list of groupings of the Indian sub-continent. While the main category 'Bengalis and Other Natives of India not particularized' remained, the term 'Hindoo' and 'Kling' were removed and the term 'Tamil' was introduced. The *1891 Census of the Straits Settlement* showed a substantial change in the main category which grouped together various Indian ethno-cultural sub-groups. The main category now termed 'Tamils and Other Natives of India' contained sub-groups of Bengalis, Burmese, Parsees and Tamils. The Sinhalese were shifted to another main category called 'Other Nationalities', reflecting their national origin in British Ceylon. The major shift from 'Bengali' to 'Tamil' as the majority in the main category 'Natives of India' coincides with the 1890s mass arrival of the Indian Tamil plantation labour who began to form a majority among the Indians. The British colonial officers, faced with the task of categorising an increasing number of ethno-linguistic groups such as the Malayalis, the Telugus and the Punjabis,[7] whose only commonality was their national origin as the people of British India, adopted the main category 'Natives of India' to alleviate the administrative struggle to make sense of this increasingly heterogeneous group.

In 1901, two separate census were made for the Straits Settlements and the Federated Malay States, and in 1911, the term 'Indian' was first coined in order to replace the nationalistic category of 'Tamils and Other Natives of India'. While the *1911 Straits Settlements Census* contained categorical differentiation in terms of place of birth, for example whether the individual was born in India or in the Straits Settlements, the census of the Federated Malay States itemised the main Indian category by 'race' which referred to ethno-cultural sub-groups, for example the Tamils, Telugus and Punjabis. From 1921 onwards, a consolidated census for the Straits Settlements and the Federated Malay States maintained the category 'Indian' with a breakdown of ethno-cultural sub-groups referred to in the census as 'race'. One could argue that, by 1921, the formal *racial* identity of people from the Indian sub-continent was fixed as being 'Indian'.

Despite the fixation of the main census category as 'Indians', there were frequent changes in the sub-categories of the ethno-cultural Indian sub-groups. On the one hand, the colonial administration's perception of race as a homogeneous entity did not fit the Indian population which was clearly diverse. On the other hand, many of the sub-categories were the result of internal fractures among the Indian community itself. For instance the 'Ceylon Tamil' sub-category first appeared in the *1947 Census* but was put under the main category called 'Others', which clearly distinguished the Ceylon Tamils from the 'Indian' Tamils. This was a reflection of the internal or self-conceived identity of the Ceylon Tamil sub-group who distinguished themselves from the Indian Tamils.

Notwithstanding the constant changes *within* the Indian census category, the main census categories in British Malaya were, nonetheless, fixed into three main categories due to the colonial labour policy, which maintained a strict division between the natives of Malaya, the natives from China and the natives of India. The process of formal categorisation simply shifted from nationality (or national origin) to race and the three main nationality-based groups were racialised into the Malays, Chinese and Indians. As such, the colonial racial ideologies and colonial economic perceptions of labour groups were formalised into the census categories. These census categories had, in turn, *racialised* the three main national groups in Malaya, including the Indians. Hence, this shows a dialectic process between legal formalities such as census classifications and racial ideology.

### 3.2.2   *Colonial laws, policies and the racialisation of space*

The colonial labour policy in Malaya was instrumental in structuring ethno-cultural groups in two ways: first, through the overarching 'divide and rule' policy which created racialised spaces that physically and socioeconomically segregated the Malays, Chinese and Indians; and second, through a socioeconomic hierarchical structure of specific ethno-cultural sub-groups within each of these larger groups. For instance, the plantation labour and clerical employees from the Indian sub-continent were spatially as well as economically segregated within the rubber plantations. The British planters had utilised pre-existing horizontal and vertical cleavages of the Indians to construct a hierarchical labour structure which exacerbated inequalities between Indian sub-groups and discriminated against the lower-class plantation labour. This will be discussed further in Section 3.2.3.

The role of the law in the socioeconomic/race structuring of the three main ethno-cultural groups in Malaya is evident from the colonial immigration ordinances and legal enactments, as well as the labour codes and policies which constructed racial as well as class-based segregation. The main colonial labour policy in Malaya was to separate the three main ethno-cultural groups spatially, economically and socially. The Malays who were native to Malaya lived in rural villages and were left to survive on agricultural activity like paddy planting and fishing, while the migrant Chinese were mostly set to work the tin mining industry, and the Indians (particularly the Indian Tamils) were recruited for specific work in the rubber plantations. The British were in economic control of the tin and rubber industries and safeguarded their position by placing legal and policy restrictions on the ethno-nationalist characteristics of labour for each industry.[8] As described in Chapter 1 (Section 1.2), the *1884 Indian Immigration Ordinance* effectively transferred the control of Indian emigration from the Government of British India to the Straits Settlements Government (British Malaya). The Government of British India was noted to have partially

*Table 3.1* Racial Classification of Indians in the Colonial Census from 1871 to 1947

| Census of the Straits Settlements | | | | | Consolidated Census | | |
|---|---|---|---|---|---|---|---|
| *1871* | *1881* | *1891* | *1901* | *1911* | *1921* | *1931* | *1947* |
| Bengalees and other Natives of India not particularized | Bengalis and other Natives of India not particularized | Tamils and other Natives of India | Tamils and other Natives of India | Indians | The Indian Pop. by Race | Indians by Race | Indians by Specific Community |
| • Hindoos<br>• Klings<br>• Parsees<br>• Burmese<br>• Singhalese | • Burmese<br>• Parsees<br>• Singhalese<br>• Tamils | • Bengalis<br>• Burmese<br>• Parsees<br>• Tamils | • Bengalis<br>• Burmese<br>• Parsees<br>• Tamils<br><br>Census of the Federated Malay States<br><br>Tamils & other Natives of India<br>• Bengalis etc.<br>• Burmese<br>• Not particularized<br>• Tamils | • Indian-born<br>• Straits-born<br>• Born Elsewhere<br><br>Indian Pop. by Race<br>• Tamil<br>• Telugu<br>• Punjabi<br>• Bengali<br>• Malayali<br>• Hindustani<br>• Afghan<br>• Gujerati<br>• Maharatta<br>• Burmese<br>• Other Indians | • Tamil<br>• Telugu<br>• Malayali<br>• Punjabi<br>• Bengali<br>• Hindustani<br>• Pathan<br>• Gujerati<br>• Maharatta<br>• Burmese<br>• Gurkha<br>• Other and Indians Unspecified | • Tamils<br>• Telugu<br>• Malayalam<br>• Punjabi, etc.<br>• United Provinces<br>• Burmese<br>• Bengal, etc.<br>• Bombay, etc.<br>• Bihar & Orissa<br>• Nepal<br>• Other and Unidentified | • Tamil<br>• Telugu<br>• Malayali<br>• Other unspecified or indeterminate South Indian peoples<br>• Sikh<br>• Bengali<br>• Gujerati<br>• Maharatti<br>• Marwari<br>• Pathan<br>• Punjabi<br>• Rajput<br>• Sindhi<br>• Other unspecified or indeterminate Indian peoples |
| | | | Other Nationalities/ Other Races | The 'Other' Pop. by Race | The 'Other' Pop. by Race | Others by Race | Other Communities |
| | | | • Sinhalese/ Singhalese | • Singhalese | • Sinhalese | • Ceylon Peoples | • Ceylon Tamil<br>• Sinhalese<br>• Other unspecified or indeterminate Ceylon peoples |

Source: Extracts from the 'Ethnic Classifications of Census from 1821' in Hirschman (1987).
Note: The shaded boxes show the main census categories, whereas the unshaded boxes show the census sub-categories.v

relinquished their paternalistic function over the Indian migrants and had taken a 'grandmotherly' role in handing over Indian emigration to the British Straits Settlements.[9]

The change of power meant that Indian labour emigration into Malaya became more straightforward, faster and cheaper in comparison to Chinese labour emigration, which required negotiations with Chinese agents and brokers. The legal control of Indian emigration provided the British planters in Malaya the lobbying power to demand for the 'suitable' type of Indian labour (the agricultural peasantry from Tamil Nadu) and stipulate contractual terms of labour as well as emigration (e.g. the indentured or *kangany* contracts described in Chapter 1). As the docile and submissive Indian Tamil agricultural peasantry were specifically chosen for rubber plantation work, the Straits Settlement passed the *1908 Tamil Immigration Fund Ordinance* (which was re-enacted as the *1910 Indian Immigration Fund*). Under *Section 7(1)* of the *1908 Ordinance*, British planters and rubber plantation employers in Malaya were provided with financial incentives in the form of assessment rebates and recruitment allowances for the importation of Indian Tamil labour into Malaya, while the Indian Tamil 'coolies' were provided with return tickets to Malaya.[10] It was quite clear that the Tamil immigration fund was not meant to provide any particular socioeconomic assistance to Indian Tamil plantation labourers, as under the indentured contract transportation of labour costs were legally shouldered by the British planters. However, the colonial Indian emigration laws had, through financial incentives, facilitated the importation of specific Indian Tamil labour for British Malaya's rubber industry.

In order to retain full control of the rubber economy in Malaya, the British planters had pressured the colonial administration to enact legal restrictions on the rubber industry as well as land alienation. After a series of heavy lobbying by the British Rubber Growers Association, the British Parliament established laws and sanctioned policies which would stabilise the price of rubber.[11] For instance, the Stevenson Restriction Schemes from 1922 to 1928 and later from 1934 to 1941 were established under the *Export of Rubber (Restriction) Enactment 1922* and the *International Rubber Regulation Agreement 1934*. These rubber restriction schemes constructed racial/economic divisions as they legally prohibited native Malays from planting rubber. The schemes enabled British monopoly of rubber in Malaya but also reinforced existing colonial laws which racially segregated the three main ethno-cultural groups according to colonial economic needs. For instance, the *1913 Malay Reservation Enactment* legally defined a Malay as 'a person belonging to any Malayan race who habitually speaks the Malay language or any Malayan language and professes the Moslem religion'. Under the *1913 Enactment*, a Malay was legally prohibited from selling or leasing reserved land to a non-Malay. Further to land alienation, the *1917 Rice Lands Enactment* placed a legal prohibition on growing rubber in Malay reserved lands and only allowed paddy plantation stipulated as the cultivation of 'wet rice'.[12] Hence, by using the law, the colonial administration ensured that the Malays would continue with traditional agricultural pursuits such as paddy planting, which also ensured a steady supply of inexpensive staple food for the Chinese and Indian migrant labourers in the tin and rubber industries.[13]

The discussion above shows that the colonial laws were instrumental in constructing a type of 'raced space'[14] where the three ethno-cultural groups were racialised and segregated within the socioeconomic and spatial layout of colonial Malaya. Although within the rubber plantation sector, British planters had the choice of native Malays, Javanese migrant labourers from the Dutch colony of Indonesia, the Indian Tamil peasantry and the Chinese migrants, Indian Tamil labour from British India was preferred; the Chinese migrants were inexpensive but were more prone to rebellion due to communal links with Chinese clans and secret societies while the Javanese labourers were considered an expensive choice as emigration required negotiations with the Dutch colonialists. The Malay peasantry were mostly unwilling to work under the harsh conditions of the rubber plantations, while the Indian Tamil peasantry from British India were clearly an inexpensive, willing and submissive group.

The communal separation of the Malays, Chinese and Indians through this 'divide and rule' policy was also useful in instilling mistrust between the groups. The enforcement of racial cleavages between the three ethno-cultural groups ensured that there would be no opportunity for any collective labour demands or collective resistance against the British colonial power. For instance, in order to keep these potential labour groups in a weak bargaining position *vis-à-vis* wages and other employment terms, the British planters were advised to play up racial differences and stoke scepticism between the groups. A colonial practice direction for British planters stated,

> To secure your independence, work with Javanese and Tamils and, if you have sufficient experience, also with Malays and Chinese; you can then always play the one against the other. In case of a strike, you will never be left without labour, and the coolies of one nationality will think twice before they make their terms, if they know that you are in a position that you can do without them.[15]

Although the colonial creation of raced space was meant to disrupt any non-communal *class*-based mobilisation, it also sowed the seeds for collective *race*-based resistance. For instance, the treatment of Chinese and Indian indentured labour was particularly harsh and grievances were easily shared among the labourers of each respective group who lived in close quarters. The pooling of grievances arose naturally from the similar situation labourers of the same ethno-cultural group found themselves in.

However, in order to minimise the possibility of race-based resistance, the British industrialists and administration constructed a hierarchical class-based structure *within* each ethno-cultural group. The British colonial administration was particularly concerned about resistance by Chinese labour who were more ethno-culturally unified. In order to impede Chinese resistance, the colonial administrators negotiated with the heads of Chinese clans known as the *kongsi* and the Chinese secret societies to control and place physical restrictions on Chinese labourers who were cordoned within their '*kongsi* houses or barracks'.[16] Despite the physical and repressive nature of control, Chinese resistance occurred in the form of labour strikes in the 1930s (discussed in Section 3.4). The native Malay peasantry on the other hand was controlled by a Malay feudalistic aristocracy. The British administration provided land and financial incentives for the Malay land-owning class in order to restrain Malay economic activity to paddy. The land concessions and paddy planting restrictions had subsequently led to a Malay preferential policy in the 1920s which was meant to legally protect Malay interests.[17] However, the Malay preferential policy constructed a new Malay administrative class who were chosen from the traditional Malay aristocrats and landlords. In return for colonial economic control of Malaya, the Malay aristocrats were given political and administrative power to control the Malay peasantry who were economically reliant on the paddy plantations. Furthermore, the political power given to the Malay aristocrats also assisted the British in keeping the Chinese and Indians politically subordinate. This set the stage for the legal reinforcement of the Malay preferential policy in the post-independence *Federal Constitution* and the political supremacy of the Malay aristocrats in post-colonial politics which will be discussed in Chapter 4. As the discussion to follow shows, the British planters similarly created a tightly controlled hierarchical structure that separated the diverse Indian sub-groups into particular economic roles in the plantation industry in order to impede a unified Indian resistance, especially in the rubber plantations.

### 3.2.3 Discrimination and inequality among Indians in Malaya

Pre-existing Indian intra-group fragmentations based on caste, linguistic and regional differences became useful to construct a pecking order within the rubber plantation layout. As discussed in Sections 3.2.1 and 3.2.2, the British were familiar with the hierarchical division of the caste system and its manifestation in labour-based or class cleavages in British India. Furthermore, as Chapter 1 had iterated, the British were familiar with the antagonism between the Indian Tamils and the Ceylon Tamils from their earlier tea plantation ventures in British Ceylon. In fusing caste and regional intra-group cleavages, the rubber plantations in Malaya were able to construct a complex chain of command which would maintain or even fuel antagonism between Indian sub-groups. The class cleavages safeguarded the rubber plantation industry from a collective 'Indian' labour strike. This resulted in socioeconomic or class inequality between Indian sub-groups and discriminatory treatment against the Indian Tamil plantation labour.

The role of the law in constructing the division of Indian labour in Malaya begins from the control of Indian emigration, as discussed in Section 3.2.2. However, specific legal restrictions on the Indian Tamil plantation labour emerged through the Indian indentured and *kangany* labour systems. These two forms of labour control were essentially contractual debt mechanisms that kept the British planters in a position of economic and physical control of the Indian Tamil plantation labour, as explained in Chapter 1 (Section 1.3.2). While both systems entailed a contractual relationship, the terms and conditions contained in the indentured contract were considered to be particularly unjust and inequitable towards the Indian Tamil plantation labourer.

The indenture was essentially between the British planter and the Indian Tamil plantation labourer for a fixed five year contract during which time the labourer was prohibited from changing jobs or employers and wages were fixed at extremely low levels. In most cases, the labourer would be prepared to enter into a contract that compromised his autonomy in order to gain employment in British Malaya. The uneven nature of the contractual bargain was evident from the restrictions on the type of Indian labour recruited, who were mostly uneducated and in most cases illiterate agricultural peasantry from Tamil Nadu. The Indian indentured labour system seemed close to a legalised system of slavery.

In the 1870s, the British parliament was beginning to recognise the unfair nature of the indentured contract and the slave-like conditions of the Indian indentured labour in all of Britain's colonies. One British law-maker, Lord Stanley of Alderly had in an 1875 House of Lord session of the British Parliament emphasised the need to establish a regulatory officer within the British Raj to oversee and supervise all contractual engagements of Indian 'Coolies'.[18] Lord Stanley had pushed forth his argument against the indentured system based on the debt-associated problems which not only exacerbated poverty among the Indian indentured labourers but also legally bound the labourer to a single employer without providing any legal remedies for breach of contract. He further quoted the Governor of Goldcoast, who explained the dilemma of a debt-based contract:

> But besides slavery proper there is a species of slavery called "pawning," which has its origin in contract, and the chief feature of which is that the pawn remains in servitude to a temporary master, as a pledge for debt.[19]

Although the British Parliament had since 1875 acknowledged that the indentured system was a type of slavery which led to severe debt as well as poverty of the indentured labourer, the British Parliament failed to take any legal measures to remedy the system. In fact, the *1884 Indian Immigration Ordinances* had transferred the control of Indian immigration to the Straits Settlements Government that failed to regulate the contractual Indian indentured system. It was not until the 1920s that the British

Raj administration banned the indentured system and replaced it with the Indian *Kangany* system.

The *Kangany* system removed the direct contractual relationship between the British planter and the Indian Tamil plantation labourer, instead establishing a third-party 'middle-man' in the form of the Indian recruitment mediators known as the *kangany*. The British administration in Malaya issued *kangany* licences to particular individuals who were always Indian Tamils of a slightly higher caste than the labourers. The *kangany* agents being Indian Tamil enabled the agents to solicit Indian Tamil labour from the hinterland of Tamil Nadu in British India. This system created a long-term contractual agreement between the British planter and the *kangany* who was paid a one-off commission for the number of Indian Tamil labourers recruited but was also paid a portion of the labourer's wages. This meant that the *kangany* had a separate employment agreement with the Indian Tamil labourer. Hence, there was no direct contractual link between the British planters and the labourers themselves, who were treated by the British planters as sub-contracted or freely contracted labourers. The system also meant that the *kangany* had a financial interest in ensuring that the labourers did not breach the contract. Through the double layer of contracts, the first contract between the British planter and the *kangany*, and the second contract between the *kangany* and the Indian Tamil plantation worker, the system was able to construct a hierarchical order in the rubber plantation. The *kangany* was not only contractually bound as a recruiter of Indian Tamil workers but also required to act as a foreman otherwise known as the *mandore* and was put in charge of supervising the labourers as well as paying their wages.[20] This meant that Indian Tamil plantation labour were only able to channel their grievances through the *kangany* foreman who usually placated the workers and settled minor issues. The *kangany* contractual system allowed the British planter to evade any direct legal responsibility between the employer and the labour, and at the same time enabled the British planter to exploit the labour without any legal repercussions.

The British planters did, however, directly employ Indians who were usually non-Tamils and Ceylon Tamils as administrative staff in the plantations, such as the estate clerks or *kranies* and estate 'runners' or the *oodumpillai*. Besides staffing of plantation administration, there was also Indian recruitment in the urban areas for the service sectors like land transport (e.g. the railway and road building), ports and telecommunications. This set of Indian workers and administrative staff were employed under different contractual terms. They were directly employed for particular skills and education as they were usually British trained. Hence, the direct contractual relationship between the British employer and the Indian employee was clearly distinct from the case of the Indian Tamil plantation labour. The differential treatment between the two classes of Indians had constructed new economic and status-based cleavages among the people from the Indian sub-continent. The different contractual terms and conditions resulted in the discrimination of the Indian Tamil plantation labour.

From the perspective of the colonial employer, direct contractual relationships between the upper-class Indian employee and the British planter or colonial employer did not risk any form of collective race-based action. This was because the Indian administrative staff as well as Indian urban workers were more ethno-culturally diverse, in comparison to the somewhat homogeneous Indian Tamil plantation labour. In other words, the horizontal cleavages among the 'upper-class' or 'middle-class' Indians were more severe in comparison to the 'lower-class' Indian Tamil plantation labour. Further to this, the vertical division of migrant labour from the Indian sub-continent, that is, Indian Tamil plantation labour, *kanganies*, clerks and managers within the plantation system created a complex ethno-cultural and socioeconomic inequality that impeded both race-based and class-based resistance.

The differential treatment of the two socioeconomic classes of Indians was also apparent in the colonial labour laws and labour policy in Malaya. For example, the breach of employment contract was treated differently between the upper-class Indians and the Indian Tamil plantation labour. Before the 1923 *Labour Code* was enacted, a breach of contract by an Indian Tamil plantation labourer would lead to a criminal allegation of 'vagrancy' and criminal offence of an act of desertion from the plantation.[21] The criminalisation of purely industrial-type offences and breach of *kangany* labour contracts portrays the utility of the law as a discriminatory and repressive tool. Such vagrancy laws with punitive repercussions were not extended to the upper-class Indians who were employed in managerial and administrative roles.

Furthermore, the standard wage system under the indentured and *kangany* contracts that was imposed on Indian Tamil plantation labour was non-negotiable and did not provide for a minimum wage threshold. In 1884, the colonial government had passed the *Straits Settlement Ordinance* which created a wage structure particularly for the Indian Tamil plantation labour in Malaya. However, the rubber commodity market was always prone to wide price fluctuations and heavily affected the livelihoods of plantation labour.[22] The standard wage was also discounted for the housing and other facilities such as basic schooling and medical services provided for the labourers in the rubber plantation. This meant that a breach of contract resulted in automatic eviction and repatriation to British India without any wages.[23] Hence, the Indian Tamil plantation labourers were exploited under the colonial wage system, which was also subject to the constant fluctuations of the rubber economy and the regular influx of Indian Tamil labourers until the Great Depression of the 1930s.[24]

These differences in treatment and the inequality between the two Indian socioeconomic groups laid the foundation for vertical cleavages that reinforced pre-existing caste differences. The literature reviewed in Chapter 1 suggests that the Indian Tamil plantation labour were specifically taken from the lower-caste agricultural peasantry in British India and were discriminated by the upper-caste Indian sub-groups in Malaya. Despite the role of legal formalities such as census and the colonial laws as well as policy that racialised the Indians as a homogeneous group, the internal social identity of Indians was fragmented by a caste consciousness that even superseded ethno-cultural cleavages.

There are no studies on the linkage between caste identity and mobilisation among the Indians in Malaya, but there is evidence to suggest that the social perception of caste identity among Indians in colonial Malaya was a significant factor in the prolonged acquiescence and lack of ethno-cultural unity. For instance, Manickam, a contemporary Indian activist wrote in a historical commentary that the Ceylon Tamil administrative staff in the rubber plantations often displayed contempt towards the Indian Tamil plantation labour who they viewed as lower caste and remained unconcerned with their grievances.[25] In essence, despite linguistic commonality between these two Indian sub-groups, the perception of caste-based differences had driven the two sub-groups apart.

The social perception of caste among 'upper-caste' Indians in colonial Malaya constructed an external social identity of the Indian Tamil plantation labourers as 'lower-caste'. The former Indian sub-group, which perceived its own internal social identity as 'upper-caste' used the hierarchical practice of the caste system to physically segregate themselves from the Indian Tamil plantation labourers in terms of separate housing, schooling and medical facilities as well as justified their own punitive treatment of the 'lower-caste' Indian Tamil plantation labourers. The colonial layout of the rubber plantation and the hierarchical structure of Indian labour reinforced the caste-based stigmatisation of the Indian Tamil plantation labour and social perceptions of caste difference in order to maintain antagonism between the Indian sub-groups. A post-colonial Indian novel entitled *The Immigrant* aptly describes the dialectic process of colonial policy and caste cleavages in the rubber plantations of Malaya:

> "Didn't they employ Indian clerks and supervisors? Didn't they help? Couldn't they have helped to ease the situation?"
>
> "Thooi," the old man spat on the ground loudly.
>
> "Yes, they did," Marimuthu said quietly. "The British used the divide and rule policy even in the estates. They stratified the working community just to ensure that the workers remained controllable. They did this in hiring Telugus, Malayalees, Bengalis, Punjabis and Ceylon Tamils as clerks, male nurses and supervisors. These people were encouraged not to "mix with the riff-raff" – namely the rubber tappers. It worked very well. At times, these so called Indians were even more cruel than the white managers. Some of them thought nothing of slapping or kicking the workers on the slightest pretext."
>
> "If you consider the white men animals for their cruelty and exploitation, then you can only consider these so-called Indians mangy

dogs for what they did to us. They would kick us in front of the manager just to suck up to the white men. Don't mention the names of these people. Don't call them Indians, you do great injustices to the term Indian."[26]

Interviews of Indian activists and Indian leaders conducted as part of this study further confirm that the social perception of inequality and discrimination within the hierarchical structure of the rubber plantation was linked to the caste-based identity of the various Indian sub-groups.[27]

Hence, the construction of a formal identity of Indians as a homogeneous race by the British administration did not lead to the social unification of the Indians, as the internal social identity of the group was severely fractured by caste and other ethno-cultural differences. By basing the labour hierarchy on caste, the colonial administration was able to easily maintain law and order as well as ensure the maintenance of an inexpensive, submissive and acquiescent Indian labour force. In the meantime, the colonial process of controlling Indian labour in Malaya had constructed severe grievances pertaining to socioeconomic, cultural and political status. Section 3.3 discusses further the escalation of grievances of the Indian Tamil plantation labour and finds that despite the grievances, the Indians remained a divided and acquiescent community until the 1941 Klang Strikes.

## 3.3 The pooling of grievances and differential treatment of Indians in Malaya

The grievances associated with the Indian Tamil plantation labour revolved around the debt-based indentured system, the later *kangany* system and the differential treatment as well as inequality experienced by the group. The most serious concern was poverty which was linked to the contractual debts owed to the British planters and the *kangany* as well as the standard low wage system. Further to poverty-related issues, the differential treatment of the Indian Tamil plantation labour constructed socioeconomic and cultural grievances. For instance, the segregation of the Indian Tamil plantation labour living quarters, schools as well as medical amenities meant that housing and facilities were constantly sub-standard or in some cases totally ignored by the British planters. Segregation of 'lower-caste' Indian Tamil plantation labour also meant that the housing, often called 'lines' were plagued by poverty-related issues such as poor sanitation and overcrowding. Many labourers were prone to illness due to the hard labour in the plantation and the unhygienic living conditions, but received marginal medical aid.

The situation led to serious concerns among the British parliamentarians about the state of plantation labour health, but no changes were made in terms of providing better living conditions and health facilities for the labourers. Hugh Tinker explains the living condition of the labourers in a rubber plantation in Province Wellesley (present day state of Penang) situated in the Straits Settlement:

> In 1874, the manager of one of the largest estates in Province Wellesley, Malakoff, reported that one hundred of his Indians were sick. An inquiry was ordered, and two government doctors and an assistant superintendent of police investigated conditions at Malakoff. They reported: "The lines we visited formed two sides of an open square. The huts were sadly dilapidated and dirty, the open ground in front being a perfect mess of clay, thoroughly permeated with filth, which gave forth a most putrescent stink." They found the hospital: "The ground surrounding it was a swamp ... It consisted of a large attap hut, dimly lighted by a small lamp ... The smell was strong and the temperature high, with a great feeling of closeness." All this created a scandal, whose echoes were heard in England. Yet, nothing fundamental changed.[28]

Tinker's description of the rubber plantation in Province Wellesley not only provides a snapshot of the poor conditions but also indicates that the British administration was aware of the gravity of the situation but chose to disregard it. The official indifference is attributed to the lobbying power of the British planters and industrialists who strove to maintain an inexpensive labour force for their profit-driven enterprises. The British planters were indifferent to the grievances of the Indian Tamil plantation labour not due to ignorance or a lack of capacity to respond but rather because they were unwilling to incur the higher costs of providing better accommodation and health facilities. Furthermore the biased nature of the indentured as well as the *kangany* contracts, and the legal control of Indian immigration meant that the cheap labour was easily replaceable. Hence, the disregard of the Indian Tamil plantation labour's grievances was maintained by a legally repressive colonial power. Although the segregation of labour facilitated the pooling of grievances among the Indian Tamil plantation labour, the weak or non-existent bargaining power of the labour either in their employment contract or through existing laws meant that the group was unable to push forth its claims.

Another major grievance of the Indian Tamil plantation labour was the harsh and cruel treatment that was accorded to the labourers by the British planters and the Indian *mandores* or managers. Labourers faced punishment that ranged from being kicked to severe flogging which sometimes led to death. For instance, in a particular case that involved the death of an Indian Tamil plantation labourer, the coroner's report showed that the labourer had been beaten by a rattan cane and whipped by a 'cat-o'-nine-tails' to death.[29] Several other similar reports often showed that the punishments were unfitting of the crime, as it involved mostly trivial actions that were construed as breaking the code of conduct. Examples of such trivial 'crimes' include failing to dismount from a bicycle when crossing the path of a British planter or an Indian *mandore*, and grooming the hair in the wrong manner.[30]

The official reports on the treatment accorded to Indian Tamil plantation labourers had subsequently reached the British Parliament and due to an emerging lobbying power of several British humanitarian societies, a call was made to enact a protective law called the *Indian Immigration Protection Act* in order to end the harsh and cruel treatment accorded to the 'Indian coolies' throughout the British colonies. In one of the House of Lords debates regarding this issue, specific mention was made of the case of two Indian Tamil plantation labourers in Malaya who had died due to the practice of flogging.[31] The Malayan case was not peculiar as several other cases reported in British Malaya as well as throughout the British colonies also showed that Indian indentured labourers were subject to physical and emotional abuse with no recourse. The urgency as well as the seriousness of the matter and the increasing lobby power of the Anti-Slavery Society in the United Kingdom had prompted the British government to ratify new legislative measures. The House of Lords debate made special mention of three critical issues to be included in a shielding law for the protection of 'Indian Coolies in the Straits Settlements': first, the need for a supervised system of transportation of Indian Coolies; second, the scrutiny of contracts entered into by the Indian Coolies with British planters; and third, the treatment accorded to the Indian Coolies both within the duration of their contract and on expiry of the contract.[32]

Despite the persuasive calls made by British civil society, the colonial government was slow in responding to the issue of the 'Indian Coolies' or the Indian Tamil plantation labour. The primary reason was the lobbying power of the British planters, who had pressured the British government to enact laws which were favourable to the planters. For instance, British planters in Province Wellesley in Malaya had lobbied for anti-crimping laws to stop the practice of crimping, which involved the enticement of Indian Coolies from one rubber plantation to another with higher wages and benefits.[33] The colonial government was quite willing to consent to the requests made by the British planters by enacting new legal penalties under the 1877 *Crimping Ordinance*. The British planters had been constantly pushing for legal changes in order to fully control the Indian Tamil plantation labour and secure the planters' economic interests. In fact, the legal changes propelled by the British planters had become too rampant to the extent that the laws had become vague and complex, as it was difficult to ascertain 'what is law and what is not'.[34]

In comparison, the issues pertaining to the aggrieved Indian Tamil plantation labourers were treated as less important. For instance, in the several cases of harsh treatment of the labourers, punitive measures meted out to the offending British planter were rare and in most cases extremely lenient. The 1875 House of Lords debate exemplifies the clemency offered to British planters with regard to the death of two Indian Tamil plantation labourers in Malakoff estate in the Straits Settlement. The debate report found that the punishment imposed on the two British planters who caused the death of the labourers was halved to three and four months' imprisonment. The reason behind the leniency was because one of the planters was urgently needed to manage the rubber plantation that was left unattended, and due to the clemency offered to the first planter, the punishment imposed on the other planter was also reduced in order to avoid differential treatment.[35] Hence, the colonial laws were favourable to British planters as well as aimed at maintaining the British colonial economy.

However, British civil society groups were agitating on behalf of the Indian Tamil plantation labour in British Malaya, while the British Raj was concerned about the poor treatment accorded to the labourers. The colonial government in the Straits Settlements enacted labour laws such as the *Labour Codes* of 1912 and 1923 and the *Health Board Enactment* in 1926 in order to placate growing concern among the British civil society groups and the British Raj. Although these laws provided a comprehensive regulation of the working and living conditions of the Indian Tamil plantation labour, in terms of housing and medical facilities, they were limited. Furthermore, the British planters formed a formidable lobby to exert political pressure on the colonial government to abandon all such schemes, or at the very least to hinder the enforcement of the schemes. One such scheme was the major proposal to establish an education system for the children of the Indian Tamil plantation labourers. Under the *Labour Code 1923*, it was compulsory for all plantations with ten or more children of school-going age to make provision for a school. A very basic Tamil education system was established but the schools were often in appalling conditions and were constructed as a sham to fool the officials. In a 1923 Federal Council proceeding on the Labour Code provision for compulsory schooling in plantations, a British planter's representative commented, '[s]o long as they let the Controller of Labour pass my smoke factory with the word 'school' written up in large letters I shall be quite happy.'[36] The British planters were concerned that providing education or skills may encourage or facilitate the social mobility of the Indian Tamil plantation labour.[37] As such, the British planters ensured that schooling facilities were inadequate so that the labourers' children remained and worked in the same plantations that their parents had worked in. Hence, the laws, administrative orders and schemes which were meant to protect the labourers were mostly toothless and left unenforced.

In contrast, the Indian and Ceylon 'managerial' workers had a more cordial relationship with the British planters, received higher wages, faced fewer restrictions in terms of freedom of movement and were able to send their children to English language schools. This facilitated social mobility of the Indian and Ceylon 'management'. The differential treatment accorded to the different Indian sub-groups due to the existing vertical (language, culture, nationality) and horizontal (caste and class) cleavages had created a sense of shared grievances among the Indian Tamil plantation labour. Despite the grievances of similarly situated Indian Tamil plantation labourers due to differential treatment they received and the inequalities they faced, the Indian Tamil plantation labour remained acquiescent and docile until the emergence of Indian activism in the 1930s, culminating in the 1941 Klang Strikes discussed in Section 3.4.

## 3.4 Indian activism, rights consciousness and mass mobilisation

The existence of grievances by itself did not lead to mass mobilisation among the Indians in colonial Malaya. The grievances described in Section 3.3 were primarily those of the Indian Tamil plantation labour and not the Indian community as a whole. This particular labour group was also placed in a weak bargaining position through the biased contractual relationship with the British planters and its low socioeconomic as well as caste status in comparison to the upper-caste Indian management. However, the author argues that these grievances of the Indian Tamil plantation labour formed the basis of a growing consciousness of injustice by this group, which led to its mobilisation in the 1930s. Why this process of mobilisation occurred is explained below.

### 3.4.1 Indian activism from the 1930s

The 1930s witnessed two major changes in the Indian community: first, the emergence of an urban Indian middle class who came into Malaya as free migrants and second, the rise of anti-imperialist ideology and anti-caste ideology in British India which was disseminated to the Indian community in Malaya by the urban Indian middle class. These were crucial factors in the process of Indian mass mobilisation that was beginning to take shape from the 1930s onwards. The 1920s had witnessed a rise in British colonial laws and regulations which was generally aimed at the suppression of all political and rebellious acts. Legal repression served to hinder the formation of any non-ethno-culturally based, class-based movement in Malaya. Most of these laws were labour laws, such as the *Labour Code 1923*, which criminalised industrial offences in order to impede labour-based collective action. The legally repressive labour laws and policies were meant to widen the gap between the three main ethno-cultural groups in Malaya and sustain the colonial economy in Malaya.

The urban Indian middle class who were an educated, professional subgroup which consisted, *inter alia*, of lawyers, journalists and teachers, were beginning to question the lack of enforcement of the few protective provisions in the labour codes and the prevalence of poverty among the Indian plantation labour.[38] The urban Indian middle-class professionals were fully aware of the antagonism that existed between the Indian management and Indian Tamil plantation labour in the rubber plantations due to caste and regional differences. The urban Indian middle class shared certain ethno-cultural commonalities with both the Indian Tamil plantation labour as well as the Indian management, and attempted to bring about a temporary unity. These commonalities included ethno-linguistic similarities as the urban Indian middle class had the ability to speak in both Tamil and English, as well as ethno-regional similarities in terms of originating from South India. The most significant factor was the ideological leanings of the urban Indian middle class, which oriented around political ideologies of anti-imperialism and nationalism, as well as social reform ideologies such as anti-casteism and socialism from India. Hence, the urban Indian middle class was committed to defeating the caste system which was utilised by the Indian management in the rubber plantations to legitimise the harsh treatment accorded to the Indian Tamil plantation labour. The urban Indian middle class was also heavily influenced by the nationalist politics in British India and sought to disseminate the idea of a unified and independent India among the Indians in Malaya.[39]

The anti-caste movement in the state of Tamil Nadu in British India was hostile to the caste system that was being practiced by particularly the *Brahmin* priestly caste as well as the landowning upper-caste group which bonded and subjugated the lower-caste agricultural peasantry. While there were few *Brahmins* among the Indians in Malaya,[40] the British planters and the higher caste Indian management in the rubber plantations were identified as subjugating the lower caste Indian Tamil plantation labour. The essence of the anti-caste ideology was to use South Indian or *Dravidian* identity in order to break the shackles of caste-based identity. For instance, by placing emphasis on a wider Tamil ethno-linguistic identity, the existing social perceptions and divisions of caste were weakened. This implies a shift from the external social identity based on caste towards a *mobilising identity* based on Tamil ethno-linguistic cohesion.

On the other hand, the anti-imperialist movement in British India was creating a wider united Indian consciousness in order to defeat British colonial rule and seek the right to sovereignty. The anti-imperialist or nationalist movement in British India sought to utilise Indian political identity in order to mobilise the hyper-diverse and fragmented Indian sub-groups within British India. The urban Indian middle class who came into Malaya in the 1930s brought with them the idea of self-rule but were confined to the nationalist politics of British India. As a migrant group, the Indians in Malaya did not have any political rights but the idea of defeating the imperialist power was gradually infused into the psyche of the Indian Tamil plantation labour in order to mobilise against the British.[41] This led to a shift from external social identities which were influenced by caste and ethno-cultural differences to a *mobilising identity* that was based on the political identity of being Indian.

The Indian identity in British India was purely a nationalist, anti-imperialist agenda as regional and ethno-cultural differences kept Indian sub-groups apart. However, in the case of the Indians in Malaya, since the

1890s, the colonial government had attempted to racialise and formalise a singular Indian identity. This facilitated a smoother transition from external social identities to an Indian mobilising identity. As the urban Indian middle class as well as the Indian management in rural plantations were more diverse in terms of ethno-cultural cleavages, the nationalist Indian identity became useful to unite these two Indian sub-groups. The Indian identity was also not biased towards any one ethno-cultural sub-group and did not alienate minority Indian sub-groups.

The ideology of nationalism was also useful for the urban Indian middle class to raise injustice and rights consciousness among the Indian Tamil plantation labour. The idea of a unified demand for rights by a migrant Indian community also brought about a temporal solidarity between various Indian sub-groups. Mitnick contends that identity and rights are bridged through the consistent experience of similarities in terms of shared grievances.[42] The Indian Tamil plantation workers were able to forge their identity as a non-rights bearing group due to the experience of repressive and discriminatory treatment in the rubber plantations. As colonial law and policy had already cemented the socioeconomic and geopolitical divisions of racial groups, the aggrieved individuals that faced these particular grievances seem to have consisted of a proportionally higher number of Indian Tamils, and the treatment that they encountered only served to strengthen their ethno-cultural identity and invoke a realisation of being sidelined. The Indian urban middle class on the other hand was more ethno-culturally diverse but mobilised to unite the group through the nationalist based identity of being Indian as well as claims for the right to sovereign rule in India.

The question is whether Mitnick's theory on the bridge between rights and identity is applicable to the temporary unity that existed between the urban Indian middle class, the Indian management in the rubber plantations and the Indian Tamil plantation labour. The three sub-groups did not share any common grievances, as the labour issues were separate and colonial hierarchical divisions in the rubber plantations had cemented ethno-cultural as well as socioeconomic cleavages. However, the anti-caste ideology that was spread by the urban Indian middle class was able to break away some of the caste-based cleavages and unite the Tamil speaking sub-group on the basis of forging a *Dravidian* identity. Further to this the nationalist identity of being Indian was essentially anti-imperialist in nature, which meant that the common adversary of the three Indian sub-groups were the British, both the British planters who controlled the Indian Tamil plantation labour and the Indian management, as well as the British colonial administration that had oversight over all constituents of British India and Malaya, which included all the Indian sub-groups. Hence, the nationalist rights agenda was a wider platform from which to forge a mobilising identity that was formidable enough to face British rule.

Interviews conducted for this study confirm that for the very first time in history the Indian community united from the mid-1930s to the 1940s due to the Indian nationalist rights agenda. Krishnabahawan, a retired school teacher and current leader of an Indian non-governmental organisation (NGO), iterated that Indian unity in colonial Malaya was mainly due to the Indian nationalist ideology which acted as a unifying cause.[43] Another interview participant for this study, a senior Indian politician in Malaysia who wished to remain anonymous, commented that the Indian nationalist agenda was not about ideological unification but was more 'cultural' in nature.[44]

However, Janakey Raman Manickam, a grassroots Indian activist and author of a historical commentary on Indians in Malaysia interviewed for this study believes that the divisions among Indians in the rubber plantations were more apparent among the 'educated class' (the Indian management) rather than the 'plantation workers' (the Indian Tamil plantation labour).[45] The Indian management in the estates had a 'friendly' or cordial relationship with the British planters, whereas the urban Indian middle class was mobilised by anti-caste and anti-imperialist ideologies.[46] Hence, the urban Indian middle class was able to form a connection with the Indian Tamil plantation labour by co-opting the latter's labour grievances as part of the anti-British campaign.

### 3.4.2 Indian activists, lawyers and leaders in colonial Malaya

The rise of urban Indian middle-class activists and leaders in the 1930s was opportune in terms of mobilising the already aggrieved Indian Tamil plantation labour. While Indian Tamil plantation labour grievances had been in existence from the 1890s, the emergence of Indian activists and identity-based ideologies were crucial in paving the way towards mass mobilisation in the 1930s and early 1940s. The Indian activist leaders consisted of educated professionals such as lawyers and journalists who raised awareness among the urban Indian middle class regarding the colonial exploitation of Indian Tamil plantation labour. The Indian activists also began to mobilise the Indian Tamil plantation labour by raising consciousness of the plantation group's labour rights and anti-caste rights. The Indian activist lawyers in particular played a significant role in using rights-based rhetoric and rights language in order to frame labour centric claims. These lawyers were thus key figures in the Indian activism that was taking place from the 1930s.

In contrast, Indian lawyers in the 1920s were not activists, but took on advisory roles and adopted a legal professional approach in voicing out the grievances of the Indian Tamil plantation labourers. For instance, in 1922, the Indian Immigration Committee appointed Mr P.K. Nambiar, a lawyer who was instrumental in advising the British Raj on the problems faced by the Indian Tamil plantation labourers in Malaya. Nambiar's discussions with the colonial officials led to the enactment of the 1922 *Indian Emigration Act* which contained strict regulations for labour recruiters in order to protect the Indian Tamil plantation labour.[47] In 1923, a former magistrate named Mr Arulanandam Pillay arrived in Malaya from India in order to take up the position of Indian Emigration Officer under the 1923 *Labour Enactment*.[48] Pillay reported on the earnestness of the colonial government in Malaya to investigate and address the grievances of the Indian Tamil plantation labour as well as to carry out legal action in the law courts on behalf of the aggrieved labourer.[49] In 1928, lawyer Mr S.N. Veerasamy was appointed to the Legislative Council of the Federated Malay States and was acclaimed as the first Indian representative in the Federal Council.[50] In essence the Indian lawyers in the 1920s were a part of the colonial civil service and took an elitist approach to the grievances of the Indian Tamil plantation labour by keeping to legal issues. As discussed above, the laws concerning labourer's grievances were limited and the bulk of the labourer's issues such as the harsh treatment accorded to labourers were not covered by any legal enactments. In some instances, the Indians lawyers were criticised for petitioning the interest of their own ethno-linguistic Indian sub-group, for example the Malayalis and Ceylon Tamils, rather than appealing the interest of the Indian community as a whole.[51] Hence, the Indian lawyers of the 1920s were unable to bring about significant changes to the situation of the Indian Tamil plantation labour.

The Indian lawyers in the 1930s were more activist in nature and in some instances took on a more radical approach compared to their predecessors. Their activism can be linked to the Indian nationalist ideology that was prevalent in the 1930s as well as the formation of new political organisations like the Central Indian Association of Malaya (CIAM). The arrival of the urban Indian middle class resulted in the formation of Indian societies, clubs and organisations which led to a flurry of networking between activists, lawyers and journalists. The coalition between legally trained actors such as the lawyers and extralegal actors such as journalists was crucial in the mobilisation of Indian Tamil plantation labour. Two prominent Indian activist leaders at that time were Mr M.N. Nair, a journalist, and Mr N. Raghavan, a lawyer.

As the grievances and claims made on behalf of the Indian Tamil plantation labour were labour-centric, this group of professional lawyers and journalists used rights-based language and rhetoric to frame the demands. Legally trained actors in social movements are known to use legal tools and legal materials that are accessible to them. As discussed in Chapter 2 (Section 2.2), Harding and Whiting's analysis of lawyers in post-colonial Malaysia revealed that lawyers mobilise by utilising the 'materials and tools of their trade', which, *inter alia*, included legal ideas like rights.[52] Halliday iterates that legally trained individuals when acting as a part of a collective define their cause through legal ideas and arguments.[53] Activist lawyers also tend to influence other activists with legal ideas, especially the right to equality and non-discrimination. Although there have been no studies done on the role of activist lawyers in Malaya during the colonial period, the theoretical point discerned by studies on activist lawyers in post-colonial states[54] can be utilised to make sense of the role of rights among the Indian lawyers in colonial Malaya. The colonial Indian lawyers of the 1930s were prominent leaders of the Indian Tamil plantation labour movement and utilised rights-based language in order to frame demands, which is analysed in Section 3.4.3.

The influence of legal ideas on activist journalists and leaders is evident from the speeches and writings produced by them. For instance, from the mid-1930s onwards, there was an escalation of speeches and publications to warn the general Indian polity against colonial discrimination, inequality and the lack of rights. The writings show a serious concern for the political status of Indians in colonial Malaya especially in relation to the unfavourable situation of other migrant Indian groups in British colonies. In 1937, M.N. Nair an activist leader and journalist wrote,

> The pro-Malay policy pursued in recent years and the policy of discrimination showed against Indians by the Government here have created suspicion in the minds of the Indian public men, that in the course of time the history of Indians in South Africa will be re-enacted here, too.[55]

The journalistic articles also incorporate both the grievances of the Indian Tamil plantation labour which was socioeconomic in nature, and the grievances of the urban Indian middle class, which were oriented around the political status of Indians in colonial Malaya. For instance, in 1940, *The Indian* in its editorial piece stated,

> The Empire is expending large sums for the persecution of this war, but what has the rubber industry done for its labour? Is it too much to hope that at last it will see reason? Will the Government of Malaya succeed in making Indians feel that they are equal partners in Malaya?[56]

Hence, the pivotal concerns during the 1930s to the 1940s did not just revolve around the socioeconomic rights of the Indian Tamil plantation labour, they also embraced the civil and political rights of the Indian community as a whole. The amalgamation of both the Indian Tamil plantation labour issues and the urban Indian middle-class problems into a single concern of political status also shows the temporal unity of Indians during this time.

### 3.4.3  Mobilising Indian identity and rights: framing socioeconomic, cultural and political rights in colonial Malaya

From the 1930s to 1941, the mobilisation strategy of the urban Indian middle-class professionals show a combination of legal tools and ideas like rights and injustice, as well as the use of journalistic reporting to create publicity and awareness of the situation of the Indian Tamil plantation labour. Using Snow and Benford's framing theory,[57] which is explained in Chapter 2 (Section 2.4.1), the framing strategies used by Indian activists from the 1930s onwards show 'diagnostic framing' which identify and attribute the Indian problems, 'prognosis framing' which provides solutions to the Indian problems and strategies to realise the solutions, as well as 'motivational framing' which engages the Indians to mobilise for collective action, or what is termed as a 'call for arms'.

An example of diagnostic framing is seen in the journalist M.N. Nair's report in 1937, which is described in Section 3.4.2. Nair draws a parallel between the status of Indians in Malaysia with the Indians in South Africa, as he attributes the problems facing the Indians to the 'pro-Malay policy' and the 'policy of discrimination against the Indians'.[58] In attributing the status of Indians to the pro-Malay policy, Nair clearly diagnoses the problem of discrimination as arising from the colonial government's Malay affirmative action policy. By making a comparison of the status of Indians to the native Malays, the core issue of the Indians had been shifted to reflect political grievances rather than the socioeconomic condition of the Indian Tamil plantation labour. The framing of Indian issues in terms of discrimination also shows that the root of the problem is differential treatment.

By 1937, the Indians had generally become more politicised and organised, which is evident from the formation of the CIAM. The CIAM's main contention was to discuss the civil rights (such as citizenship) and political rights of the Indian community in Malaya. However, CIAM had also begun championing the cause of the Indian Tamil plantation labour, which included demands for minimum wages and the prohibition of harsh treatment on labour. CIAM went to the extent of petitioning the British Raj to stop assisted Indian emigration to Malaya due to the physical and socioeconomic abuse of the Indian Tamil plantation labour. At that time, there was no political opportunity for the Indian Tamil plantation labour to air their labour-oriented grievances. The group did not have adequate representation as trade unions were restricted by the colonial administration. The *kangany* was an agent of the British planter and did not sufficiently represent the Indian Tamil plantation labourer's grievances. Hence, radical Indian lawyers and journalists who were crucial components of the Indian Tamil plantation labour movement had become members and leaders of CIAM in order to place political pressure on the colonial government in Malaya.

CIAM lobbied for legislative reform in terms of minimum wages for the Indian Tamil plantation labour, the legal recognition of Hindu marriages, educational provisions for the children of the Indian Tamil plantation workers and made public appeals to end social problems like the *toddy* ('palm liquor') drinking culture that was prevalent among the Indian Tamil plantation labour.[59] CIAM's campaign and advocacy for social, economic and cultural reforms is reflected in a 1938 report in *The Indian* news journal. The report attempted to frame the specific issues of the Indian Tamil plantation labour by relating to the 1938 ban on the Indian *kangany* system of labour recruitment and immigration. However, the report also displays prognostic framing in providing solutions to the Indian immigration problem:

> Important and far-reaching issues of policy will have to be faced before the sluice-gates of Indian emigration to Malaya are ever opened again. Questions of political status, full rights of citizenship, establishment of a minimum wage not affected by the ups and downs in the rubber market, and amenities for Indian labour, the position of non-labour immigrants and domiciled Indians – these and quite a number of other matters have to be tackled.[60]

The report suggested that Indian issues can be resolved by providing civil and political rights to Indians in general, as well as socioeconomic and labour rights to the Indian Tamil plantation labour. The mention of 'non-labour immigrants and domiciled Indians' is a clear indication of the 1930s arrival of the urban Indian middle class as well as the Indian residents already in Malaya who had come as free migrants in the past. CIAM's contention shows a wider agenda of incorporating the many Indian sub-groups and placing greater importance on the issue of citizenship.

The colonial government pointedly ignored all of CIAM's claims due to two main reasons. First, there was no genuine colonial interest in raising the socioeconomic and politico-legal status of the Indian Tamil plantation labour, as the maintenance of a temporary underclass labour was more economically favourable to the British planters. Second, the colonial government believed that the urban Indian middle class or professional group had 'neither the rapport nor the genuine sympathy' with the Indian Tamil plantation labour group in order to form its indisputable political representation.[61] The second point is supported by Michael Stenson's study of colonialism and Indian labour in Malaya, which revealed that '[t]he Indians probably had more associations but less co-operation' and most Indian Associations were simply unable to reach 'the core of the community, the labourers'.[62] This suggests that CIAM had incorporated the Indian Tamil plantation labour's grievances in order to widen its political agenda.

It was the colonial belief that the CIAM which consisted largely of the urban Indian middle class and professionals was not fully representative of the Indian Tamil plantation labour. However, this belief was based on the hyper-diverse and fragmented nature of the Indian community, which had remained acquiescent and submissive on the whole. Despite the inherent weaknesses of the Indian community, attributed to horizontal and vertical cleavages in the community, a few key Indian activists were able to mobilise the Indian Tamil plantation labour between 1938 and 1941. The pre-war period had led to severe grievances experienced by the Indian Tamil plantation labour, *inter alia* low wages and harsh treatment by the British planters. At the same time, Indian activists from the urban Indian middle-class and professional group had begun to spread radical social ideas based on the anti-caste and anti-imperialist ideologies already discussed above. The combination of rising grievances and the call for Indian as well as labour-oriented rights, reached its pinnacle in the 1941 Klang Strikes.

The Klang Strikes was a far-reaching event that involved thousands of Indian Tamil plantation labourers who organised plantation strikes and walk-outs from rubber plantations in the state of Selangor, for more than a month. The main leaders or activists of the walk-outs were not Indian Tamil plantation labourers, but Indian activists from the Klang Indian Association and the Klang District Indian Union which were affiliates of CIAM. The two main activist leaders who organised the walk-outs were Mr R.H. Nathan, the sub-editor of a Tamil newspaper called the *Tamil Nesan*, and Mr Y.K. Menon, a clerk from a rubber plantation.[63] The first ever mass mobilisation of Indian Tamil plantation labour was triggered by the initiation of wage fixing by the British planters and industrialists in order to boost the production of rubber during the Second World War.[64] The already aggrieved Indian Tamil plantation labourers now faced the prospect of low wages and all its accompanying consequences for a prolonged period.

R.H. Nathan, the leader of the Klang District Indian Union and CIAM affiliate, made a 'call for arms' of the Indian Tamil plantation labour and listed the full demands of the Indian Tamil plantation labour movement:

> Parity of pay for Indian and Chinese labourers; The removal of estate staff who were brutal and their replacement with Tamil speaking staff; The provision for proper education for children; An end to the molesting of labourers' women folk by Europeans and "Black" Europeans; The provision of proper medical facilities; The closing of toddy shops; The freedom of speech and assembly; Free access to estates for relations and friends; Permission for labourers to mount bicycles before European managers and Asian staff; The abolition of 10 to 12 hours of working day; No victimisation of those presenting grievances; Permission for the labourers to have an association to look after their interests and put forward their grievances.[65]

While the main issue was the restrictions imposed on wages, the demands included an exhaustive list of specific grievances pertaining to the Indian Tamil plantation labour as well as more general claims such as the freedom of speech and assembly. Ramasamy's research on labour resistance in colonial Malaya points to two main factors that caused the Klang uprising: first, the absence of wage increases despite huge increases in profit for the rubber companies in London and second, the influence of Indian nationalism through CIAM.[66] Although the main leaders of the strike were affiliated to CIAM and other Indian Associations, the list of demands itself does not portray a nationalist agenda. This implies that Indian nationalism served only as a motivational factor to rally the Indian Tamil plantation labourers together.

None of the claims made specifically relate to any legal rights or legislative provisions. However, most of the claims made indicate an urgent call for 'equal concern and respect', which according to Ronald Dworkin, is the most fundamental political right.[67] For example, the claims for freedom from 'brutal' treatment by staff and the 'molesting' of women, indicate the basic requirement of respect and human dignity. The list also includes claims for basic freedoms such as the freedom of movement (having access to friends and family), the freedom of association (in order for grievances to be aired) as well as the freedom of speech and assembly. The 1941 Klang Strikes clearly occurred before the promulgation of the 1945 *United Nations Charter* and the 1948 *Universal Declaration of Human Rights*. Hence, it is unlikely that the Indian activists and leaders were using the notion of human rights in its modern post-war form.

What is notable about the demand made by the Indian leaders of the strike is that the claim for more freedoms, equality and a type of moral dignity for the Indian Tamil plantation labour is associated with the anti-caste ideology that was spread through the Self-Reform Movement among the urban Indian middle class, discussed in Chapter 1 (Section 1.4.1). Donnelly in a study on non-Western concepts of human rights, comments that the principle of 'human dignity' was in existence in non-Western settings including in 'Hindu India'.[68] Despite the existence of the caste system in pre-colonial India, there were also established principles on human dignity and respect. The escalation in Indian Tamil plantation labour strikes and the growth of Indian associations in Malaya which has been attributed to the urban Indian middle class and the rise of *moral rights* consciousness is therefore linked to the wave of anti-caste philosophy in colonial British India which advocated the right to human dignity.[69]

Despite the sudden mobilisation of thousands of Indian Tamil plantation labourers in the Klang strikes, the colonial authorities quickly subdued the uprising by physically crushing the strikers using military troops. The colonial authorities completely ignored the grievances and the list of demands made, while taking repressive action against the strikers and activists. A few of the Indian Tamil plantation labourers and Indian activists were deported back to India and the remaining labourers were restricted within their rubber plantations and districts. The colonial authorities misrepresented or 'covered up' the strikes and walk-outs as an agitation caused by Indian nationalists. The authorities were clearly more concerned for the welfare of the British planters rather than the Indian Tamil plantation labour, and as such refused to conduct an investigation into the strikes.[70] The High Commissioner is said to have reported that 'all the strikes were subversive and violent, and the strike demands were ridiculous'.[71] The reaction of the colonial authorities to the claims made by Indian activists was repressive in terms of the use of physical force.

Stenson reports that the strikes, which took place in a few rubber estate plantations in Klang, were, in fact, conducted in an organised manner, 'with few allegations of intimidation and little or no damage to property'.[72] In fact, the Agent of the Government of India, found the legal persecution of the strike leaders to be unduly excessive. In his letter to the Government of the Federated Malay States, he writes that the criminal prosecution of the Indian strikers and the union leaders initiated by the British planters was malicious and in bad faith.[73] The Agent of the Government of India further argued that the aim of the prosecution was to intimidate the strikers and put an end to the Indian Tamil plantation labour movement, which was viewed by the public in India as a gross abuse of the courts of justice. Clearly, the legal prosecution of the strikers and activists operated as legal repression in order to suppress future direct action tactics.

While the representatives of the British Raj were appalled at the treatment accorded to the strikers, the colonial government in British Malaya viewed the strike as a threat to the British rule of Malaya itself. The colonial government in Malaya feared that the Klang Strikes were a precursor to a growing anti-imperialist uprising. The dread of a nationalistic rebellion was evident in the caution issued by the Director of Criminal Intelligence, Mr John Dalley to the Controller of Labour in Malaya that the 1941 Klang strikes would inevitably lead to widespread civil disobedience throughout colonial Malaya.[74] Dalley warned that if CIAM as well as other political and labour-based organisations were not scrutinised and forced to withdraw from making labour-based claims, they will eventually mobilise the Indian Tamil plantation labour all throughout Malaya. However, the colonial authority's concern of further strikes and protests instigated by the nationalistic fervour of India soon turned into awareness that Malaya itself was ready for independence.

Although CIAM was able to mobilise the Indian Tamil plantation labour, its involvement with nationalist politics in British India meant that much of the Indian Tamil plantation labour grievances were heavily politicised. The grievances were of grave concern but the lack of adequate representation of Indian Tamil plantation labour issues meant that it became a part of the wider nationalist agenda. The nationalist ideology of India was able to forge a united Indian identity among the various Indian sub-groups in Malaya and was also helpful to Indian activists seeking civil and political rights of Indians in Malaya. However, the question remains as to the status of the Indian Tamil plantation labour, whose' grievances were not addressed through nationalist and identity-based politics.

The colonial government's stance on restricting trade unionism and labour representation in order to avoid class-based collective action had inevitably led the way for a race-based collective action. As discussed in Section 3.2.3, the divide and rule policy in Malaya based on racial divisions of the main ethno-cultural groups had itself served to construct a race-based resistance. Although the laws and policies were geared towards creating racial and class-based divisions (such as the hierarchical divisions in the rubber plantations) in order to impede resistance, the race-based identity held a stronger affinity. Hence, racial kinship offered stronger social capital that could be utilised to mobilise the Indian ethno-cultural group in Malaya.

Nevertheless, the issues faced by the Indian Tamil plantation labour are clearly class-based, and the attempt to solve these problems by way of an Indian nationalist movement in Malaya was not fruitful. Race-based mobilisation inevitably dilutes class-based issues. By incorporating the Indian Tamil plantation labour grievances into the Indian nationalist agenda of seeking sovereign rule in India, these specific grievances were swept aside, especially when Malaya was facing its own path towards independence in the 1950s. These particularistic concerns soon shifted towards political concerns about the status of Indians as a community within the Malayan polity.

## 3.5 Conclusion

The serious grievances among the Indians during the colonial period have largely been class-based problems which come from the colonial exploitation of the Indian Tamil plantation labour. Despite the persistence of grievances from the 1890s, through the Indian indentured labour system and the Indian *Kangany* system, the Indian Tamil plantation labour did not mobilise until the 1941 Klang Strikes. In the 1930s, the urban Indian middle-class professionals organised and formed associations based on anti-caste and anti-imperialist ideas that had influenced the key leaders of these Indian associations. It was the journalists and lawyers affiliated to these Indian associations who coopted the grievances of the Indian Tamil plantation labour and *mobilised* the labour group. Hence, the rhetoric of *moral* rights was useful for the mobilisers or in this case, the leaders of the plantation labour strikes, rather than for the plantation labourers themselves.

## Notes

1 Sally E Merry, 'Law and Colonialism' (1991) 25 *Law and Society Review* 889, 890.
2 See Charles Hirschman, 'The Meaning and Measurement of Ethnicity in Malaysia: An Analysis of Census Classifications' (1987) 46(3) *The Journal of Asian Studies* 555; Charles Hirschman, 'The Making of Race in Colonial Malaya: Political Economy and Racial Ideology' (1986) 1 *Sociological Forum* 330. See also Benedict Anderson, *Imagined Communities: Reflections on the Origin and Spread of Nationalism* (University of Michigan, 2006) 64; Timo Kortteinen, 'Embedded Ethnicity: On the Narratives of Ethnic Identity in Malaysia and Sri Lanka' (2007) 32(3) *Journal of the Finnish Anthropological Society* 62.
3 The Straits Settlements (the first British settlement in Malaya) included the states of Malacca, Penang and Singapore in Malaya. The Federated Malay States (British protected states) included Selangor, Perak, Negeri Sembilan and Pahang.
4 Hirschman (1987), above n 2, 564.
5 Anderson (2006), above n 2, 165.
6 Judith A Nagata, 'What Is a Malay? Situational Selection of Ethnic Identity in a Plural Society' (1974) 1 *American Ethnologist* 331, 336.

7  Hirschman (1987), above n 2, 571–578.
8  Palanisamy Ramasamy, 'Labour Control and Labour Resistance in the Planta-tions of Colonial Malaya' (1992) 19(3–4) *Journal of Peasant Studies* 87, 90.
9  See 'The Indian Immigration Ordinance', *The Straits Times (British Straits Settlement)*, 23 October 1875 <http://newspapers.nl.sg/Digitised/Article.aspx? articleid=straitstimes18751023.2.8>. See also 'Indian Immigration: How Labour Supplies are Raised', *The Straits Times (British Straits Settlement)*, 8 July 1913 <http://newspapers.nl.sg/Digitised/Article/straitstimes19130708.2.64.aspx>
10 See 'Tamil Labour Fund: Additional Rules By Immigration Committee', *The Straits Times (British Straits Settlement)*, 4 December 1908 <http://newspapers. nl.sg/Digitised/Article/straitstimes19081204.2.67.aspx>
11 Jess N Parmer, *Colonial Labor Policy and Administration: a History of Labor in the Rubber Plantation Industry in Malaya* (Locust Valley: New York, 1960).
12 See 'Rice Cultivation in the Federated Malay States (FMS): Conditions for Cer-tain Alienated Lands', *The Straits Times (British Straits Settlement)*, 25 January 1917 <http://newspapers.nl.sg/Digitised/Article/straitstimes19170125.2.57.aspx>. See also Paul Kratoska, 'Rice Cultivation and the Ethnic Division of Labour in British Malaya' (1982) 24(2) *Comparative Studies in Society and History* 280.
13 Michael Stenson, *Class, Race and Colonialism* (University of Queensland Press, 1980) 4. See also S Nair, 'Colonial "Others" and Nationalist Politics in Malaysia' (1999) 54(1) *Akademia* 55.
14 The term was used to describe the Jim Crow Laws in the United States which spatially segregated the Blacks from the White populace (See Frances L Edwards and Grayson B Thompson, 'The Legal Creation of Raced Space: The Subtle and Ongoing Discrimination Created Through Jim Crow Laws' (2010) 12 *Berkeley Journal of African American Law and Policy* 145).
15 Quoted in Collin E R Abraham, 'Racial and Ethnic Manipulation in Colonial Malaya' (1983) 6(1) *Ethnic and Racial Studies* 18, 24.
16 P Ramasamy, above n 8, 93.
17 See Callistus Fernandez, 'Colonial Knowledge, Invention and Reinvention of Malay Identity in Pre-Independence Malaya: A Retrospect' (1999) 55 *Akade-mika* 39, 49–50.
18 United Kingdom, *Parliamentary Debates*, House of Lords, 19 July 1875, vol 225 col 1630 (Lord Stanley of Alderly).
19 Ibid.
20 Sinappah Arasaratnam, 'Indian Society of Malaysia and its Leaders: Trends in Leadership and Ideology among Malaysian Indians, 1945–1960' (1982) 13(2) *Journal of Southeast Asian Studies* 236, 237–238.
21 Prakash C Jain, 'Exploitation and Reproduction of Migrant Indian Labour in Co-lonial Guyana and Malaysia' (1988) 18(2) *Journal of Contemporary Asia* 189, 200.
22 See Richard Stubbs, 'Malaysia's Rubber Smallholding Industry Crisis and the Search for Stability' (1983) 56 *Pacific Affairs* 84.
23 Amarjit Kaur, 'Plantation Systems, Labour Regimes and the State in Malaysia, 1900–2012' (2014) 14(2) *Journal of Agrarian Change* 190, 196.
24 Jomo K Sundaram, 'Plantation Capital and Indian Labour in Malaya' in Kernial S Sandhu and A Mani (eds), *Indian Communities in Southeast Asia* (Institute of Southeast Asian Studies, 1993) 312.
25 Janakey R Manickam, *The Malaysian Indian Dilemma: The Struggles and Ag-ony of the Indian Community in Malaysia* (Nationwide Human Development and Research Centre, 2012) 19.
26 B C Bhattacharjee, *The Immigrant* (DavRa Publications, 1989) quoted in Manickam, above n 25, 52.
27 Interview with Mr G. Krishnabahawan, Indian activist and leader at Malaysian Community Education Foundation (Petaling Jaya, 13 July 2012); Interview with

a senior politician in a leading Indian party (Petaling Jaya, 15 November 2012); Interview with Jiwi Kathaiah, Editor of *Semparuthi* (a Tamil online newspaper) (Kuala Lumpur, 15 March 2013).

28 Hugh Tinker, *A New System of Slavery: The Export of Indian Labour Overseas, 1830–1920* (Oxford University Press, 1974) 199.

29 Quoted in Sunil S Amrith, 'Indians Overseas? Governing Tamil Migration in Malaya 1870–1941' (2010) 208 *Past and Present* 231, 241.

30 Ravindra K Jain, *South Indians in the Plantation Frontier in Malaya* (Yale University Press, 1970) 290.

31 United Kingdom, *Parliamentary Debates*, House of Lords, 19 July 1875, vol 225 col 1630 (Lord Stanley of Alderly).

32 Ibid., col 1630.

33 'The Late Debate', *Straits Times Overland Journal*, 30 November 1876, pg 2 <http://newspapers.nl.sg/Digitised/Article/stoverland18761130-1.2.8.aspx>

34 Ibid.

35 United Kingdom, *Parliamentary Debates*, House of Lords, 19 July 1875, vol 225 col 1635 (Lord Stanley of Alderly).

36 Quoted in P Jain (1988), above n 21, 199.

37 See T Marimuthu, 'The Plantation School As an Agent of Social Reproduction' in Kernial Singh Sandhu and A Mani (eds), *Indian Communities in Southeast Asia* (Institute of Southeast Asian Studies, 1993) 489.

38 See Rajeswary Ampalavanar Brown, *Class, Caste and Ethnicism Among Urban Indians in Malaysia, 1920–1941* (Kuala Lumpur: Nusantara 2, 1972) 209.

39 See generally Muzafar Desmond Tate, *The Malaysian Indians: History, Problems and Future* (Strategic Institute of Research and Development, 2008).

40 See Rajakrishnan Ramasamy, *Caste Consciousness Among Indian Tamils in Malaya* (Pelanduk, 1984).

41 Ghosg quoted in Tayyab Mahmud, 'Migration, Identity and the Colonial Encounter' (1997) 76 *Oregon Law Review* 633, 653.

42 See Eric J Mitnick, *Rights, Groups, and Self-Invention: Group Differentiated Rights in Liberal Theory* (Ashgate, 2006).

43 Interview with Mr G. Krishnabahawan, Malaysian Community Education Foundation, an Indian education NGO (Petaling Jaya, 13 July 2012).

44 Interview with a senior politician in a leading Indian party (Petaling Jaya, 15 November 2012).

45 Interview with Janakey Raman Manickam, Indian activist and author of *The Malaysian Indian Dilemma: The Struggles and Agony of the Indian Community in Malaysia* (Nationwide Human Development and Research Centre, 2012) (Klang, 8 August 2012).

46 Ibid.

47 Stenson, above n 13, 41.

48 'Labour in Malaya: Arrival of Indian Emigration Officer', *The Straits Times* (British Straits Settlement), 29 October 1923, pg 10, <http://newspapers.nl.sg/Digitised/Article/straitstimes19231029.2.67.aspx>

49 Ibid.

50 'Indians Acclaim Council Appointment', *The Straits Times* (British Straits Settlement), 4 March 1934, 12, <http://newspapers.nl.sg/Digitised/Article/straitstimes19340304.2.82.aspx>

51 Rajeswary Ampalavanar Brown, *The Indian Minority And Political Change in Malaya, 1945–1957* (Kuala Lumpur: Oxford University Press, 1981) 6.

52 Andrew Harding and Amanda Whiting, 'Custodian of Civil Liberties and Justice in Malaysia: The Malaysian Bar and the Moderate State' in Terence C Halliday et al (eds), *Fates of Political Liberalism in the British Post-Colony: The Politics of the Legal Complex* (Cambridge University Press, 2012) 247, 297.

53  Quoted in Harding et al, above n 52, 297.
54  See Harding et al, above n 52.
55  M.N. Nair, *Indians in Malaya* (1937), 47–48, quoted in Manickam, above n 25, 76.
56  *The Indian*, Editorial 12th September 1940, quoted in Manickam, above n 25, 84.
57  Robert Benford and David Snow, 'Framing Processes and Social Movements' (2000) 26 *Annual Review of Sociology* 611, 615.
58  M.N. Nair, *Indians in Malaya* (1937), 47–48, quoted in Manickam, above n 25, 76.
59  P Jain, above n 21, 198.
60  Editorial, *The Indian* (1938), quoted in Stenson, above n 13, 50.
61  Sinappah Arasaratnam, 'Malaysian Indians: the Formation of Incipient Society' in Kernial Singh Sandhu and A Mani (eds), *Indian Communities in Southeast Asia* (Institute of Southeast Asian Studies, 1993) 190, 198.
62  Stenson, above n 13, 54.
63  Harold E Wilson, *The Klang Strikes of 1941: Labour and Capital in Colonial Malaya* (Singapore: Institute of Southeast Asian Studies, 1981) 6.
64  P Ramasamy, above n 8, 103.
65  K B Subbiah, *Yuttatal Vantha Yutham* (Because of War a War) (Kuala Lumpur, 1946) quoted in Manickam, above n 25, 87.
66  P Ramasamy, above n 8, 103.
67  See Ronald Dworkin, *Taking Rights Seriously* (Harvard University Press, 1977).
68  Jack Donnelly, 'Human Rights and Human Dignity: An Analytic Critique of Non-Western Conceptions of Human Rights' (1982) 76(2) *The American Political Science Review* 303, 308–309.
69  See Gail Omvedt, *Reinventing Revolution: New Social Movements and the Socialist Tradition in Indian* (M.E. Sharpe, 1993).
70  Wilson, above n 63, 9.
71  Quoted in Stenson, above n 13, 61.
72  Ibid., 61.
73  Letter from C.S. Venkatachar, ICS, Agent of the Government of India to Adrian Clark, Legal Advisers, FMS, 27 March 1941, CO 77/145, quoted in Wilson, above n 63, 11.
74  John D. Dalley, Director of Criminal Intelligence to C. Wilson, Controller of Labour Malaya dated 4 April 1941, quoted in Wilson, above n 63, 15.

# 4 The quiet minority
## Indians and legal repression in an illiberal democratic Malaysia (1957–1989)

### 4.1 Introduction

The previous chapter showed how the presence of mobilisers – the lawyers and journalists – played a key role in converting the shared grievances of the Indian Tamil plantation labour into action in the form of the 1941 Klang Strikes. In this story, the law played an important role in a number of ways: a constitutive role by constructing identity and shared grievances; a repressive role which also contributed to grievances; and a mobilising role through the use of legal and rights claims. This chapter takes the analysis into the post-Independence period and examines not Indian mobilisation but rather why they did not mobilise for over thirty years despite persistent and escalating grievances during this period. This chapter will analyse the role of the law as a repressive tool of an increasingly authoritarian state, which was not only used to maintain an illiberal political system but also used by the state as a coercive and ideological instrument that deepened racial cleavages. The chapter begins therefore by considering how the law played a role in constructing the politico-legal identity of Indians in post-colonial Malaysia.

### 4.2 The racialisation of Indian identity in post-colonial Malaya

As Chapter 3 showed, the colonial ideology of race and the capitalistic nature of colonial control in British Malaya had racialised the native Malays and the main sources of colonial labour: the Chinese in the tin mines and the Indians in the rubber plantations. Although Social Darwinism was a paternalistic ideology of race which placed the British as a superior people and protectorate of the native Malays, the remnants of colonial ideology was still to be seen in post-independence census categorisation, registration formalities, the *1957 Federal Constitution* as well as the 1970 affirmative action policy in favour of the Malays, the *New Economic Policy* (NEP). However, the main thrust of the post-colonial Malaysian government's political ideology is the notion that the special position of the Malays and other natives who are collectively and legally identified as the *Bumiputera vis-à-vis* the non-*Bumiputera* communities of ethnic Chinese and Indians, acts as a political and legal trump. This notion impinges on the cardinal principle of equality before the law and has become the source of not only racial inequalities but also severe intra-group class inequalities, as will be shown in Section 4.2.3. However, race was the underpinning political ideology. Hence, the theoretical argument of critical race theorists on the mutually constitutive link between the law and race discussed in Chapter 2 (Section 2.4.2) is useful in analysing the way in which legal formalities, laws and policies in Malaysia have been used as tools of racial construction. Formalities and official instruments which use racial or ethnic markers in order to reference and categorise the Malaysian polity include the demographic and population census as well as the obligatory process of identity registration.

### 4.2.1 Formal registration of racial identity and census categories of ethnicity

The legal categorisation of race in Malaysia begins from birth, whereby *Section 7* of the *Births and Deaths Registration Act 1957 (Act 299)* provides that '... the birth of every child born in Malaysia shall be registered by the Registrar ...' The only ethno-cultural or racial reference in the Act is in *Section 7(3)* which states that '[i]n the case of a child of the Chinese race the Registrar may ... permit ... to insert ... the name of such child ... in Chinese characters.' However, the act authorises the National Registration Department which comes under the purview of the Ministry of Home Affairs to regulate and monitor the formalities of identity registration. The formal process of birth registration which takes place in the National Registration Department requires the racial and religious identification of the child's parents. From that point onwards the child is racially categorised.

Another mandatory procedure of identity registration is the 'national identity card' at the age of twelve. The process confirms the racial and religious identification of the child based on the birth certificate, but does not explicitly state racial identity in the identification card itself. However, it is compulsory to provide ethno-cultural information in the official forms to be filled at both the registration of birth and in the registration for the national identification card at the age of twelve. Both official forms require information on *keturunan* ('descent') and *agama* ('religion') to be submitted.[1] Although 'descent' is not defined the term loosely refers to parental lineage, and based on the official census classifications analysed below, it is a reference to the ethnic/racial group that the individual is categorised as. Hence, due to the obligatory and binding nature of the formal process of identity registration, the individual Malaysian's ethno-cultural attributes become a permanent aspect of his/her legal identity.

The legal process of establishing one's racial identity is significant as it shows how the law constructs race. However, the registration formalities also indicate the arbitrary nature of classifying race which is loosely conceived from social perceptions of parental lineage and ethnicity. It can be said that while the law constructs race, socially conceived notions of race in turn construct legal categories of ethno-cultural identity. In the interviews conducted for this study, participants responded to the interview question 'Who is an Indian person?' by stressing birth registration as the source of racial identity.[2] However, racialisation in Malaysia is deeply rooted in social perceptions, political ideology as well as legal formalities. In fact, the relationship between the law and racial identity is not linear or unidirectional, but rather fluid and dynamic. The mutually constitutive nature of formalities and socially perceived notions of racial identity was exemplified by another interviewee in this research. S. Arutchelvan, a political and grassroots activist in response to the interview question, 'Who is an Indian person' responded with, 'Who is an Indian? Actually it's very easy ... from birth they are given a birth certificate saying you are Chinese, Indian, Malay.'[3] These interview responses suggest that internal social identity or the self-perceived identity of ethno-cultural groups in Malaysia is heavily influenced by *racial* identifications that are enforced through legal formalities. Mitnick describes this process: '[e]ven more ominously, because we so readily internalise legally constructed categories, values and definitions, we are rarely specifically conscious of their influence on our perceptions'.[4]

The political ideologies of race and social perceptions of racial identity are especially evident in the Malaysian census classifications, which is authorised under the *Census Act 1960*. The manner in which the population census was devised is based on the colonial methodology, while the census categories of ethno-cultural groupings have gradually evolved from the colonial taxonomy of *race* described in Chapter 3. However, there have been two major shifts in the procedure. First, the post-colonial method of obtaining ethno-cultural information was based on self-identification or self-perception of which 'community' or 'ethnicity' the individual felt (s) he belonged to. This shift in census method suggests that the post-colonial census categorisation is moving away from *race* towards self-perceptions of *ethnicity* as the classification criteria. In other words, the categories of ethnicity in the census are constructed from the internal social perceptions of ethno-cultural identity. In fact, Hirschman has challenged the common misconception among some commentators that census classifications on ethnicity conform to criteria set by governmental policy or the Constitution, by pointing out that the matter on who decides and how it is decided is vague.[5]

However, the author argues that the social perceptions of ethno-cultural identity have been intrinsically influenced by the formal identities devised during the colonial period and hold remnants of the British racial ideology. As discussed above, the social perception of ethno-cultural identity and the legally imposed racial identity are mutually constitutive. This is further shown in the formal classification of the heterogeneous Indian community under one census race-code, but subdividing the code into as many as nine to ten sub-codes to accommodate the diverse nature of Indian self-perceived identity (see Table 4.1 below). While the single racial code of 'Indian' reflects the racialisation of the term during the colonial era, the numerous sub-codes reflect the internal social identity of the various Indian ethno-cultural sub-groups.

The second major shift relates to the terminologies used to refer to the ethno-cultural category in the census. Previous colonial census reports had shifted from the term 'nationality' to the term 'race', but the 1947 colonial census report had coined the word 'community' to replace 'race'. However, the first post-colonial Malaysian census in 1957 at the time of the Malaysian Independence preferred to utilise the old colonial term 'race'. This suggests that the post-colonial census categorisation of ethno-cultural identity reflected the politico-legal ideology of the Social Contract, the constitutional definition of the Malay race and administrative references to the three main races. Furthermore, in 1957, there was a need to consolidate the three different races into a single nation, based on the familiarity of colonial categorisations and divisions of ethno-cultural groups. However, in 1970, another major shift in terminology occurred whereby the census report returned to use the more neutral term 'community'.[6] This particular shift in terminology relates to the 1969 racial riots that created racial tension between the majority Malays and the minority Chinese. In fact, the 1977 Census Report stated, 'A complete break was made in 1970 when respondents were asked the question: "To what community do you belong? No reference to "race" was made in any of the documentation.'[7] The Malay version of the census even coined a brand-new word (*komuniti*) in order to accommodate the major shift.

Later census classifications became more diverse in terms of recognising the different ethnic, linguistic, religious and cultural groups and subgroups. For instance, the 1980 census asked the question 'To what ethnic group, community or dialect group do you belong?', with the Malay version asking '*Apakah kumpulan keturunan, komuniti atau loghet anda*?'[8] Thus, the Malay term '*kumpulan keturunan*' directly relates to the term 'ethnic group'. This change in terminology relates to the previous discussion on birth and identification registration forms, which found that the term '*keturunan*' or 'descent' relates to the individual's ethnicity. However, the fluctuating changes of terminology in formal instruments indicate an inherent difficulty in measuring and classifying an ethno-culturally disparate and diverse Malaysian populace. Hence, the construction of census codes according to rigid categories such as Malays, Chinese and Indians, displays the subjective and discretionary manner in which an ethno-culturally diverse population is force-fitted into neat racial categories. As Holst commented, '[i]n order to create a feeling of belonging to an ethnicized group ... the census turned out to be a powerful and normative, yet at the same time often arbitrary, tool.'[9]

The arbitrary nature of race-based or ethnicity-based classification in formal instruments such as the census is shown in the way the Indians have been categorised from the first colonial census in 1871 (see Table 3.1 in Chapter 3) to the current 2010 census (see Table 5.1 in Chapter 5). As Chapter 3 denoted, Indians are not a race or ethnic group, but a nationality. However, the colonial ideology as well as the perception of race and colonial labour policy in

Malaya was driven by the capitalist need to racialise and divide the labouring masses. While the term 'Indian' itself is a colonial construct, the Indians are an extremely heterogeneous ethno-cultural group which is also reflected in the sub-categories in the census classifications. However, the arbitrary nature of drawing census classifications as well as the inherent tensions between the formal Indian identity and the ethno-culturally diverse social identities, is shown in the census classifications from 1957 to 1980 (see Table 4.1 below).

Table 4.1 shows that in 1970, the Indian category became wider and more diverse, when the sub-groups 'Ceylon Tamil', 'Other Ceylonese' and 'Pakistani' which were previously categorised under 'Others' in the 1957 census, were absorbed into the main 'Indian' category. The 1957 census reflected the colonial census arrangement which separated the Ceylon Tamils from the

*Table 4.1* Ethnic Classification of Indians in the Census from 1957 to 1980

| 1957 | 1970 | 1980 |
|------|------|------|
| Indians<br>• Indian Tamil<br>• Telugu<br>• Malayali<br>• Other Indian | Indian<br>• Indian Tamil<br>• Telugu<br>• Malayali<br>• Punjabi<br>• Other Indian<br>• Pakistani<br>• Ceylon Tamil<br>• Other Ceylonese | Indian<br>• Indian Tamil<br>• Malayali<br>• Telugu<br>• Sikh<br>• Other Punjabi<br>• Other Indian<br>• Pakistani<br>• Bangladeshi<br>• Sri Lankan Tamil<br>• Other Sri Lankan |
| Others<br>• Ceylon Tamil<br>• Other Ceylonese<br>• Pakistani | Others<br>- | Others<br>- |
| Malays<br>• Malays<br>• Indonesian<br>• All Aborigines<br>  • Negrito<br>  • Semai<br>  • Semelai<br>  • Temiar<br>  • Jakun<br>  • Other Aborigines | Malays<br>• Malay<br>• Indonesian<br>• Negrito<br>• Jakun<br>• Semai<br>• Semelai<br>• Temiar<br>• Other *Orang Asli*<br>  • Other Malay Community | Malays<br>• Malay<br>• Indonesian<br>• Negrito<br>• Jakun<br>• Semai<br>• Semelai<br>• Temiar<br>• Other Indigenous<br>• Other Malay race |

Source: Extracts from the 'Ethnic Classifications of Census from 1821' in Hirschman (1987).

Note: The category 'Others' contains a list of communities, but for the sake of brevity this table only includes the communities who were from the Indian sub-continent and in 1980 categorised under the main 'Indian' category.

Indian Tamils due to intra-group tensions. As discussed in Chapter 1, the colonial planters had specifically chosen the labouring class/caste of Indian Tamils to work in the rubber plantations, while the administrative staff was selected from British Ceylon. This had created an antagonistic relationship between the two sub-groups, which continued to exist during the fervour of Indian nationalism in the 1930s. While both sub-groups share a common language and similar *Dravidian* customs, the class/caste wedge had kept them apart socially and politically. Hence, the 1957 classification mirrored the separation. However, the 1970 consolidation of the two sub-groups under the main category of Indian was made in response to the 1969 race riots that witnessed major changes in the way race and racial groups were categorised.

Another notable difference in the census categories is the introduction of the sub-category of 'Punjabi' in the 1970 census.[10] While past census categories had absorbed the Punjabis into the sub-category 'Other Indian', the 1970 census reflected the rising consciousness of the Punjabi community as a distinct ethno-cultural group. In 1980, the Punjabi group split into two separate sub-categories: 'Sikh' and 'Other Punjabi'. The creation of a separate 'Sikh' sub-category reflected the religious cleavages within the complex Indian ethno-cultural identity as well as the internal social identity of the Sikh as a distinct ethno-religious community. Hence, not only is religion a crucial aspect of racial identity, but the sheer diversity of Indian sub-groups was becoming more apparent. From 1957 to 1980, the number of Indian sub-groups in the census classification had increased and included diverse nationalities (namely Indian, Ceylonese/Sri Lankan, Pakistani, Bangladeshi), regional-linguistic groups (Tamils, Telugus, Malayalis, Punjabis) and religious groups (Sikh), reflecting the horizontal cleavages and the increasingly fragmented nature of the Indian community in Malaysia.

The census categories, census reports and registration formalities provide valuable data in making sense of the mutually constitutive relationship between legal categorisation and social perceptions of Indian identity. In order to make sense of the way in which the law not only racialises Indian identity but also constructs Indian-centric grievances, the discussion to follow will investigate the legal exclusion of Indians from particular rights.

### 4.2.2 The constitution (positive law) and government policy (soft law) as tools of racialisation

As expounded by critical race theorists, racialisation is a political as well as a social phenomenon, which is reinforced by legal institutions and legal enforcement (see Section 2.4.2 in Chapter 2). Examples of this process include the United States' racial segregation policy and the later affirmative action programmes, which were meant to remedy past racial discrimination against the Black community. These laws and policies were a legal reinforcement of existing social divisions, which were fortified through the legislature, the judiciary and in some cases the police (law enforcement officials). In the case of post-colonial Malaysia, the existing social divisions were largely due to the colonial 'divide and rule' labour policy and the special reservation policy for the Malays, especially in terms of offering them land concessions but also stopping them from planting rubber. Hence, during the 1956 negotiations for Independence and the Social Contract, the colonial version of the Malay reservation policy was enacted into *Article 153* of the *Federal Constitution*, which states,

> (1) It shall be the responsibility of the *Yang di-Pertuan Agong* ('the King or Ruler') to safeguard the *special position* of the Malays and natives of any of the States of Sabah and Sarawak and the legitimate interests of other communities in accordance with the provisions of this Article. (emphasis added)

In exchange for the Malay special position, the 'other communities' consisting of the minority Chinese and Indians were given the right to citizenship. The above constitutional provision legalised the Social Contract, outlined in Chapter 1 (Section 1.4.2). The Malays were given a 'special position' under *Article 153* as a privileged or rights-bearing race, while the descendants of the Chinese and Indian migrants were given rights to Malayan citizenship.[11] *Article 153* specifically entitles the privileged group to a reservation of quotas in public sector employment and scholarships, as well as licences and permits for any trade and business. To entrench the privileges accorded to the Malays, *Article 160(2)* defined a Malay as,

> a person who professes the *religion* of Islam, habitually speaks the Malay *language*, conforms to Malay *custom* and – (a) was before Merdeka Day born in the Federation or in Singapore or born of parents one of whom was born in the Federation or in Singapore, or is on that day domiciled in the Federation or in Singapore; or *(b)* is the issue of such a person. (emphasis added)

Hence, by virtue of the racialised categorisation of the Malays in the constitutional provision, the Chinese and Indians were characterised as the 'other communities' in *Article 153*.

The implicit racialisation of the Indians as a racial group begins from the constitutional provision which defines the Malays. The legal construction of a Malay person in Malaysia is based on particular ethno-cultural markers such as the Malay language and custom, as well as the Islamic religious criterion, which are emphasised in the provision above. The constitutional definition of a Malay person is purposeful and was meant to describe the 'investitive criteria'[12] to qualify for Malay special rights contained in *Article 153*. As already noted, the 'special position' of the Malays as a rights-bearing group provides a list of entitlements and privileges such as quotas in public institutions of higher education, public sector employment and business or trade licenses. However, the rights-bearing group was extended in 1963 to accommodate the joining of two states (Sabah and Sarawak) in Northern Borneo to form the

Federation of Malaysia. Hence, *Article 153*'s special rights now apply to both the Malays as well as the native groups in Sabah and Sarawak.

The legal inclusion of the native and indigenous groups in Northern Borneo as rights-bearers under the special rights provision also led to the racialisation of group identity. *Article 161A(6)* (a constitutional amendment made in 1963) provided a legal definition of a native of Sabah and Sarawak:

> In this Article "native" means (a) in relation to Sarawak, a person who is a citizen and either belongs to one of the *races* specified in Clause (7) as indigenous to the State or is of mixed blood deriving exclusively from those races; and (b) in relation to Sabah, a person who is a citizen, is the child or grandchild of a person of *a race indigenous* to Sabah, and was born (whether on or after Malaysia Day or not) either in Sabah or to a father domiciled in Sabah at the time of the birth. (emphasis added)

*Article 161A* racialises the indigenous groups in Northern Borneo by referring to the native tribes and ethno-cultural groups in Sabah as 'races' as well as categorising the various indigenous tribes in the state of Sarawak into 'races'. *Article 161A(7)* indicates a list of races in Sarawak who are qualified to be rights-bearers:

> The races to be treated for the purposes of the definition of "native" in Clause (6) as indigenous to Sarawak are the Bukitans, Bisayahs, Dusuns, Sea Dayaks, Land Dayaks, Kadayans, Kalabits, Kayans, Kenyahs (including Sabups and Sipengs), Kajangs (including Sekapans, Kejamans, Lahanans, Punans, Tanjongs and Kanowits), Lugats, Lisums, Malays, Melanos, Muruts, Penans, Sians, Tagals, Tabuns and Ukits.

Although the constitution or the law is instrumental in racialising the various tribes and ethno-cultural groups in Northern Borneo into neat racial categories, there is an obvious differentiation even among the rights-bearers of *Article 153*. The 1957 legal definition of the Malay race contained detailed investitive criteria or ethno-religious markers, whereas the 1963 legal definition of the native races in Sabah and Sarawak do not contain any specific ethno-cultural markers for the specific tribes. While it is arguable that the 1957 definition of a Malay conforms to the colonial definition of a Malay as constructed under the *Malay Reservation Enactment 1913*, the constitutional definition homogenises the Malays. In contrast, the natives in Northern Borneo are kept heterogeneous and diverse.

The homogenisation of the Malays through the *Federal Constitution* is further reinforced by judicial description, as seen in the case of *Lina Joy*. In the High Court decision of *Lina Joy*,[13] a case involving a Malay woman's application to convert from Islam to Christianity, the court quoted *Article 160(2)* of the Malaysian *1957 Federal Constitution* which laid out the legal definition of a Malay and stressed on the ethno-religious criteria of being a Malay (discussed further in Section 5.2.2 of Chapter 5). Hence, the legalisation of the ethno-religious criteria of being a Malay constructs another layer of differentiation between the rights-bearers, that is, of being Muslim and non-Muslim. The homogeneity of the Malays arises mainly from the religious criteria and not the ethno-cultural markers per say (see discussion below on the hybrid Malay cultural groups).

In any case, by exerting a race-based criterion on the constitutional right to higher educational opportunities, public service jobs as well as access to business and trade licences, the law has directly constructed an exclusive rights-bearing group and indirectly produced a non-rights-bearing group. The ethno-cultural minorities in Malaysia such as the Chinese and Indians, who were constitutionally lumped together as the 'other communities' under *Article 153*, have been clearly excluded from the special rights provision. In fact, *Article 153* clearly defines a two-tiered process of citizenship and racialisation. The first tier which consists of 'the Malays and natives of any of the States of Sabah and Sarawak' explicitly defines the racial characteristics of rights-bearing Malaysian citizens. The second tier which is the 'other communities' are citizens of Malaysia who have been excluded from specific rights but not explicitly racialised. This shows that the law defines the ethno-cultural group identity of the Malays as well as the natives of Sabah and Sarawak more rigorously than it does the ethno-cultural identity of the Chinese and the Indians. However, the legal exclusion implicitly racialises the Chinese and the Indians due to the racial discrimination and racial inequalities that it creates (this point is analysed in Section 4.2.3).

Another example of the legal process of racialisation in Malaysia is the stipulations of the 1971 NEP and the 1971 *National Cultural Policy* (NCP), which were established after the 1969 race riots (see Section 1.4.2). The NEP is a form of soft law as it operates as the policy arm of the special rights provision in the *Federal Constitution*. As a policy extension of the provision, the NEP makes references to socioeconomic programmes which aim to 'correct racial economic imbalance' and 'eliminate the identification of race with economic function'.[14] The racial economic imbalance is in reference to the racial and economic divisions constructed by the colonial British, which led to the segregation of Malays, Chinese and Indians according to their economic activity.

However, a key objective of the affirmative action programme introduced under the NEP was 'the creation of a Malay commercial and industrial community', which would equalise the economic status of the Malays with the other races.[15] The NEP outlined an array of programmes which were exclusively meant to remedy the social and economic backwardness of the Malays, particularly the circumstances of the Malay peasantry in the rural agricultural sector. In pursuing the policy objective of redressing the socioeconomic backwardness of the Malays, the NEP implicitly worsened the social and economic backwardness of non-Malay communities. While one of its policy objectives was to eradicate poverty regardless of race, the poverty reduction programmes bypassed the private agricultural sector, which encompassed rubber plantations. As described in Chapter 1 (Section 1.3.2), the majority of

Indians living under conditions of rural poverty were the Indian Tamil plantation labour, who had been marginalised along horizontal (racial) and vertical (caste/class) lines. The Indians were already excluded from constitutional special rights and the affirmative action programme, which made them part of the non-rights bearing group. By circumventing the privately held rubber plantations, the NEP explicitly discriminated against class-based groups such as the plantation labour. Hence, the NEP not only racialised the socioeconomic programmes but reinforced class divisions among the non-rights bearers.

Furthermore, Malaysian administrative practice had coined a new term to refer to the beneficiaries of the affirmative action programme. The term *Bumiputera* (Sanskrit word for 'sons of the soil') amalgamated the Malays and the natives of Sabah and Sarawak, effectively constructing a pseudo-racial group. While the *Federal Constitution* had constructed special rights in order to remedy the backward circumstances of the Malays, the Reid Commission during the negotiations concerning the constitutional provision had expressly stated that any special rights should have a time limit (see Section 1.4.2 in Chapter 1). In other words, the special rights were meant to be temporal in nature as it explicitly violated the fundamental right to equality. However, the construction and utility of the term *Bumiputera* in public administration and legal formalities (see Chapter 5, on how the term has now been utilised in census and registration) shows the creation of a permanent rights-bearing group based on the investitive criteria of indigenousness. The term has been extensively used in public administration, for example in the case of public university entrance requirements (see Table 4.2 below).

However, the *Bumiputera* criteria are not fixed but rather arbitrary and vague. First, as Table 4.2 shows, the definition of a *Bumiputera* differs

*Table 4.2* The Definition of Bumiputera in a Malaysian Public University

Definition of Bumiputera – Peninsula
If a mother OR father candidate (sic) is a Malay who is a Muslim/*Orang Asli* as defined in Article 160(2) of the Federal Constitution, the child is considered a Bumiputera.

Definition of Bumiputera – Sabah
If the father of the candidate is a Malay Muslim/Indigenous Peoples of Sabah as defined in Article 161A(6)(b) of the Federal Constitution, the child is considered as Bumiputera.

Definition of Bumiputera – Sarawak
If the father and mother is a Native Sarawak (sic) as defined in Article 161A(6)(a) of the Federal Constitution, the child is considered a Bumiputera.

Source: Admission requirements for Universiti Teknologi MARA, a wholly *Bumiputera* university. (Website: <http://online.uitm.edu.my/takrif_bumi.cfm>, 4 March 2014.)

Note: The definition of indigenous people adopted was based on the Federal Constitution for the processing and selection into universities.

radically between the regions in Malaysia. In the case of Peninsular Malaysia, the *Bumiputera* person is one who is born to a Malay or *Orang Asli* parent (either mother or father), whereas in the state of Sabah, the *Bumiputera* person is one who is born to a Malay or native father only. In the state of Sarawak, the discrimination is more apparent, as both parents must be a native. The different interpretations of a *Bumiputera* between the regions reveal the administrative understanding of the constitutional provisions which define the Malays and the natives of Sabah and Sarawak. Second, the subjective and fluid nature of the *Bumiputera* identity is reflected in the status of ethno-culturally mixed 'indigenous' groups such as the Indian Chitty community. The Indian/Melaka Chitty people are descendants of fifteenth century Indian traders who married local Malays (see Section 1.2 in Chapter 1). Although the Indian Chitty follow Malay customs and speak the Malay language, they are not constitutionally or formally classified as Malay as they are adherents of the Hindu religion. Other hybrid communities, for example the Baba and Nyonya Chinese/Malay community are also not recognised as Malay. In comparison, Muslim hybrid communities such as the Arabs and the Indian/Muslims have been assimilated into Malay society due to their shared religious affiliation.[16] Hence, the Malay investitive criteria is not ethno-cultural or based on indigenousness but based on the ethno-religious condition.

The *Bumiputera* criteria, however, raises the question of whether non-Muslim indigenous communities should qualify as *Bumiputera*. As natives of Sabah and Sarawak do not have an Islamic criterion to fulfil, the non-Muslim hybrid groups should also qualify on the basis of their indigenousness. However, in a recent study of the Indian Chitty community, Moorthy laments that the Indian Chitty community has been unable to obtain *Bumiputera* status and its associated socioeconomic entitlements.[17] The ambiguity of the *Bumiputera* status and the stress on the ethno-religious criteria rather than indigenousness, at least for those from the Peninsular, indicates the discriminatory nature of the special constitutional rights and affirmative action programmes.

Another policy or soft law instrument that stresses on the criterion of indigenousness and has led to ethno-cultural discrimination is the 1971 *National Cultural Policy* (NCP). The NCP and the *Rukunegara* ideology (the political doctrine of Malaysian nationhood) was meant to facilitate national unity after the 1969 race riots by stressing the ethno-culturally plural Malaysian society. However, the NCP declared that Southeast Asia's indigenous Malay culture and the Islamic religion were the basis of Malaysian national culture. In defining the indigenous Malay culture, the NCP drew on the point that the Malays were a part of the wider Southeast Asian region beyond Malaysia. The NCP states that

> The national culture must be based on the *indigenous culture of this region*: The region involved covers Malaysia, Indonesia, Philippines, Singapore, Brunei, Thailand and Cambodia, as well as the South Pacific

islands (Polynesia, Melanesia and Oceania) and Malagasy. This whole region has been an important part of *Malay civilization and culture*. During the height of the Malay civilization era based in Malacca, the *Malay language* has been used as an international language in trade relations (lingua franca). The culture of this region showed several similarities, in the language used, which was basically the Malay language – Austronesia, the geographical location, historical experience, natural resources, arts and moral values. The Malay culture today is a way of life and symbol of *identity* of more than 200 million people who speak the same language. As such, the culture of the indigenous people from this region, which, in a wider or narrower sense, refers to the Malay culture, forms the basis of the National Culture Policy.[18] (emphasis added)

Thus, the NCP clearly indicates the ethno-cultural markers of what amounts to the 'indigenous culture of this region', which includes the Malay culture, the Malay language and the Malay identity. While the NCP acknowledges a clear distinction between indigenous/ethnic culture and national culture, it makes a contradictory statement in its general aim to 'transcend the boundaries of race and religion' and 'create a united Malaysian race'. This contradiction is evident in the specific policy aim which is to uphold Malay culture and Islamic principles and values. Indian and Chinese minority group culture is acknowledged but only to provide additional 'suitable elements' to enrich the base national culture. The suitability of minority culture to the national culture is based on 'the provisions in the Constitution and the principles of *Rukun Negara*, as well as national interest, moral values and the position of Islam as the official religion of the country'.[19] The NCP, however, does not elaborate on which provision of the *Federal Constitution* it draws on or define what it means by 'national interest' and 'moral values'. However, it clearly introduces Islam as a criterion of national culture and differentiates the status of Islam *vis-à-vis* other minority religious beliefs. The importance of Islam as a component of national culture is based on its position as the official religion of Malaysia. Hence, the NCP can be regarded as the policy arm of two provisions in the *Federal Constitution*: *Article 3* that stipulates Islam as the 'religion of the Federation of Malaysia' and *Article 152* that formalises the Malay language as the 'national language'. The NCP policy uses the constitutional provisions to legitimise its main aim of upholding the dominant position of Malay culture and language, as well as the Islamic religion *vis-à-vis* the minority cultures, languages and religious beliefs. However, the use of law and policy to accord secondary status to the ethno-cultural identity of minority groups has given rise to minority group grievances.

### 4.2.3 Discrimination and inequality under the law

The dominance of the Malay culture and language became evident in the *1971 National Educational Policy* as well as the 1981 landmark case of

*Merdeka University Berhad v. Government of Malaysia* (see Section 1.4.2 in Chapter 1). The National Educational Policy incorporated the political ideologies declared in the NCP and the *Rukunegara* into the post-1971 education system. This meant that education in national schools which received aid from the government used Malay as the medium of instruction and adopted an approach to moral values centred on Islam. While the system worked to nationalise education, which was previously a product of the colonial administration (including English mission schools), the Chinese and Tamil minority language schools were discriminated. The Chinese and Tamil primary schools were only partially funded by the government, which led to the need for additional funding from private citizens. While the economically vibrant Chinese community were able to pool resources to maintain Chinese language education, the Indian community was fragmented, poorer and unable to fund Tamil schools.

The problem of Tamil schools reflected both horizontal and vertical cleavages of the Indians. The majority of Indians, as explained in Chapter 1, were of Tamil origin, and the majority of Tamil schools were situated in the rubber plantations to cater for the children of the Indian Tamil plantation labour. This class-based group lacked the economic clout to sustain the Tamil school structure, which was ultimately taken under the wings of the Indian political elites in the Malaysian Indian Congress (MIC). However, after the 1990s, the grievances related to the Tamil schools were taken over by Indian non-governmental organisations (NGOs) and civil society groups who mobilised the Indian community to support the Tamil schools (see Chapter 5). The grievances that were related to the Tamil school were mostly framed as the loss of ethno-cultural identity and the right to minority language education. In an interview conducted for this study, the president of Malaysia Hindu Sangam (an Indian Hindu but Tamil-centric NGO) stated, 'When the English brought us [the Indian Tamil plantation labour] here, they gave us the three T's: temple, Tamil school and *toddy* [a type of liquor] shop … the identity of the Indians is in the temple and the Tamil school'.[20] Hence, the internal social identity of the Indian Tamil plantation labour in particular hinges on the Tamil language and ethno-religious forms of education. This is different from the internal social identity of the Indian urban middle class who were ethno-linguistically diverse and were more inclined to educate their children in the former English mission schools in the cities. However, both of these Indian groups were affected by the acculturation of the national education system, which was utilised to construct a Malay-centric national identity and culture.

The contestation between the internal social identity of ethno-cultural minority groups and the politicised national identity manifested in the legal case of *Merdeka University*.[21] The plaintiffs who were part of the Chinese education movement (*Dong Ziao Jong*) formed a company in order to establish and manage a private Chinese-medium university in Malaysia. The company known as Merdeka University Berhad filed a suit against the government of

Malaysia for rejecting an earlier petition for a university incorporation order under *Section 6* of the *Universities and University Colleges Act 1971*. The *1971 Act* specifies that the King (*Yang di-Pertuan Agong*) can declare an order to establish a university if it is 'expedient in the national interest'. The petition was rejected and the Ministry of Education reasoned that the university would be 'contrary to the national education policy'. The ministry's reasoning rested on three specific grounds: first, the utilisation of Chinese language as the teaching language; second, that the university would only be useful for students who came from Chinese schools; and third, it is a private university.

The plaintiffs who were part of the Chinese education movement had made diplomatic attempts to resolve the matter such as requesting a dialogue with the minister. However, civil society attempts did not bring about any response from the government. The plaintiffs then resorted to using the legal avenue and sought a declaration from the courts that the denial of the petition was in contravention of the *Federal Constitution* (in particular the equality clause in *Article 8(2)* and the constitutional proviso to *Article 152(1)* which allows for teaching and learning in non-Malay languages). Further to this the plaintiff sought another declaration for judicial review that the Ministry's act was 'an unreasonable and improper exercise of the discretion' under the *1971 Act*. A purely legal analysis of the case found that the plaintiffs had attempted to utilise human rights principles, especially *Article 26* of the *Universal Declaration on Human Rights* which gave parents the right to choose their children's education.[22] Hence, both legal rights, that is, the constitutional right to equality and non-discrimination as well as moral rights, that is, the human rights declaration, were utilised to seek minority language education in Malaysia.

The High Court decided that the *National Education Policy* did, indeed, fail to provide for parental rights to choose their children's education, but the matter was a 'moral, social or political' issue and as such was not a legal issue which is justiciable by the courts.[23] The court also found that both a fully or partially Chinese medium university was contrary to the 'national interest' which was to uphold the national language and the national culture. The judicial decision had swept aside the minority rights issues which included language rights, educational rights and cultural rights on the basis that they were components of international law and hence not binding on the national courts. However, the peculiarity of the court's decision came from its interpretation of *Article 152(1)* which states,

> The national language shall be the Malay language ... Provided that –
> (a) no person shall be prohibited or prevented from using (otherwise than for official purposes), or from teaching or learning, any other language ...

The court found that 'official purposes' was defined by the *Federal Constitution* as 'any purpose of a public authority', and proceeded to interpret 'public authority' as a 'statutory authority' which included Merdeka University.[24] As such Merdeka University was deemed to be outside the ambit of *Article 152(1)* which protects the rights of non-Malay ethno-linguistic groups to teach and learn their language.

The decision shows that the NEP and the NCP are racialising tools, which have led to the discrimination against ethno-linguistic minority groups. The judge in the *Merdeka case* affirms the racial differentiation when he states that *'bumiputeras* ... literally meaning autochthons and in popular use in recent times as a composite term to denote Malays ... and indigenes of the soil ...' are the sole beneficiaries of special reservations in public university education.[25]

While Thio's analysis centres on the legal case, it does not elaborate on the minority movement's extralegal strategies. Lee, in a study of the Malaysian cultural policy, focusses on the mobilisation of the Chinese minority in Malaysia and the Chinese education movement's campaign to secure minority language rights.[26] Lee contends that the movement was in response to the 1971 NEP and the affirmative action programme for the Malays which reduced the Chinese quota for public universities in Malaysia.[27] While the NEP, NCP and National Educational Policy has affected both the Chinese and Indian minorities, especially in terms of minority language rights,[28] the Indian minority did not mobilise around language like the Chinese *Dong Ziao Jong*. The absence of Indian group mobilisation around the language and education issue can be attributed to the fragmented nature of the community, particularly in terms of the group's linguistic diversity and the limited interest of the urban Indian middle class towards Tamil language education. Thus, in this case, the grievance was not fully shared by the larger Indian community.

However, the urban Indian middle class had briefly mobilised on a limited scale due to an escalating ethno-religious issue involving religious hate crimes in the mid to late 1970s. In this instance, the religious grievance, which was shared by a wider swathe of the Indians, prompted a limited mobilisation but did not lead to mobilisation of Indians *en masse*. In 1979, the urban Indian middle class rallied around the high-profile criminal case of *Jayaraman & Ors v Public Prosecutor*.[29] The case concerned a few Islamic extremists killed by Indian security guards near the premises of a Hindu temple in the district of Kerling in the state of Selangor (hence it was known as the 'Kerling Incident'). The trial itself concerned the charge of culpable homicide not amounting to murder, as it was recognised by the courts that the accused were defending the temple from attacks. Then Lord President[30] Tun Suffian in describing the Kerling Incident stated in the appeal case,

> Some Malays went one night to destroy idols in a Hindu temple in Kerling. Some Indians had been expecting the attack and were guarding the temple, and as a result there was a fight. Four of the Malays were killed and the eight applicants were convicted ... under sections 304 and 34 of the Penal Code and sentenced to various terms of imprisonment.[31]

The background to the case concerned a succession of previous assaults by Islamic extremists on various Indian Hindu temples which rallied a number of Indian Hindu NGOs as well as the MIC leaders to seek government intervention. However, due to a lack of response from the government, the NGOs and the MIC resorted to taking self-protective measures in order to secure the Hindu temples. The security guards that were placed at the Kerling temple were the response to previous attacks on the temple. The incident had affected in particular the Hindus and the urban Indian middle class, who responded by mobilising resources in order to legally protect the security guards who were arrested. Although there was no direct action, mobilisation was confined to lobbying of MIC leaders to take action.

The judge in the *Kerling Case* was aware of the limited mobilisation of the Hindu community and the sensitive nature of the case. The courts duly recognised the anguish of ethno-religious and ethno-cultural minority groups in cases of hate-crime, and took this into consideration at the sentencing phase of the case. The judge contended that if a heavy sentence were to be passed on the eight accused of the crime, it may encourage 'would-be temple desecrators'; on the other hand, if the sentence were to be light, it may encourage vigilantes to 'take the law into their hands'. In fact, the judge in the case found that the accused were 'good citizens' who were trapped in a situation which was beyond their control.

The government had issued a media blackout on the incident and the Prime Minister Hussein Onn (1976–1981) made a statement calling for religious tolerance. Hence, while the incident mobilised the Hindus, particularly those of the urban Indian middle class, the government's response in quelling Islamic extremism and the lenient decision of the Kerling case reassured the affected community. However, the incident had sparked the Indian Hindu revival movements which began to mobilise from the mid-1980s onwards, and will be discussed in Chapter 5. Religious sentiments and grievances clearly invoke a more powerful response among the Indians in Malaysia, in comparison to purely ethno-linguistic issues. As the NCP was focussed on the Islamic religion and Islamisation was rising from the 1990s onwards, the religious identity of the Hindus constituted latent social capital that could be invoked by Hindu activists in order to mobilise the Indian Hindu community.

The laws (the *Federal Constitution*) and policies (the NEP and the NCP) discussed above show that the executive arm's political ideology of race centres on the supremacy of Malay culture and the Islamic religion. The ideology has been utilised to construct a Malaysian national identity which suppresses internal social identities of minority groups and reformulates the internal social identity of the majority group. The law has been an instrumental tool of racialisation, in the reinforcement of a Malay race, the creation of a pseudo-racial *Bumiputera*, as well as the construction of a Malaysian 'race'. This link between social identity and the law is circular in nature. While society constructs the legal subject, the subjects' cognition of their legal subjectivity will influence their understanding of, and relationship to, the law. This study shows that while state institutions construct the legal category of Indians, Indian perception of their social identity has, in turn, influenced their understanding of the law as being biased and unjust. Hence, the law not only constitutes the social identity of the group but also constructs the group's grievances.

## 4.3  The exclusion from rights: grievances and responses

Aside from ethno-religious and ethno-linguistic grievances, another main grievance of the Indian community from 1957 to the late 1980s lay in the socioeconomic status of the Indian Tamil plantation labour. As discussed in Chapter 1, this group has always been the most marginalised sub-group within the Indian community. Chapter 3 discussed the grievances experienced by the Indian Tamil plantation labour during colonial times, which mostly revolved around low wages and the harsh treatment meted out by the British planters as well as the Indian management in the plantations. However, these grievances did not result in any mass mobilisation despite the limited Klang Strikes of 1941. In the years leading up to independence, the focus of the Indian elites shifted towards communal bargaining and establishing political control over the Indians, while securing citizenship rights for the Indians in Malaysia. Hence, the Indian Tamil plantation labour group was forgotten but the grievances of the group persisted throughout the post-independence years.

As discussed in Chapter 1 and in Section 4.2.2 of this chapter, the NEP, which focussed on eradication of poverty, had bypassed the private plantations and as such had also neglected the socioeconomic status of the Indian Tamil plantation labour. While the grievances persisted and, in some cases, became more serious and urgent, the Indian Tamil plantation labour was too submissive and docile to mobilise, and was excluded from the socioeconomic development that was taking place in Malaysia from the 1970s. The situation became more urgent as the 1980s witnessed the fragmentation and subdivision of rubber plantations in Malaya. Many families of the Indian Tamil plantation labourers who had, since the colonial time, been living in the same rubber plantation were threatened with retrenchment and eviction. The disruption to the plantation social system and the general lack of education and skills beyond the rubber plantation had propelled the emergence of an urban Indian underclass. The Indian Tamil plantation labour was being pushed into the urban areas where the group mostly found itself in urban squatters and slums.

The education system in the rubber plantations was less than mediocre, as the early colonial control of the plantations had railed against a better schooling system. The post-independence era witnessed race-based identity politics which privileged the Malay language and Malay culture in the newly formed national education system. As such the ethno-linguistic language schools of minority groups like the Chinese and the Indians were neglected by government policy and funding. While the Chinese were able to sustain the Chinese language schools (as discussed above on the *Dong Jiao* movement), the Indian Tamil plantation labour did not have the economic or political clout to develop a better schooling system. At the same time, the urban Indian middle class had drifted towards the national education system and had ignored the cultural value of Tamil education. Since the NCP and national education policy was also Malay-centric, the Tamil schools were in a pathetic state.

The Indians believed that the constitutional references to the 'special position' of the Malays and the active affirmative action policy exemplified by the NEP were the primary source of grievances of the Indian Tamil plantation labour. Indian civil society leaders and Indian activists who were interviewed for this research confirm that both law and policy were the main source of Indian grievances. While some interview participants referred to the absence of similar 'positive help for the Indians as for the Malays', others criticised the race-based affirmative action policy for not offering impartial 'distributive justice'.[32] Although the MIC attempted to develop a self-help scheme for Indian Tamil plantation labour, the scheme did not have the political backing or the economic resources to take off.[33]

In 1974, four years after the NEP was put in place, the then MIC President Tan Sri V. Manickavasagam initiated a gathering of elites and professionals for an Economic Conference to discuss the possibility of extending socioeconomic protection for all plantation labour, who were excluded from poverty eradication programmes under the NEP. The result of the conference was the MIC Blueprint or MIC Bluebook, which contains proposals for an affirmative action policy specifically for the rubber plantation labourers regardless of race or ethnicity. A senior politician in a leading Indian party who was interviewed for this study, and who wished to remain anonymous, emphasised that the MIC Bluebook comprised carefully worded recommendations for an affirmative action policy for all plantation labour, but the underlying purpose was to target Indian Tamil labour who were outside the scope of the NEP.[34] The MIC Bluebook includes case studies on the rubber plantation industry and analysed foreseeable socioeconomic effects of the fragmentation of estates such as rural displacement, forced urbanisation and urban poverty. The recommendations are broadly defined under four main issues: 'the economic position of Malaysian Indians, employment issues and problems, land development and education problems'.[35]

The Bluebook recommendations include the following:

- To increase Indian share capital, ownership and control of productive assets and reservation of 10% new share equity;
- To achieve racial balance in public employment, to offer training programmes, to grant citizenship or work permits to Indians who were restricted under the *Employment (Restriction) Act 1968* and abolish the Contract Labour System;

- To allot new land schemes for plantation families and modernise rural area housing;
- To introduce a systematic academic scheme for Tamil schools as recommended under the Aziz Commission Report.[36]

The Bluebook proposals were made for the approval of the government, but emphasised the role of the Indian community and the MIC in advancing the proposals. The Bluebook declared,

> it would not be consonant with Indian *dignity* and *self-respect* to be merely content with asking for assistance from the Government. The MIC feels very strongly that the community in general and the MIC in particular should contribute towards the advancement of Indians in the education sector.[37] (emphasis added)

The MIC Bluebook is a diplomatic policy response from the Indian political elites to the NEP which is focussed on the *Bumiputera* group. The suggestions made indicate a concern for the economic, social and educational welfare of Indians, particularly the Indian Tamil plantation labour and their future in a society that was being constructed by the race-based NEP. The wordings in the Bluebook suggest that the approach was tactful and cautious, so as not to stoke racial tensions. The inherent tension between the seriousness of the Indian grievances and the diplomatic approach is apparent in the MIC President Manickavasagam's foreword:

> Almost half the Malaysian Indian community has lived in virtual isolation in plantations and smallholdings, while a good many others have their livelihood on the fringes of urban life. This has affected the manner and extent of their involvement in the vast changes and progress in the nation. More serious, it has also affected the performance and prospects of the younger generation of Malaysian Indians. If permitted to continue, this situation will do serious damage to the image, standing and welfare of the community. *It will deprive the community of its rightful place and role in the New Malaysian Society that is being fashioned under the Rukunegara and the New Economic Policy.*[38]

The MIC Bluebook proposals were, however, not implemented and the reasons are unclear as to why it was not taken forward, either in Parliament or through political lobbying. Interview participants who mentioned the MIC Bluebook also lamented on the 'unknown' and 'mysterious' reasons for the failure to implement the recommendations, but a few of them suggested a number of reasons for this, among them the sudden change in the MIC leadership after President Manickavasagam and President Sambanthan passed away in 1979, as well as the lack of political clout and leverage of the MIC leadership itself within the *Barisan Nasional* (BN) coalition.[39]

For these reasons, the MIC had not succeeded in advancing the Bluebook recommendations.

The senior politician of a leading Indian party who was interviewed iterated that '[i]f they had done this [the Bluebook recommendation] in all the estates, you would not have had these people [the Indian Tamil plantation labour] flooding into Kuala Lumpur and turning out to be criminals.'[40] The statement implies that the social problems faced by Indians today are a result of neglect by the NEP and the non-implementation of the Bluebook recommendations. As Chapter 5 will elaborate further, the socioeconomic issues predicted by the Bluebook became a reality in the 1990s, especially after the implementation of the *National Development Policy* which replaced the NEP. The MIC Bluebook recommendations became an issue of contention among Indian activists during and after the 2007 Indian mobilisation.

Apart from the grievances of the Indian Tamil plantation labour, the urban Indian middle class was also facing grievances that were linked to the NEP and the NCP. These grievances revolved around tertiary educational opportunities and public service employment. The NEP had sought to change the system in order to ensure a fair distribution among all the races. However, many Indian civil servants were bypassed for promotions in government service, while the shift from English to Malay as the formal language of the government impeded the recruitment of Indian civil servants.[41] Furthermore, the higher education system had since the 1957 *Federal Constitution* imposed a quota system in order to encourage the entry of Malays into public university.

The NEP in the 1970s also increased the number of Malay-only higher educational institutions which discriminated against non-Malay students. Even though the quota system had generally allocated university places for Indians in line with the population proportion, these places were mostly taken up by the urban Indian middle class who had the benefit of urban national schools.[42] The Indian Tamil plantation labour group whose children were in the Tamil school system therefore faced class-based barriers to the Indian seats in higher education. The quota system not only discriminated against minority Indians and Chinese, *vis-à-vis* the Malays, but also encouraged intra-ethnic competition. Hence, the Indian underclass was unable to compete with the urban Indian middle class. Race-based quotas effectively discriminated against the Indian underclass.

While the two grievances described above pertain to specific Indian sub-groups, the constitutional inequality established by the *Federal Constitution* affected the Indian community as a whole. In fact, the qualified nature of equality, due to the Malay special rights provision, had resulted in the construction of non-rights-bearing groups and a second-class citizenry. Although *Article 8* of the *Federal Constitution* enshrines both the principles of equality and non-discrimination, it also contains within it the seeds of the inequality of citizenship when it warrants that non-discrimination can be excluded in circumstances justified by the Constitution itself. *Article 8* states that

1    All persons are equal before the law and entitled to the equal protection of the law.
2    Except as expressly authorized by this Constitution, there shall be no discrimination against citizens on the ground only of religion, race, descent, place of birth or gender in any law ...

However, a number of Indian activist lawyers and Indian politicians who are lawyers, interviewed for this study felt that the equality provision in *Article 8* was adequate, and that the problem was either a lack of judicial enforcement of the equality provision or the wrongful implementation of the special rights provision (*Article 153*) in the NEP.[43] The argument that *Article 8* lacks legal enforcement is based on the word 'special position' in *Article 153*. Fadiah Nadwa, legal activist in an NGO called Lawyer's for Liberty, stated at an interview for this study, that the government has wrongfully implemented the provisions [*Articles 8* and *153*], because the Malay 'special position' was a privilege and not a legal right, as rights were guaranteed for every citizen regardless of race under the equality provision.[44] The prevalent view among lawyers of the equality clause suggests that the judiciary has failed to uphold the original intention of the drafters of the *Federal Constitution*.

Though the Constitution does not explicitly or directly discriminate against a Chinese or an Indian, it does authorise the inequality of Malaysian citizens in constitutionally prescribed situations. This 'indirect' discrimination arises from the constitutional privilege or special position of the Malays and native groups in Sabah and Sarawak (collectively known as East Malaysia) enshrined in *Article 153* of the *Federal Constitution*. The indirect discrimination is legitimised by its purpose, which is preferential treatment, to provide special reservations for the majority Malays and the natives in East Malaysia in public service employment, educational training, scholarships, as well as permits and licenses for trade and business. However, as argued in the previous section, there is an implicit division between the Malays and the natives in East Malaysia, where the Malay legal identity includes being a Muslim. In taking into account the religious dimension of the Malay identity, Amanda Whiting argues that '[c]itizenship rights have a social and ethnic dimension; equality before the law has a different meaning as between Muslims and non-Muslims ...'.[45] The Constitution thus indirectly constitutes a two-tiered citizenship divided along ethno-cultural and ethno-religious lines. The Indians and Chinese minority groups, being neither Malays nor natives of East Malaysia, are constitutionally discriminated against.

This implicit legal division of citizenship is mirrored in the self-perceived or internal social identity of Indians as 'second-class citizens' and even as a marginalised 'third-class' citizenry. Jiwi Kathaiah, editor of an Indian Tamil online newspaper, in an interview for this study, compared the inequality of legal rights to the legal duties owed by all citizens irrespective of race. He stated,

> Indians in this country today, are virtually the third class citizens. Third class! And they are branded as minorities, classified as minority, which I don't agree, because as a citizen, an Indian, but as a citizen, I'm entitled to all the rights, as a citizen equal to anyone in this country, as I have my legal duties to this country that is to die for this country. I have a duty, and my right must be equal to that, which is not the case here.[46]

Jiwi Kathaiah's view of the correlation between rights and citizenship duties reflects Dworkin's theory on rights as political trumps. As discussed in Chapter 2, Dworkin postulates that the most fundamental right is the right to equality, or as he terms it, the right to 'equal concern and respect' which cannot be denied by any 'collective goal'.[47] In the Dworkinian sense, the right to equality is a political right which acts as a trump against the law. Hence in that sense, the qualification imposed on the legal right to equality by the collective goal of Malay special rights cannot be justified. Although most of the lawyers who were interviewed for this study[48] challenged the legality and legitimacy of the qualified equality provision on the basis that the judiciary had failed to interpret the law's original meaning, the Indian activist Jiwi Kathaiah, a journalist,[49] found that the constitutional right to equality must be connected to the right to citizenship which was perceived as a *political right* rather than a legal right. The difference in approach to rights between the activist Indian lawyers and the Indian activists who had no legal training exemplifies the multifaceted role of rights in mobilisation, especially after the 1990s. However, despite the serious grievances that arose from the lack of equality before the law, the Indians remained an acquiescent community until the 1990s.

## 4.4 Quiescence under an illiberal polity

The quiescence of the Indians despite their grievances can be attributed partly to the divisions within this community as described in Chapter 1. The horizontal and vertical cleavages appear to have prevented any mobilisation effort. However, Chapter 3 has shown that the temporary mass mobilisation of the Indian Tamil plantation labour in the 1941 Klang Strikes came about because of the Indian nationalist and anti-caste ideology that helped to forge a unifying identity and sense of common purpose or shared rights. In the colonial case, the mobilised identity was political in nature, which cut across the internal social identities as well as the external social identities of the various Indian sub-groups. The discussion above on the *Kerling case* also shows that particular internal social identities for instance as a Hindu religious community can act as a mobilising identity that brings the Indian community together.

The Indian Tamil plantation labour is by and large, ethno-culturally homogeneous; the group consisted of Tamil speaking Indians who had for generations lived and worked in the rubber plantation system. The group had developed its own social system and remained submissive in a fairly secluded environment in the plantations. The plantation labour also had no economic clout and very little intellectual resources to frame demands and make claims. Since the 1960s, the plantation labour has been under the patronage of the Indian political elites in the MIC. However, the MIC has far less resources and political clout when compared to UMNO and the MCA. Because of its limited electoral leverage, the MIC has not been able to place class-based issues arising from the Indian Tamil plantation labour on the government's agenda. This was evident in the failure to implement the MIC-driven Bluebook recommendations discussed in Section 4.3.

The urban Indian middle class on the other hand had far more economic and intellectual resources in comparison to the Indian Tamil plantation labour. However, the urban Indian middle class has lacked the political clout to advance any of its grievances within the identity-based Malaysian political system. The bulk of Indian activists came from Indian urban middle class and had better access to civil society groups, which they used to channel grievances. However, illiberal laws such as the *Internal Security Act 1960* (abolished in 2012) and the *Sedition Act 1948* served to suppress demands and actions by the broader public and non-governmental groups. The increasing authoritarianism was seen evident in the 1987 incident known as 'Ops Lalang'. The government used the *Internal Security Act 1960* to arrest 107 individuals consisting of key opposition leaders, NGO activists, trade union activists, university academics and even church workers, claiming that the detention was necessary to prevent a potential racial riot like the May 13 Incident.[50]

Although the mass arrests were clearly a response to the Chinese *Dong Jiao Zong* movement's demand for Chinese education, not all of the 107 arrested were connected to the *Dong Jiao Zong* movement. Those arrested included a number of Indian trade unionists and opposition leaders such as V. David and P. Patto of the Democratic Action Party (DAP) and were primarily from the urban Indian working class who rejected the race-based politics of the MIC. Civil society groups viewed Ops Lalang as a politically motivated incident by the ruling government and a deliberate utilisation of the draconian *Internal Security Act* to silence the opposition leaders as well as troublesome (or critical) social activists. The grievances of the Indian Tamil plantation labour were mostly class-based issues, and any representation of the group by urban Indian middle-class activists or leaders were ignored or repressed due to the illiberal laws in place and partisan politics. This meant that both the urban Indian middle class and the plantation labour were unable to mobilise in search of redress for their respective grievances.

Further to the 1987 clampdown on the opposition parties and civil society groups, which included the urban Indian middle class and Indian activists, in 1988 a 'constitutional crisis'[51] took place. The crisis led to the curtailment of the Malaysian judiciary's independence by an authoritarian executive. The then Prime Minister Dr Mahathir Mohamad (1981–2003) expelled five Supreme Court judges and the lord president (who was the head of the Malaysian judiciary until 1994, now known as the Chief Justice) of the Courts of Malaysia, on the grounds of judicial misconduct. As constitutional expert H P Lee noted, Dr Mahathir removed the lord president because he had presided over a few legal decisions which went against the prime minister's interests.[52] Of these legal decisions, the most crucial dealt with an appeal regarding the validity of an UMNO election which meant that Mahathir Mohamad's post as president of UMNO was also in contention. Lee writes that the case was unprecedented, in terms of the clash between the executive and the judiciary or where '[l]aw and politics intersected'.[53] Subsequent to the removal of the judges, constitutional amendments were made to restrict the civil courts and extend the Islamic or *Syariah* courts' jurisdiction. *Article 121(1A)* of the amended constitution reads, 'The courts referred to in Clause (1) [the High Court and other inferior civil courts] shall have no jurisdiction in respect of any matter within the jurisdiction of the *Syariah* courts'. The amendment created a constitutional uncertainty of whether the High Court of Malaysia was stripped of its jurisdiction over constitutional issues.[54]

As already noted in Chapter 1, the law in Malaysia was illiberal. In addition to the draconian laws, there were no specific legal rights for minority groups. The single exception is the constitutional provision of *Article 153* which says 'other communities' have 'legitimate expectations'. However, 'other communities' have not been judicially defined; neither has the phrase 'legitimate expectations', which therefore remains vague. Furthermore, several changes to the constitution and other legislative measures in 1988 impede minority groups from seeking remedies through the courts. The most significant legal change was the legislative curtailment of judicial review of some administrative decisions. In 1988, the *Internal Security Act* introduced a new provision, *Section 8B* which stated,

> There shall be no judicial review in any court of, and no court shall have or exercise any jurisdiction in respect of, any act done or decision made by the Yang di-Pertuan Agong [the King] or the Minister in the exercise of their discretionary power in accordance with the Act, save in regard to any question on compliance with any procedural requirement in this Act governing such act or decision.

The *Internal Security Act* already allowed the minister to detain individuals without any need to present them at court, which meant that the legislation allowed for detention without trial. The new *Article 8B* meant that the minister's decision to detain without trial could not even be legally challenged in the courts. Further to this provision, the amendment of *Article 121* of the *Federal Constitution* in 1988, when literally interpreted, restricts the jurisdiction of the High Court to that which is allowed by federal statutory provisions. The High Court was thus usurped of its inherent constitutional jurisdiction. Therefore, judges were impeded from interpreting the law by referring to 'constitutional norms', which include non-discrimination and equality, while Parliament was now empowered to enact legislation that could completely evade the interpretation of the law by the courts.[55] The use of ouster clauses, which sought to oust judicial review, in legislation was common. Hence, the executive branch of government which is controlled by the ruling *Barisan Nasional* party, achieved command over the judiciary and the legislature. The Indian activists and the opposition Indian leaders were constrained in this illiberal setting, and hence were unable to effectively mobilise the Indians.

Due to the cleavages of the various Indian sub-groups and the illiberal nature of Malaysian politics, the Indians could not mount a unified demand for political rights. Their electoral numbers were too low to be effectively represented under the identity-based political system, while the urban Indian middle class was more inclined towards a non-communal class-based political approach. Furthermore, the BN government only recognised the MIC as the legitimate political representative of the Indians in Malaysia. This means that politics is also a major divider of the Indians. From the 1980s, the Indian political elites in the MIC, entrenched within the identity-based political system, could not afford to 'shake the boat' if they wished to retain their position within the BN. This is evident from the self-help schemes the MIC had adopted to address Indian socioeconomic grievances and the party's overly submissive or diplomatic manner in approaching serious grievances. On the other hand, the opposition political parties of the day were more socialist and class-oriented, and hence were not willing to take up race-based issues or frame grievances in race terms. While there have been efforts by opposition parties to bring together the former Indian Tamil plantation labour as a class-based group, the MIC has constantly railed against such attempts. Any issue that was framed as an Indian issue was dominated by the MIC. Hence, the division between the Indian political elites in the MIC and the urban Indian middle class also explains the absence of mobilisation among Indians as a whole, and among the former Indian Tamil plantation workers or the Indian underclass to seek redress for the group's mounting grievances.

Nevertheless, in the late 1980s, human rights awareness was beginning to seep into Malaysian civil society in general, while lawyers and legal activists had begun to mobilise against the government clampdown of the judiciary. A number of Indian lawyers were also emerging as activists, a combination which had last been seen in the colonial period from the 1930s to the 1940s and which had culminated in the 1941 Klang Strikes. These developments gave rise to a growing rhetoric of legal rights and human rights (moral rights) which was beginning to infuse into the consciousness of the urban Indian middle class. However, rights consciousness was easily repressed by draconian laws, while the prevailing counter-ideologies of the Malaysian government, specifically the communitarian Asian Values and *Rukunegara*, challenged the emerging human rights ideology. Furthermore, as Malaysia is not a signatory to the international human rights conventions, the government is not legally bound by international human rights laws. However, human rights activism was beginning to play a crucial role in the 1990s in forging minority rights claims and in accentuating the ethno-cultural *identity* of the Indians as a minority group.

## 4.5 Conclusion

Indian collective grievances persisted between 1957 and 1989, but mobilisation *en masse* only occurred in 2007. Hence, pooling of grievances alone does not predict mobilisation although the *type* of grievances seems to matter. When the grievance is ethno-religious, touching the heart of the Indian identity, collective mobilisation has occurred. The Kerling case illustrates this, but even here, the mobilisation was limited, possibly because the grievance had not yet been perceived as a threat to *all* Indians who profess a variety of faiths although predominantly Hindu. In addition, the absence of mobilisers – akin to the lawyers and journalists of the 1941 Klang Strikes – in the 1957 to 1989 period suggests another explanation for the absence of mobilisation. The next chapter will show how the coming together of both these factors – a shared sense of threat to ethno-cultural self-identity, taking the form of denial of fundamental religious rights and safeguards, *as well as* a mobilising force made up of mostly lawyers and activists led to a series of mobilisations that culminated in the unprecedented 2007 Hindu Rights Action Force (HINDRAF) rally.

## Notes

1 See Form JPN.LM01 and Form JPN KP01 at the National Registration Department website <www.jpn.gov.my>. The words are in Malay and were translated using the *Oxford Fajar Malay-English Dictionary* (Oxford Fajar, 2008).
2 Interview with K. Shanmuga, lawyer and activist in Loyarburok (Kuala Lumpur, 7 July 2012); Confidential Interview with a senior Indian politician in a leading Indian party (Petaling Jaya, 15 November 2012).
3 Interview with S. Arutchelvan, secretary-general of Socialist Party of Malaysia and JERIT (grassroots NGO) activist (Kuala Lumpur, 6 July 2012).
4 Eric J Mitnick, 'Law, Cognition and Identity' (2006–2007) 67 *Louisiana Law Review* 823, 828.
5 Charles Hirschman, 'The Meaning and Measurement of Ethnicity in Malaysia: An Analysis of Census Classifications' (1987) 46(3) *The Journal of Asian Studies* 555, 566.
6 Ibid., 562.

7 Ibid.
8 Ibid.
9 Frederik Holst, *Ethnicization and Identity Construction in Malaysia* (Routledge, 2012) 36.
10 Another notable difference in the 1980 census is the change from 'Ceylon Tamil' and 'Other Ceylonese' to 'Sri Lankan Tamil' and 'Other Sri Lankans' to reflect the change in the name of British Ceylon to Sri Lanka in 1972.
11 In 1971, the *Constitutional (Amendment) Act* (Act A30) incorporated the natives of Borneo (States of Sabah and Sarawak in East Malaysia) as a privileged group under *Article 153*. See Section 1.4.2 for the historical background on *Article 153*.
12 Eric J Mitnick, 'Constitutive Rights' (2000) 20(2) *Oxford Journal of Legal Studies* 185, 189. The term was used by Mitnick to describe the qualifying conditions attached to particular legal rights. See Section 2.4.2.
13 *Lina Joy v. Majlis Agama Islam Wilayah & Anor* [2004] 2 MLJ 119.
14 'Chapter 1: The New Development Strategy' *Second Malaysia Plan (1971–1975)*, clause 2.
15 Ibid.
16 Ravec Raghavan, 'Ethno-Racial Marginality in West Malaysia: The Case of the Peranakan Hindu Meleka or Malaccan Chitty Community' (1977) 133(4) *Bijdragen tot de Taal-, Land- en Volkenkunde* 438, 440–441.
17 Ravichandran Moorthy, 'The Evolution of the Chitty Community of Melaka' (2009) 36 *JEBAT: Journal of History, Politics and Strategy* 1, 14.
18 1971 NCP (see Ministry of Tourism and Culture, Malaysia website: <www.jkkn. gov.my/en/national-culture-policy>).
19 Ibid.
20 Interview with Datuk Mohan Shan, president of Malaysia Hindu Sangam (Petaling Jaya, 20 November 2012).
21 *Merdeka University Berhad v. Government of Malaysia* [1981] 2 MLJ 356 [hereinafter referred to as the *Merdeka University case*].
22 Li-Ann Thio, 'Beyond the "Four-Walls" in an Age of Transnational Judicial Conversations: Civil Liberties, Rights Theories, and Constitutional Adjudication in Malaysia and Singapore' (2005) 19 *Columbia Journal of Asian Law* 428, 437.
23 *Merdeka University case*, 366.
24 Ibid., 360.
25 Ibid., 358.
26 Lee Hock Guan, 'Ethnic Relations in Peninsular Malaysia: The Cultural and Economic Dimensions' (2000) *Social and Cultural Issues* 1.
27 Ibid., 8.
28 Joshua Castellino and Elivira Dominquez Redondo, *Minority Rights in Asia: A Comparative Legal Analysis* (Oxford University Press, 2006) 24.
29 [1979] 2 MLJ 88 (Sessions Court); [1982] 2 MLJ 306 (Federal Court). The case is hereinafter referred to as the *Kerling case*.
30 Title for the head of the Malaysian judiciary until 1994, when it was changed to Chief Justice.
31 [1982] 2 MLJ 306 (Federal Court) paragraph 1.
32 Based on the interviews conducted from May 2012 to March 2013.
33 Confidential Interview with a senior Indian politician in a leading Indian party (Petaling Jaya, 15 November 2012); Confidential Interview with an Indian civil servant (Kuala Lumpur, 21 September 2012).
34 Confidential Interview with a senior Indian politician in a leading Indian party (Petaling Jaya, 15 November 2012).
35 *Dasar Ekonomi Baru dan Malaysian Indian: Rantindak MIC* ['The New Economic Policy and the Malaysian Indian: MIC'] (1974, MIC HQ); MIC's National

Seminar on 'The New Economic Policy, the Second Malaysia Plan, and the Mid-term Review, and the role of the MIC' held on 11–12 May 1974.
36 The Aziz Commission or the Teacher's Salaries Commission was set up in 1967 to make recommendations on the appointment of teachers and other issues pertaining to the teaching staff in schools.
37 Ibid., 38.
38 Ibid., Foreword.
39 Confidential Interview with a senior Indian politician in a leading Indian party (Petaling Jaya, 15 November 2012); Interview with Dato' Haji Thasleem Mohamed Ibrahim, president of National Indian Action Team (Kuala Lumpur, 31 January 2013).
40 Confidential Interview with a senior Indian politician in a leading Indian party (Petaling Jaya, 15 November 2012).
41 Confidential Interview with an Indian civil servant (Kuala Lumpur, 21 September 2012).
42 Ibid.
43 Interviews with N. Surendran, lawyer, activist in Lawyers for Liberty and vice president of the *People's Justice Party*, a leading opposition coalition (Kuala Lumpur, 12 November 2012); K. Shanmuga, lawyer and activist in Loyarburok (Kuala Lumpur, 7 July 2012); M. Kulasegaran, lawyer and member of parliament (MP) (Kuala Lumpur, 1 October 2012); K. Ravin, lawyer and human rights desk executive in ERA Consumer (Petaling Jaya, 9 May 2012); K. Arumugam, lawyer and chairperson of Malaysian Human Rights NGO SUARAM (Petaling Jaya, 9 October 2012).
44 Interview with Fadiah Nadwa Fikri, lawyer and activist at Lawyers for Liberty (Petaling Jaya, 3 September 2012).
45 Andrew J Harding and Amanda Whiting, 'Custodian of Civil Liberties and Justice in Malaysia: The Malaysian Bar and the Moderate State' in T C Halliday et al (eds), *Fates of Political Liberalism in the British Post-Colony: The Politics of the Legal Complex* (Cambridge University Press, 2012) 247, 297.
46 Interview with Jiwi Kathaiah, Editor of *Semparuthi* (a Tamil online newspaper) (Kuala Lumpur, 15 March 2013). *Semparuthi* is the Tamil name for the hibiscus, which is the national flower of Malaysia.
47 Ronald Dworkin, *Taking Rights Seriously* (Harvard University Press, 1977) 6.
48 Interviews with N. Surendran, lawyer, activist in Lawyers for Liberty and vice president of the *People's Justice Party*, a leading opposition coalition (Kuala Lumpur, 12 November 2012); K. Shanmuga, lawyer and activist in Loyarburok (Kuala Lumpur, 7 July 2012); M. Kulasegaran, lawyer and MP (Kuala Lumpur, 1 October 2012); K. Ravin, lawyer and human rights desk executive in ERA Consumer (Petaling Jaya, 9 May 2012); K. Arumugam, lawyer and chairperson of Malaysian Human Rights NGO SUARAM (Petaling Jaya, 9 October 2012).
49 Interview with Jiwi Kathaiah, editor of *Semparuthi* (a Tamil online newspaper) (Kuala Lumpur, 15 March 2013). *Semparuthi* is the Tamil name for the hibiscus, which is the national flower of Malaysia.
50 The Malay word 'lalang' connotes a type of weed grass; hence, Ops Lalang was the Weeding Operation. See Nicole Fritz and Martin Flaherty, 'Unjust Order: Malaysia's Internal Security Act' (2002) 26(5) *Fordham International Law Journal* 1345, 1357. See also Julian C H Lee, 'The Fruits of Weeds: Taking Justice at the Commemoration of the Twentieth Anniversary of *Operasi Lalang* in Malaysia' (2008) 97(397) *The Round Table: The Commonwealth Journal of International Affairs* 605.
51 Andrew Harding, 'The 1988 Constitutional Crisis in Malaysia' (1990) 39 *International Comparative Law Quarterly* 57; See Tun Mohamed Salleh Abas and

K Das, *May Day for Justice: The Lord President's Version* (Kuala Lumpur: Magnus Books, 1989).

52  H P Lee, 'A Fragile Bastion Under Siege – The 1988 Convulsion in the Malaysian Judiciary' (1989) 17 *Melbourne University Law Review* 386.

53  H P Lee, 'Judiciaries in Crisis – Some Comparative Perspectives' (2010) 38 *Federal Law Review* 371, 378.

54  Vanitha S Karean, 'The Malaysian Constitution and its Identity Crisis: Secular or Theocratic' (2006) 27 *Lawasia Journal* 47, 56.

55  Ratna R Balasubramaniam, 'Has Rule By Law Killed The Rule of Law in Malaysia?' (2008) *Oxford University Commonwealth Law Journal* 211, 213.

# 5 The unquiet minority

## Legal mobilisation of Indians in illiberal Malaysia (1990–2018)

### 5.1 Introduction

Although the 1987 Ops Lalang and the 1988 judicial crisis reflect the growing authoritarianism and illiberalism in Malaysia, they may have inadvertently sparked off greater activism among non-governmental organisations (NGOs) and among lawyers especially the Malaysian Bar Council. From the 1990s onwards, Malaysian non-communal civil society groups, activist lawyers and opposition political parties were also forming coalitions in order to advance a subtle agenda for democratisation in Malaysia. As lawyers and the Malaysian Bar Council became increasingly activist, there grew understated linkages between legal activists and NGOs to advocate on non-communal issues such as fundamental human rights and environmental rights. Despite the illiberal nature of the state, there was a 'subaltern non-state public sphere'[1] that was being constructed in the shadows. The law and rights as a tool of empowerment was beginning to emerge in these subaltern spaces but utilised in a subtle form of human rights advocacy and human rights education. The urban Indian middle class, which consisted of professionals like lawyers and journalists, had access to this emerging subaltern public sphere and used it to focus attention on class-based issues of the urban Indian underclass (the former Indian Tamil plantation labour), as well as rights-based and ethno-religious issues which by this time were affecting *all* Indians in Malaysia.

### 5.2 The legal construction of ethno-religious identity, grievance and rights

Since the 2000s, ethno-religious differentiation between Muslims and the minority non-Muslim groups was becoming more apparent in the legal, social and political domains. For instance, from 2000 onwards there was a rise in legal battles for custodial rights between newly converted Muslim fathers and non-Muslim mothers. These custodial battles brought to the fore the contestation between the civil courts and the *Syariah* or Islamic courts over legal jurisdiction in such cases, discussed further in Section 5.2.2.

In addition, the state was emphasising Islamic culture and identity beyond the ambit of the *Federal Constitution* and the 1971 National Cultural Policy (NCP). The 1970 emphasis on race in Malaysian laws, policies and identity politics was in the 2000s shifting towards incorporating religious elements as part of race, especially in relation to the majority Malay Muslims. This is exemplified by the changes made in the legal identities of the three main ethno-cultural groups in Malaysia through legal formalities such as census categorisations.

### 5.2.1  Racialising rights-bearing and non-rights-bearing groups through legal formalities

The period of the 1990s to 2013 has witnessed several changes to the legal identity as well as the internal social identity of Indians in Malaysia. Chapter 4 showed how census categories reflected the internal social identity of various Indian sub-groups but also how legal formalities concerning ethno-cultural identity have reinforced political ideologies of race. A similar pattern is observed in the census categories from 1991 to 2010 but with three new features. First, new religious-based sub-groups have been introduced as pseudo-ethnic sub-categories, such as the Indian Muslims. Second, in contrast to the diversity of Indian sub-categories as well as the Chinese sub-categories, the Malay sub-categories which were visible in previous census, have been consolidated into a single Malay census category. Third, a new pseudo-ethnic category was introduced into the census: the *Bumiputera* ('sons of the soil') which incorporated the 'Malays' and constructed a new category of 'Other Bumiputera' that includes a list of non-Malay native groups, which is shown in Table 5.1 below.

In the *2010 Population Census* which is shown in Table 5.1, the breakdown of the census category for Indians displays the current diversity and cleavages of Indian sub-groups. Although from the 1890s, the colonial ideology attempted to racialise Indians and from the 1960s, the post-colonial census practices attempted to record the self-perceived or internal social identity of Indian sub-groups, the current census shows a more disparate and complex division of the Indian community. According to the latest 2010 categorisation, Indians consist of *ethno-religious* sub-groups (Indian Muslims, Malabari and Sikh), *ethno-linguistic* sub-groups (Malayali, Sinhalese, Punjabi, Tamil and Telugu) as well as *ethno-regional* sub-groups (Punjabi, Indian Tamils and Sri Lankan Tamils). The use of religious, linguistic and regional markers has created overlapping sub-categories, which indicate a more fluid and dynamic Indian ethno-cultural identity rather than a rigid category of Indians. In comparison to previous classifications, the introduction of ethno-religious sub-category 'Indian Muslim and Malabari', which includes Indians who are Tamil Muslims and Malayali Muslims (known as the Malabaris), shows that religious identity is becoming more significant as an ethno-cultural marker. The 2010 Indian sub-categories further indicate the removal of two ethno-national categories, the Pakistani and the

*Table 5.1* Ethnic Classification of Indians in the Census 1991–2010

| 1991 | 2000 | 2010 |
|---|---|---|
| *Indians* | *Indian* | *Indian* |
| • Indian Tamils | • Indian Tamils | • Indian Muslim/ |
| • Malayali | • Malayali | Malabari |
| • Sikh/Punjabi | • Sikh/Punjabi | • Malayali |
| • Telugu | • Telugu | • Punjabi except Sikh |
| • Sri Lankan Tamil | • Sri Lankan Tamil | • Sikh |
| • Sinhalese | • Sinhalese | • Sinhalese |
| • Bangladeshi | • Bangladeshi | • Indian Tamil |
| • Pakistani | • Pakistani | • Sri Lankan Tamil |
| • Other Indians | • Other Indians | • Telugu |
| | | • Other Indians |
| *Chinese* | *Chinese* | *Chinese* |
| • Divided into sub-categories[2] | • Divided into sub-categories | • Divided into sub-categories |
| *Bumiputera* | *Bumiputera* | *Bumiputera* |
| • Malays | • Malays | • Malays |
| • Other Bumiputera[3] | • Other Bumiputera | • Other Bumiputera |
| • (listed) | • (listed) | • (listed) |

Source: Malaysian Population Census (1991, 2000 and 2010); Saw (2007).

Bangladeshi. Since the Pakistani and the Bangladeshi are predominantly Muslim, the removal of these sub-groups indicates that they have been absorbed into other sub-categories, such as the Indian Muslim/Malabari sub-category. The formation of a pseudo-ethnic 'Muslim' sub-category under the Indian ethnic group is indicative of a new trend in Malaysian administrative practice of ethnicising religious identity, which is discussed in Section 5.2.2.

The second major shift in the *2010 Population Census* is the amalgamation of all Malay sub-groups into a single racial category. Previous census categories, depicted in Table 4.1 in Chapter 4, divided the Malays into several sub-categories. The sub-categories include *inter alia* the Indonesians which is an ethno-*nationalist* group as well as the Negrito, Jakun, Semai, Semalai and Temiar, which are mostly *indigenous* groups. These sub-groups have, since the 1991 census, been shifted from the Malay category to other categories such as the *Orang Asli* or indigenous groups category, shown in Table 5.2 below. In the 1970 census, Nagata found that the Malay category included sub-categories such as non-Muslim indigenous people and 'persons of Indonesian decent', which did not resemble the constitutional definition of a Malay.[4] *Article 160(2) Federal Constitution* defined a Malay as 'a person who professes the religion of Islam, habitually speaks the Malay language, conforms to Malay custom ...'. Although the constitutional definition technically embraces Indonesians and groups that arise from 'intra-religious intermarriage'[5] such as the Indian/Muslims, Arab/Malay and Indian/Malay mixed groups known as the *Peranakan*, the census classifications failed to reflect these internal ethno-cultural identities. The consolidation of the Malays into a monolithic ethnic or racial group is the result of the state's political ideology of homogenising the Malays as a distinct race while formally differentiating the Malays from other ethno-cultural groups. In contrast, the Indians and Chinese groups continue to see a range of sub-categories, which in some cases have increased in number.

Since 2010, the different approaches taken in the census classification of the Malay and non-Malay groups have become a point of contention among Indian activists and Indian civil society groups who claim that the

*Table 5.2* An extract of the Ethnic Census Codes and Classifications, Population Census, Department of Statistics, Malaysia

| *Variable Etnik*<br>*KOD DAN KLASIFIKASI* | | | *DEFINISI*<br>*Kumpulan Etnik:*<br>*Sekumpulan orang yang*<br>*terikat bersama-sama*<br>*oleh hubungan bahasa,*<br>*adat resam, agama yang*<br>*sama dan sebagainya.* |
|---|---|---|---|
| 1100 Melayu | 4100 Bumiputera<br>Sarawak<br>4110 – 4998 (list) | **6100 India**<br>**6110 India**<br>**Muslim/**<br>**Malabari**<br>**6120 Malayali**<br>**6130 Punjabi**<br>**(kecuali Sikh)**<br>**6140 Sikh**<br>**6150 Sinhala**<br>**6160 Tamil India**<br>**6170 Tamil Sri**<br>**Lanka**<br>**6180 Telegu/**<br>**Telugu**<br>**6998 Orang India**<br>**Lain** | |
| 2100 Orang Asli<br>Semenanjung<br>2110 Negrito<br>2121 – 2126 (list)<br>2120 Senoi<br>2121 – 2126 (list)<br>2130 Melayu Asal<br>2131 – 2136 (list) | | 7100 Bangsa Asia<br>7110 – 7998 (list)<br>8100 Bangsa<br>Eropah<br>8110 – 8998 (list) | |
| 3100 Bumiputera<br>Sabah<br>3110 – 3998 (list) | 5100 Cina<br>5110 – 5998 (list) | 9100 Lain-lain<br>Bangsa<br>9110 – 9998 (list) | |

Source: Department of Statistics website (1 March 2014) <http://www.statistics.gov.my/portal/images/stories/files/otherlinks/etnik.pdf>.

sub-division of 'Indians' into nine sub-categories is politically motivated in order to further fragment the Indian community. The social perception that the census sub-divisions of the non-Malay ethno-cultural groups operates as an intra-group 'divide and rule' instrument of the state was reinforced by the state's move to administratively homogenise the Malays. Dato' Thasleem, an Indian rights activist and president of the National Indian Rights Action Team (NIAT), claims that the government had used the 2010 census to officially and 'statistically' (*sic*) break down the Indians as well as the Chinese but portrayed the Malays as a single united group.[6]

The state's political agenda of merging the Malays into a homogeneous race through administrative practice has been confirmed by Sadiq's findings that the government had utilised 'census practices and documentation' in the Malaysian state of Sabah in order to 'Malayise' or homogenise the Malays and incorporate Filipino Malay immigrants as well as Indonesian immigrants into the Malay census category.[7] The reason behind this was to inflate the number of Malay voters in Sabah who, in return for new 'documentary citizenship', would vote for the dominant Malay political party in the state, thereby reinforcing the political dominance of the ruling *Barisan Nasional* (BN) coalition federal government.[8] Sadiq's study confirms how the census was manipulated for political gains, and the homogenisation of the Malays in Sabah, was primarily a political exercise.

The political importance of constructing a unified Malay group is reflected in the legal decision known as the *Lina Joy* case, where a Malay Muslim person was not allowed to convert out of Islam on the basis that a Malay is constitutionally defined as being a Muslim in *Article 160(2)* of the *1957 Federal Constitution*.[9] Fadiah Nadwa Fikri, a Malay human rights lawyer and legal activist, in an interview for this study, iterated that the constitutional classification of a Malay person has often been utilised to socially and politically unite the Malays as a homogeneous race.[10] Hence, census formalities have been utilised to construct consolidated racial blocs, while judicial decisions have reinforced existing political racial ideologies.

Nevertheless, the Indian activists who have railed against the government's political motives of uniting the Malays and dividing the Indians have implicitly recognised that the Indians are already a diverse and fragmented group. Dato' Thasleem clarified at the interview conducted for this study that the government's response to the query over the sub-division of Indians was that cleavages already existed in the Indian community.[11] Therefore, the sub-division of Indians reflects the *internal* social identity of the various Indian sub-groups. However, despite the pre-existing internal social cleavages between Indian sub-groups, Indian activists have utilised the census classifications as a site of contention, where ethno-cultural categories have been contested and negotiated. The NGO known as NIAT incorporated the census classification of Indians as a major Indian grievance in a list of grievances which was published and distributed to other Indian NGOs, Indian community leaders and Indian activists in 2012.[12] Furthermore, NIAT made proposals that in future census categorisation, the Indians should be 'unified under one code to strengthen unification for national unity' and assimilated as a 'race' that originated from the Indian sub-continent.[13]

Although race and ethnicity in Malaysia are political constructions which are reinforced by state-controlled legal formalities such as the census, Indian movement activists seem to have utilised these racial categories in order to unite and mobilise a diverse and fragmented Indian community. This displays the dialectic process of the law, race (ethno-cultural identity) and mobilisation, where the prevalent *legal* identity of Indians is utilised to construct an Indian *mobilising* identity. S. Retnaguru, an Indian film-maker who was involved in producing documentaries on contemporary Indian issues, agreed that the Indian community is internally fragmented and insular but also pointed out that they *can* become united when 'provoked' to defend an 'Indian cause'.[14] Retnaguru's view reveals how a disunited and diverse set of internal social identities of the various Indian sub-groups could be transformed into a united and homogeneous mobilising identity as Indians. In this way, Indian activists were able to use the formal identity of Indians that was constructed by the political ideology of race in order to formulate a mobilising identity.

However, the Indian activists' political use of a racialised Indian identity is not just in response to a fragmented Indian community, but also as a reaction to the expanding population of the majority rights-bearing Malay/*Bumiputera* race in Malaysia. The 2010 *Population Census Survey*, states that 'Malaysian citizens consist of the ethnic groups *Bumiputera* (67.4%), Chinese (24.6%), Indians (7.3%) and Others (0.7%).'[15] Previous population census have always itemised the majority race as the 'Malays', but the introduction of a new pseudo-ethnic category (*Bumiputera*) incorporates the Malays and the indigenous groups in East Malaysia. Sadiq found that the 1980 population census of the state of Sabah, had collapsed the Malays and other native groups into a single census category known as 'Pribumi' (similar to the 'Bumiputera') in order to camouflage the various immigrant groups incorporated.[16] Clearly, the *Bumiputera* is not a homogeneous ethno-cultural group, but a political construction for the purposes of the affirmative action policy. Previous laws such as the 1957 *Federal Constitution* and policies such as the 1971 NEP merely listed the rights-bearing groups, but new policies such as the 1990 New Developmental Policy and the 2000 New Vision Policy and their associated administrative practices show that the special rights clause and/or or the affirmative action policy is instrumental in constructing a permanent rights-bearing race.

In view of its bigger majority, the *Bumiputera* holds a larger electoral leverage, and this makes it difficult for ethno-cultural minority groups like the Indians to seek remedies for their grievances. Under the identity-based partisan politics, the opportunities for the Indian minority to make claims are weak to the point that grievances are often ignored. This has been exemplified by the socioeconomic situation of the Indian Tamil plantation labour described in Chapter 4. The lack of legal protection for vulnerable minority groups and the lack of equality before the law under the *Federal Constitution* as well as governmental policies had led to serious grievances without any legal remedy. A recent example of legal discrimination against the Indian minority group and the experience of differential treatment is portrayed in a series of legal cases concerning ethno-religious identity and the lack of remedy before the courts.

### 5.2.2 Formalising ethno-religious identity and differential treatment before the law

While Chapters 3 and 4 discussed the role of the law in constructing race in Malaysia, this chapter introduces an additional element in the formal process of racialisation in Malaysia – religion. Religious identity was not a factor that was taken into account in the American-centric critical race and sociolegal theorists on the mutually constitutive link between law and race, which was discussed in Chapter 2. This was because religion was not a crucial factor in the racialisation of the Black, Native American and Chicano minority groups in the United States. In the Malaysian context, ethno-religious identity has increasingly become a crucial cultural marker of race, especially in relation to the majority Malays who are Muslims.

The formalisation of ethno-religious criteria as race complicates the definition of the rights-bearer group known as the *Bumiputera* which comprises the Malays and other natives of Malaysia. The affirmative action policy was meant to remedy the economic backwardness of the Malays and other natives without explicitly discriminating the rights of 'other communities' as indicated in *Article 153* of the *Federal Constitution*. Furthermore, *Article 8(2)* of the *Federal Constitution* provides a qualification to the equal status of the non-Malays in order to accommodate the special position of the Malays. Other than for the purposes of the affirmative action policy, the Malays and non-Malays are equal before the law. Hence, the constitution explicitly disallows the legal discrimination of a non-Muslim.

As discussed in Section 1.4.2 of Chapter 1, from the 1990s onwards the government took control of matters relating to Islam in order to contain Islamic resurgence instigated by the opposition *Parti Islam Se-Malaysia* (the Pan-Malaysian Islamic Party or PAS) and the *Dakwah* ('Islamic Missionary') movement.[17] In the mid-1970s, an emerging group of Malay middle class had come together to form an Islamic revival movement called the *Dakwah* movement which encouraged Muslims to return to the fundamental and traditional principles of the Islamic religion.[18] The government was threatened by the Islamic revival as it posed a threat both to the government's development programme which emphasised Malay economic growth and to United Malays National Organisation (UMNO). In the 1980s, another Islamic resurgence came in the form of the *Angkatan Belia Islam Malaysia* (Muslim Youth Movement of Malaysia) or ABIM, which encouraged Muslim youth to return to Islamic teachings and mobilised for an Islamic society and an Islamic state. The government's main concern at this time was the links between the *Dakwah* movement or ABIM to the opposition party PAS, which could create a formidable threat to the ruling BN's hold on the Malays.[19] In order to curb the influence of the two Islamic movements and PAS, the government placed federal bureaucratic control over Islamic activities by establishing government departments in charge of Islamic affairs and restricted or in some cases banned several Islamic associations by amending the *Societies Act 1966*.[20] Prime Minister Mahathir coopted the ABIM leader Anwar Ibrahim into the UMNO party and iterated the three objectives of upholding Malay rights, Islam and protecting the country.[21] Hence, the 1980s onwards witnessed a gradual 'creeping' of a politically motivated Islamisation programme.

In 2001, the Prime Minister Mahathir declared that Malaysia was already an Islamic state and this led to several challenges by lawyers, civil society groups as well as the opposition political parties, many of whom rallied against a politically motivated Islamic discourse.[22] The political declaration was not constitutionally viable, as *Article 3* of the *Federal Constitution* merely indicates that Islam is the religion of the Federation of Malaysia while *Article 11* provides the right to profess and practice any religion. These two provisions were the cornerstone of the 1957 constitutional bargain and *Social Contract* between the Malays, the Chinese and the Indians. The status of Islam within *Article 3* of the *Federal Constitution* was to secure the 'socio-political status' of the states-based Malay monarchy as custodians of Islam within the federation and was only meant for 'socio-cultural' observances and state ceremonies.[23] In other words, the legal status of Islam was not meant to override the constitutional rights of non-Muslims in Malaysia.

In the middle of the 2000s, a spate of legal cases which concerned the rights of non-Muslim Indians was decided in favour of the Muslim party in the cases, thereby creating a legal limbo for non-Muslim rights in Malaysia. These cases deal with two major issues of deep significance to Indians in Malaysia: the legal status of alleged religious conversions from Hinduism to Islam, and the custodial rights of non-Muslim Indian mothers to their children who had been unilaterally converted to Islam by the father newly converted to Islam. While there are many cases involving the rights of non-Muslims, this discussion will focus on aggrieved non-Muslim Indian plaintiffs and legal cases which were instrumental in mobilising the Indian community in 2007.

The first major case involving alleged conversion from Hinduism to Islam that caught the public eye was the 2005 case of a deceased Indian man named Moorthy. In this case, the Department of Islamic Affairs in the Federal Territory of Kuala Lumpur had made legal claims that Moorthy had allegedly converted to Islam and as such his body should be handed over to the Islamic authorities for Islamic burial. Moorthy's widow, Kaliammal, challenged the claim made by the Department of Islamic Affairs with evidence that Moorthy was a practicing Hindu and had never converted into Islam.[24] The Department of Islamic Affairs had successfully applied to the Islamic *Syariah* Court for an *ex parte* order (a legal proceeding brought by one party without the presence of the other parties) for Moorthy's body. Kaliammal, on the other hand, had sought a declaration from the High Court that Moorthy was not a Muslim. The High Court held that it had no jurisdiction over the matter as it concerned the subject-matter of Islam which was within the jurisdiction of the *Syariah* Court under *Article 121(1A)* of the *Federal Constitution*.[25] Kaliammal, a Hindu was clearly not a Muslim person and as such did not have *locus standi* to seek legal remedy from the *Syariah* Court. The High Court's decision in rejecting her claim for legal remedy essentially meant that Kaliammal was discriminated due to her status as a non-Muslim.

The legal conundrum created by the High Court decision led to a furore among the Hindu community; Indian activists and Hindu NGOs viewed the court's decision as a gross injustice against the Hindu community. Datuk Vaithilingam, then president of the *Malaysia Hindu Sangam* (Malaysian Hindu Association), interviewed for this study explained that Kaliammal's case had prompted a gathering of Indian and Hindu NGOs as well as Indian lawyers to support the aggrieved Kaliammal in her legal battle.[26] Another interviewee, K. Shanmuga, a lawyer and legal activist at the NGO Loyarbu-rok, pointed out that although Kaliammal's case was the 'spark-up' of the Hindu Rights Action Force (HINDRAF) Movement, previous legal decisions concerning similar issues on religious conversion were instrumental in creating a sense of shared religious grievances among the Indian Hindu community.[27] Kaliammal's case exemplified the preference given by both the civil and Islamic courts to the Islamic authority and the blatant disregard of the aggrieved non-Muslim person's right to be heard. As Kaliammal was an Indian Hindu person, the court's decision constructed a perception of differential treatment among the Indian Hindu community and a self-perceived or internal social identity as a discriminated Indian Hindu minority.

The second line of legal cases which propelled the mobilisation of the Indians, especially the Indian Hindus, in 2007 concerned the custody rights of non-Muslim Indian mothers against the unilateral rights of their newly converted Muslim husbands to convert their children to Islam. The two significant cases, which were *Shamala's case (2003)*[28] and *Subashini's case (2007)*,[29] concerned the conversion of the originally Hindu husband to Islam and the latter's subsequent attempt to convert their children into Islam without the non-Muslim wife's legal permission. In essence, they were cases concerning the custodial rights of a Muslim father and a non-Muslim mother, which were being fought in two separate jurisdictions – the non-Muslim mother's case in the civil High Court and the Muslim father's case in the *Syariah* court.

Similar to the situation of Kaliammal, both Shamala and Subashini, as the respective aggrieved non-Muslim parties did not have *locus standi* in the

*Syariah* court. Even though the non-Muslim women were crucial parties to the case, the *Syariah* court did not grant them the right to be heard and proceeded to decide the matter in favour of the Muslim fathers. Both the Shamala and Subashini cases together with the 2005 decision of Kaliammal's case had propelled a coalition of Indian lawyers, Indian activists and Indian politicians as well as several non-communal NGOs, to use the courts as well as political lobbying in order to raise publicity regarding the status of non-Muslim rights. Key non-communal NGOs that took up the matter were the National Council of Women's Organisations and the Women's Aid Organisation (who championed the rights of women), Article 11 (a coalition of lawyers who fought for the constitutional right to the freedom of religion) and the Malaysian Consultative Council of Buddhism, Christianity, Hinduism, Sikhism and Taoism (a coalition of non-Muslim minority group representatives).

The Indian Hindu women in the cases were portrayed by the Indian NGOs as victims of a discriminatory legal system and the jurisdictional tension between the civil courts and the Islamic courts. Indian Hindu NGOs and Indian activists perceived a double discrimination, which was the discriminatory treatment against non-Muslims as well as women. Indian activists and the Indian Hindu community came to perceive non-Muslim women as an aggrieved collective trapped in a legal vacuum and outside the protection of the law. This subaltern understanding of the law was based on the clear lack of legal opportunity for the aggrieved non-Muslim women to seek constitutional rights, *inter alia*, the right to equality, the right to freedom of religion, the right to personal liberty and legislative custodial rights over their children. In an interview for this study, Madam S. Meenachy, the National Women Leader at the *Malaysia Hindu Sangam*, iterated that the custodial rights cases concerning the Indian Hindu women was sending a clear message to non-Muslim women that 'if you convert into Islam, you will get your rights. But if you refuse to convert like your husband did, you get nothing.'[30]

While the legal cases concerning child custody and conversion into Islam became a site of resistance for Indian Hindu mobilisation, another contentious religious issue in the 2000s that was affecting the Indian Hindu community was the demolition of Indian Hindu temples. During the colonial period, British planters had allocated land on the rubber plantations for the building of both Hindu temples and Tamil schools as ethno-religious, cultural and educational amenities for the Indian Tamil plantation labour. Due to a shift in rubber estate ownership to Malaysian plantation corporations in the 1970s and fragmentation as well as rapid redevelopment of plantation land in the 1990s, most of the temples were demolished. Andrew Willford's anthropological study of Indians in Malaysia found that since the 1990s there has been a revivalism of Hindu temple rituals and sacred spaces in Malaysia, which he attributes to the increasing awareness of Indian Hindu displacement and the escalating Malay-Islamic pressure in politics and over the Malaysian landscape.[31] Hence, the seeds of a mobilising identity were already being planted from the 1990s onwards. The ethno-religious identity of the majority Hindu Indians constituted, as Garcia-Bedolla terms, a latent identity resource or 'social capital'[32] that existed within the Indian Hindu consciousness. The temple demolitions in the 2000s touched the ethno-religious sensitivities of the Indian Hindu community which was already enraged at the manner in which the court system was disregarding non-Muslim issues. Hence, the perception of discrimination against the Indian Hindu community through the legal cases discussed above and the temple demolitions were triggers that produced a 'positive affective attachment'[33] to the Indian Hindu community and inspired the community to make demands in the interest of the Indian Hindu collective. The mobilising identity as a Hindu collective was strategically sparked off by Indian activists under the prevalent sociolegal and political environment. The ethno-religious dimension of the grievance touched the urban Indian middle class deeply unlike the socioeconomic grievances discussed in Chapters 3 and 4.

The creation of a mobilising identity as a discriminated Hindu community was also significant in uniting the Indian underclass (the former Indian Tamil plantation labour) as well as the urban Indian middle class. As the incidents had stoked the emotional sensitivities of both Indian sub-groups, it was akin to the 1978 Kerling Incident that had mobilised the Indian Hindu community as whole. However, unlike the 1978 Kerling Incident which was a result of Islamic fundamentalists going on a rampage (discussed in Chapter 4), the temple demolitions of the 2000s were authorised by the state government and conducted by state agencies. Also, in the Kerling Incident, the prime minister had quickly intervened to stop the demolitions, reprimanded the religious fundamentalists who were responsible and placated the Indian Hindu community. In the 2000s temple demolitions in contrast, the state governments legitimised the acts of demolition by insensitively referring to the Hindu temples as illegal structures and in unlawful occupation of government or private land, which enraged the Hindu community even more.[34]

The state had framed the issue as a purely land ownership issue by making references to Malaysian land laws (especially *Section 425* of the *National Land Code*) which authorises the demolition of unauthorised structures and legislative measures which allow for the clearance of squatter buildings such as the *Emergency (Essential Powers) Clearance of Squatters Regulation 1969*. Under the *1969 Regulation*, state land may be alienated to a development corporation without the need to issue a notice to the squatters. Hence, by treating the Hindu temple on former rubber plantation land as a squatter, the state government was able to legitimise the demolition.

The refusal by the state government to discuss the matter with the affected parties led to mounting anger among the Indian Hindu community. The Indian Hindu NGOs, Indian activists and Indian lawyers responded to the temple demolition incidents by accusing the government of pursuing an Islamisation agenda to eliminate Hindu places of worship. While the state governments cited the pro-development land laws to legitimise the acts of demolition, Indian civil society group responded in similar fashion, by citing other laws, specifically various constitutional rights and international human rights provisions. P. Uthayakumar, an Indian lawyer and one of the key leaders of the HINDRAF movement,[35] had even filed a legal suit in 2006 against various state governments and state agencies for breaching *Article 11* of the *Federal Constitution*, which is the provision for freedom of religion, as well as criminal law provisions in the Malaysian Penal Code (*Section 295* for the defilement of a place of worship, *Section 296* for the disturbance of a place of religious worship and *Section 298A* for causing racial disharmony).[36] Uthayakumar in a report stated that '[t]his is our last resort, we have exhausted all other avenues',[37] signifying the lack of political opportunity to air grievances and the weak political clout of the Indian political elites in the Malaysian Indian Congress (MIC) in addressing the issue. Justice Lim Yee Lan of the Kuala Lumpur High Court (Criminal Division) had rejected Uthayakumar's criminal suit on the basis that it was a civil case which incorporated allegations of criminal action.[38]

Other than the legal suit, HINDRAF movement leaders and Indian legal activists framed the temple demolition issue as an elimination of minority rights to protect religious structures or sacred space and a breach of ethnic minority rights. In an interview for this study, P. Waythamoorthy, Indian lawyer and a key leader in the HINDRAF movement challenged the state's rhetoric that the Hindu temples demolished were 'illegally' built by iterating that temple demolitions were a violation of the '[human] right to traditional life' as well as a breach of the *National Heritage Act 2005* which protects structures and buildings which were more than a century old.[39] Waythamoorthy contended that many of the Hindu temples that were demolished were structures built during the colonial period and hence should be recognised as part of national heritage. While the state's legal framing of the issue was based on pro-development land laws, the HINDRAF movement leaders were resorting to national heritage laws as well as human rights provisions to re-frame the issue although the temples were not expressly listed on the National Heritage Register. Hence, the law clearly became a space of contestation between the state and the Indian activists, with the Indian activists employing legal notions of equality as well as moral rights to challenge the state's line of reasoning.

The legal suit that was filed in 2006 by Uthayakumar was, however dismissed by the High Court on the ground that it combined civil and criminal claims.[40] Although the HINDRAF activists had filed an appeal over the High Court's decision within a few months of the High Court decision in March 2007, they still went ahead with the HINDRAF rally which took place in November 2007. Although HINDRAF's leaders were not able to expound their legal arguments in the courts, they were able to utilise rights rhetoric in their civil disobedience strategies. One of the key issues which HINDRAF leaders had constantly focussed on was the Indian community's constitutional right to equality and the discriminatory treatment against the

Indians. For instance, in a human rights conference in New Delhi, P. Waythamoorthy, one of the main HINDRAF leaders and a lawyer, stressed that the government's refusal to grant land and gazette land for Hindu temples in the same way they had done for Islamic places of worship was discriminatory.[41] Hence, even though technical legal arguments were required to argue the temple demolition case in court, the HINDRAF leaders utilised the principle of equality before the law as a political right in its extralegal strategies.

The utility of political rights as trumps against a 'collective goal' reflects Dworkin's premise of the fundamental right to equality.[42] The temple demolition issue as well as the lack of legal recourse concerning the custodial rights cases came down to one significant political right, which was the right to equal concern and respect. While Indian activists and lawyers in the HINDRAF movement were utilising the legal tools that were available to them in order to make sense of the various ethno-religious grievances, they also framed the overarching grievance of the Indian community in terms of the lack of respect from the state, the courts and the Indian political elites in the MIC. The framing and perception of disrespect towards Indians is evident from various online media reports which described the temple demolition incidents. The reports highlighted the emotional outcry of the temple patrons of the 'disrespectful manner' in which the demolitions occurred, for instance, the breaking of temple statutes while ritual ceremonies were being conducted and while devotees were worshipping.[43] The perception of disrespect among the Indian community was utilised by Indian activists in order to mobilise the community and seek the fundamental right to equality. Hence, although the technicalities of the law mattered to the Indian activists, the Indian community itself was only concerned about the disrespect and apathetic treatment that was being shown by the state towards them.

Nevertheless, the law was useful for Indian activists to challenge the state's legal claims and to expose the state's legitimisation of its actions. The use of legal rights as well as moral rights helped to structure emotive ethno-religious grievances into dispassionate legal claims. Indian activists were attempting to move the focus of the grievances away from a focus on the private land and squatter related laws towards fundamental constitutional rights, such as the right to freedom of religion. The structuring of claims based on constitutional rights also created awareness among the Indian community, especially the urban Indian middle class who began to see the serious nature of the grievances that were being exposed. Although the Hindu temple demolitions did not affect the urban Indian middle class directly, the demolitions contributed to the pooling of ethno-religious grievances through the legal cases discussed above which had made the urban Indian middle class aware of the serious implications of rising Islamisation in Malaysia.

Although HINDRAF activists began by advocating ethno-religious issues of the Indian Hindu community, the premise of inequality before the law and the need for wider Indian support led the HINDRAF leaders to widen the Indian agenda. The mobilising identity and claim for rights was quickly shifted from *Hindu* rights to *Indian* rights. This is evident from the 2007 HINDRAF 18-point memorandum that contained a list of Indian grievances, which were generally framed into two main claims, first, the inequality of citizenship and second, the discriminatory treatment which was said to result from Malaysian laws and policies.[44] Although the temple demolition issue was urgent and required immediate action from the Indian activists in order to put a stop to further demolitions, the prevalent core issue has always been the socioeconomic status of the Indian Tamil plantation labour or the Indian underclass. This is reflected in the claims made in the HINDRAF 18-point Memorandum regarding colonial exploitation and the threat of litigation against the British government. Hence, in addition to the ethno-religious grievances among the Indians, the persistent issue of the ethno-*class* grievance of the 'Indian poor' marginalised under postcolonial laws and socioeconomic policies were also emphasised.

## 5.3   The legal construction of ethno-class identity, grievance and rights: the lingering case of the 'Indian poor'

The 1990 *National Development Policy* or the NDP described in Chapter 1 was instrumental to the construction of grievances of the former Indian Tamil plantation labour. The two major ethno-class grievances relate to first, the retrenchment and eviction of Indian Tamil plantation labour from the rubber estates; and second, the social problems of the Indian underclass in the urban squatter settlements. The forced relocation of the Indian Tamil plantation labour group to the urban squatter settlements not only shifted the socioeconomic grievances of the group from the rural to the urban but also constructed new social problems like overcrowding, high unemployment and escalation of crime. The congestion of the Indian underclass in urban spaces led to two significant elements of ethno-cultural mobilisation: first, the pooling of grievances which constructed an internal social identity as an aggrieved minority group, and second, the access to Indian NGOs and Indian activists who were framing the grievances in terms of class and/ or race, as well as rights.

### 5.3.1   The pooling of ethno-class grievances in the rural rubber plantations, the framing of grievances as class-based rights and the utility of the law as a political tool

The main ethno-class grievances which were pertinent in constructing an internal social identity as an aggrieved Indian underclass relate to the treatment accorded to the former Indian Tamil plantation labour on legal retrenchment and eviction from the rubber plantations. Since the 1980s, the private corporations that owned the rubber plantations were fragmenting, subdividing and redeveloping the rubber plantations into other economic ventures, such as oil palm plantations and housing development. The availability of cheap immigrant labour from Bangladesh and Indonesia meant that there was no longer a need for the Indian Tamil plantation labour who had since the colonial era been the main workforce of the rubber industry in Malaysia. As such, the private corporations, most of whom were Malaysian-owned multinational corporations, were utilising the pro-employer labour laws and policies as well as pro-development land laws in order to retrench and evict the Indian Tamil plantation labour. Since the 1980s, most of the multinational corporations that owned the rubber plantations were intimately linked to the federal government through *Permodalan Nasional Berhad* (PNB) a Malay trust agency.[45] As such, the complicity between the private corporations and the government established an unequal bargaining position between the plantation corporations and the Indian Tamil plantation labour. The plantation labour did not have adequate representation or in many cases no representation at all during negotiations with the plantation corporations. Hence, civil society groups mostly consisting of non-communal NGOs and grassroots activists who were oriented around socialist ideas were providing social and legal support for all plantation labourers regardless of race. Although the NGOs were non-communal in terms of their ideological stance, the majority of the activists and leaders were of Indian origin and were familiar with the ethno-class problems of the Indian Tamil plantation labour.

In the following cases of retrenchment and eviction discussed below, it will be shown that the state and the plantation corporations utilised the law as a repressive tool in order to coerce and compel the Indian Tamil plantation labour to accept low retrenchment benefits as well as legitimise the nature of the evictions of the labour group. The grassroots activists who represented the plantation labourers countered the private plantation and state's legal repression by educating the plantation labourers on negotiation skills and utilised the law to delay retrenchments and evictions until negotiations could be conducted fairly. Furthermore, the grassroots activists also utilised civil disobedience tactics in order to embarrass the state as well as the plantation corporations and create publicity regarding the issue.

In the case of Strathisla Estate in the state of Perak in Malaysia, in 1997 around 178 plantation labourers received termination notices from the plantation corporation Golden Hope Plantations. The termination notice indicated that the benefits were RM65 (equivalent to USD 25) per year of service which was less than a quarter of the statutory benefit which amounted to RM280 (USD110) per year of service mandated by the *Employment (Termination and Lay-Off Benefits Regulations) 1980* under the *Employment Act 1955*. The plantation labourers were represented by the National Union of Plantation Workers (NUPW) which did not have much bargaining power or influence. Although the Union was able to negotiate with the plantation corporation for the amount stipulated in the 1980

Regulations, the Union conceded by accepting a lower ex-gratia payment of RM300 (equivalent to USD117) and an option to purchase a low-cost house to be built by a company called Perak Corporation Berhad for RM32,000 (USD12,480).[46]

Strathisla estate's residents were very unhappy with the negotiated offer as most of the Indian Tamil plantation labourers were facing unemployment and the loss of homes with little or no financial prospects. With the help of a grassroots NGO called *Alaigal* ('The Waves' in Tamil), the plantation labourers formed the Strathisla Residents Committee in order to put forth their demands as a collective without union representation. Alaigal's activists duly exposed the complicit links between the plantation corporation, the Perak state government as well as the federal government. Dr Jeyakumar Devaraj, one of the activists and leaders in Alaigal found that Perak State Development Corporation owned 38.1% of Perak Corporation Berhad, which was the buyer of Strathisla Estate. Further to this, *Permodalan Nasional* (PERNAS) a *Bumiputera* holding company established by the federal government owned 17.1% of Perak Corporation Berhad. The financial links between the corporations and the state and federal governments meant that the Perak state government had beneficial interest in the sale of Strathisla Estate and had compromised its responsibility to ensure that private corporations heeded the 1980 Regulations. It would also financially benefit from the option offered to the workers to purchase newly built homes from the Perak Corporation Berhad which it partly owned.

There were additional reports that the plantation corporation was in collusion with the Union representative who had reportedly used repressive tactics on the chairperson of the Strathisla Residents Committee while the plantation corporation itself accused the residents with criminal trespass.[47] This was one example of how dominant plantation corporations were able to utilise the law to repress dissent and force the former plantation labourers into accepting retrenchment benefits on the corporation's terms. However, the NGO Alaigal was able to mobilise and empower the plantation workers by arming them with legal knowledge of the 1980 Regulations and legal information pertaining to their employment rights.

Even though the state government claimed that it was unable to intervene in a private legal matter between the plantation corporation and the plantation labourers, Alaigal pointed out that the Perak State Government had failed to invoke *Section 214A* of the *National Land Code 1965* which authorised the state government to intervene in the workers' matter. *Section 214A(1)* of the *National Land Code* states,

> … no estate land is capable of being transferred, conveyed or disposed of in any manner whatsoever, to two or more persons unless approval of such transfer, conveyance or disposal has first been obtained from the Estate Land Board ….

Under *S. 214 (5)* of the *1965 National Land Code*, the Estate Land Board can refuse or cancel any approval if it is not in the public interest. This provision arms the state government with power to force plantation companies to be responsible to the plantation labourers *before* they sell the land. In fact, the purpose of the enactment in 1969 was to prevent the fragmentation of estate land in order to protect the livelihood of plantation labourers.[48] Hence, legal protection could have been enforced if the state had used *Section 214A*, but it deliberately did not. On the contrary, the state with its political authority and the plantation corporation with its economic clout had both used the law as a repressive tool against the Indian Tamil plantation workers.

With the help of Alaigal, the plantation labourers were able to confront the plantation company, the Union, the purchaser Perak Corporation Berhad and the Perak State Government. They did this in two ways: one, the Resident's Committee filed a legal suit against the developer which delayed the evictions and gave the plantation labourers time to mobilise and strategise a legal and political defence. By invoking the *National Land Code* and organising a massive campaign to petition the public in the state of Perak, they were able to channel their grievances and create publicity for the issue. Two, in 1999 the Alaigal activists and plantation labourers used direct action strategy by demonstrating in front of the chief minister of Perak's office and handed in a petition. In 2002, after a long legal battle, the Perak Corporation Berhad finally agreed to an out of court settlement with the plantation labourers to provide free housing lots, RM650 (USD250) per year of service and seven acres of land for relocation of the Tamil school and temple. Hence, even though it was not a legal victory in the courts, the legal strategy coupled with the political tactic of direct action had led to political victory for the plantation labourers.

Although the private corporation resorted to using repressive laws like criminal trespass and land law to forcefully evict the plantation labourers, Alaigal activists and an organised plantation labour were able to utilise particular legal provisions to delay evictions and challenge the corporation in court. The utility of the law went hand in hand with civil disobedience tactics such as holding demonstrations to embarrass the state government's complicity in the matter. In any case, the Alaigal activists were also able to utilise the *National Land Code* in order to place legal responsibility on the state government and to ensure that the state was acting in the interest of the plantation labourers rather than the private corporations. Clearly, the law has been utilised by activists as a political tool. In an interview for this study, Dr Jeyakumar Devaraj, the grassroots leader and activist in Alaigal, iterated,

> [w]e use the legal avenue as part of our strategy, not the only strategy. If we only kept to the legal thing we would have lost. It's because of the other things, we won. The legal thing gives you time.[49]

What is also evident from the Strathisla Estate case is that racial identity was not employed to mobilise the plantation labourers, who were all Indian Tamil plantation labourers. The Indian political elites in the MIC who consider themselves as the political patrons of the Indian Tamil plantation labour and have links to the National Union of Plantation Workers did not have sufficient political influence to represent and bargain on behalf of Strathisla Estate plantation labourers. Indian activists and Indian opposition politicians from *Parti Sosialis Malaysia* (Socialist Party of Malaysia) or PSM who have taken a class-based approach on this have commented at interviews conducted for this study that the race-based identity politics of the BN discriminates ethno-cultural communities like the Indians who do not have strength in electoral numbers.[50] This is confirmed by Nagarajan's study on the displacement of Indian Tamil plantation labourers, which found that Indian grassroots leaders in the MIC had been unable to raise issues pertaining to the Indian Tamil plantation labour at MIC state and national assemblies because the elites at the helm of the MIC exercised control over party agendas and over the grassroots leaders.[51] Hence, class-based contentious politics had been far more useful for the marginalised Indian Tamil plantation labourers in comparison to a wholly race-based partisan politics.

The rubber plantation eviction cases were clearly issues of class, but there was an implicit racial dimension to the issues as a majority of the plantation labour affected were Indians. The issue of race becomes pertinent in the differential treatment accorded to the Indian Tamil plantation labour in comparison to the legal eviction against the indigenous *Orang Asli*. As part of the National Development Policy, state governments as well as the federal government had resorted to clearing and developing rural land that has traditionally housed various indigenous groups in Malaysia. These indigenous groups have also suffered the complicity between the government and private development corporations, but in comparison to the Indian Tamil plantation labour, they were able to obtain better compensation due to their native land rights. This is confirmed by a senior civil servant who was interviewed for this study but wished to remain anonymous.[52]

The differential treatment accorded to the Malay rural workers compared to the Indian Tamil plantation labourers had been an explicit part of the NEP. As discussed in Chapter 4, the NEP's poverty eradication programme for the rural agricultural sector explicitly excluded the private agricultural sector, thereby also excluding the Indian Tamil plantation labour from its ambit. In an interview for this study, P. Kamalanathan, an MIC leader and then member of parliament (MP), explained that the Indian Tamil plantation labourers lived on the rubber estates due to their contractual obligations as a 'willing employee' and hence did not own the land unlike the Malay settlers in the rural villages and agricultural programmes like 'FELDA' who were able to own the land.[53] The explicit differential treatment between the Indian Tamil plantation labourers and the Malay agricultural workers is

linked to the NEP which provided land and financial incentives to the Malays. The existing labour or employment laws including the *Employment Act
1955* and the *Employment (Termination and Lay-Off Benefits Regulations)
1980* were insufficient to protect the interest of the Indian Tamil plantation
workers. This reduced their bargaining position with the private corporations. In fact, the Indian political elites in the MIC concede that they were
not in a position to provide any governmental assistance. P. Kamalanathan,
the MIC leader iterated that when rubber plantations are sold the workers
should 'technically' be the responsibility of the employers and not the government, as it is a 'business venture' between a 'willing employer-willing
employee' and as such '[t]he government is not to blame.'[54] Thus, the race-
based political system clearly does not enable Indian political elites who are
part of the government to bargain on behalf of vulnerable sections of the Indian community. Furthermore, despite the issue being class-oriented, race
still matters in relation to the explicit legal discrimination and inequalities
against non-Malay or non-*Bumiputera* groups such as the Indians.

Nevertheless, in several Indian Tamil plantation labour eviction cases,
including the Strathisla case discussed above and others which are discussed
below, NGOs and grassroots organisations focussed on class rather than
race as a mobilising element. They also resorted to the use of rights in their
mobilisation. Although most of the plantation workers were of Indian Tamil
origin, the plantation labourers formed a mobilising identity as a labouring
class as most of the grievances were based on their employment contracts,
for example, in relation to retrenchment. However, after 2007, HINDRAF
activists and the Indian political elites in the MIC tend to highlight the
race-dimension of these grievances. For example in the eviction case of
Bukit Jalil Estate in the state of Selangor, JERIT (short for *Jawatankuasa
Jaringan Rakyat Tertindas* or 'Oppressed People's Network') which is the
NGO wing of the Socialist Party of Malaysia or PSM, HINDRAF and Lawyer for Liberty worked together to stop the eviction of forty-one families
of former Indian Tamil plantation labourers. While PSM leaders stressed
on 'natural justice' and criticised the 'inhumane treatment' accorded to the
plantation labour, HINDRAF declared it to be an act of 'ethnic cleansing'
to eliminate Indians.[55] Fadiah Nadwa Fikri, the legal counsel for the plantation labourers and legal activist at Lawyers for Liberty, spoke of the court
as 'the last bastion for the common people to seek justice' and later reprimanded the court for taking 'the government's side'.[56] Hence, the combination of race, class and rights was prominent in the Bukit Jalil Estate case.[57]

However, the involvement in these cases of Indian political elites in the
MIC complicates matters by politicising the issues instead of seeking legal
remedies. In a case concerning Indian agricultural workers and Indian petty
traders in Cameron Highlands, in the state of Pahang, activist B. Suresh
Kumar iterated in an interview for this study that press coverage of the issue
led to the intervention of the MIC leaders.[58] After a protest by the workers in front of the state government office, the chief minister of the state of

Pahang refused to meet the petitioning workers and traders as well as the NGO leaders to resolve the issue but stressed that he would cooperate only with the MIC leader.[59] However, the MIC leaders were unable to resolve the issue, which concerned land developers who were linked to the state government. Hence, race-based identity politics which compels the aggrieved Indians to channel their grievances through the Indian component party of the BN has not been useful to address the class-based issues of the Indian underclass. This finding raises the question of whether class issues matter in the courts and whether the judiciary takes into account the grievances of marginalised ethno-cultural minority groups like the Indian Tamil plantation labour (or Indian underclass).

### 5.3.2  Strategic litigation and the utility of the law as a political tool: does race or class matter in the courts?

This section will examine two legal cases concerning the eviction of Indian Tamil plantation labourers. In the 1999 case of Kamiri Estate in the state of Perak, between fifty to sixty Indian Tamil plantation labourers were retrenched by the Malaysian plantation corporation Guthrie Corporation. The plantation labourers were given the legal minimum compensation of RM 300 (USD117) per year of service, which in total amounted to almost RM 10,000 (USD3, 900).[60] Fifteen years before the retrenchment exercise, Guthrie had promised to provide alternative housing for the plantation labourers, but at the time of retrenchment failed to deliver on this promise. The plantation labourers were assisted by the NGO called JERIT which provided the labourers with legal information concerning their rights as plantation labourers. In April 2002, while negotiations were still underway, Guthrie filed for eviction proceedings to obtain vacant possession. In early 2003, Guthrie obtained a court injunction in the Ipoh High Court to evict the labourers but the plantation labourers, with the help of JERIT activists, filed a counter-claim asking Guthrie to fulfil its earlier promises.

In October 2003, the Ipoh High Court ruled in favour of Guthrie.[61] The judge, Justice V.T. Singam was reported to have said, 'Even I have to vacate my house when I retire.'[62] The judge's statement in the case showed a lack of judicial receptivity to class matters and issues concerning vulnerable groups. In an interview for this study, Dr Jeyakumar Devaraj, leader of the Socialist Party of Malaysia (PSM) and a key figure in the NGO wing JERIT which fought on behalf of the labourers, commented, 'We lost at high court, at appeal court. We kept losing all the time … The law is nothing … the law is pro-property … we had to go to court to delay the eviction order.'[63] Hence, the law was perceived as a repressive tool employed by the plantation corporation as well as the state. But despite its repressive nature, the law has also been useful as a political tool, in that the filing of appeals and counter-suing the plantation corporation was aimed at suspending the pending eviction orders.

The Kamiri plantation labourers also employed civil disobedience tactics. They demonstration in front of the Perak State chief minister's office and later in front of Guthrie's headquarters in Kuala Lumpur. Members of the Perak State assembly declared that the government was legally unable to help the evicted plantation labourers as it had no legal basis for acquiring private land for housing purposes. However, JERIT activists used the law to challenge this argument quoting *Section 3, Perak State Land Acquisition Act (Act 486)* that allowed for government intervention in the matter. The use of civil disobedience strategies served to embarrass the plantation corporation and the state government.

Since 2008, both the Court of Appeal as well as the Federal Court have rejected the plantation workers' appeals, but the delay tactic of utilising the appeal process itself was useful for the plantation labourers. Furthermore, the legal arguments presented by the Kamiri Indian Tamil plantation labourers in the appeal proceedings raised issues pertaining to constitutional rights such as *Article 5(1)* of the *Federal Constitution* on the right to life.[64] Although the plantation labourers lost the appeal at the Federal Court level, the judge was reported to be sympathetic to their cause. The Socialist Party of Malaysia reported that the judge had reprimanded the plantation corporation lawyers by asking, 'So you want to push them out to the streets do you …?' and had made the point that '[T]hese are poor workers.'[65] Despite the rejection of the appeal, the JERIT activists and the plantation labourers' *pro bono* lawyers hailed the decision as a victory for their side as it had forced the plantation corporation into an out of court settlement that provided a plot of land for thirty-three Kamiri plantation labourers. The activists reported that the alliance with lawyers had provided the impetus to 'fight back and uphold [the plantation labourer's] rights.'[66] In an interview for this study, JERIT activists iterated that rights and the law were tools of empowerment and knowledge, which formed a significant part of the political process of fighting for redress.[67] Hence, the understanding of rights among the activists was not that these were *legal* rights but rather they were *political* rights, which legitimised the cause.

Judicial perception of the legal eviction cases of the Indian Tamil plantation labour has not been uniform. While some judges have been sympathetic, others have been unreceptive to these grievances. In the 2003 case of Changkat Salak Estate in Perak, the Court of Appeal judge reprimanded the plantation corporation's lawyers by asking them, 'Leave and go where? Live on trees? Or cow sheds? Or you've got hotels for them?'[68] On the other hand, in the 2003 case of Bukit Jelutong Estate in the state of Selangor, the plantation corporation obtained an *ex parte* order (a legal proceeding brought by one party without the other party being present) for vacant possession and proceeded to demolish the plantation homes within an hour, against the legal requirement of a fourteen-day notice period. A civil society newsletter noted that the Court of Appeal rejected the workers' application for a stay order and 'the judges never asked about the plight of the estate workers, never questioned the illegal demolitions and never talked about shelter, suffering and poverty'.[69]

Judicial attitudes are significant and have a profound effect on the legal mobilisation strategies of Indian activists. In an interview for this study, B. Suresh Kumar, an Indian activist in the Socialist Party of Malaysia, iterated the perception that the judges in the lower courts are more independent and provide favourable judgements to vulnerable groups, but the judges in the higher courts like the Court of Appeal are 'controlled by the government'.[70] Other interview participants who were involved in the eviction cases expressed similar views, emphasising that the judiciary is mostly 'unsympathetic' to vulnerable groups.[71] However, Suresh Kumar also stressed that when plantation labourers are 'dragged into court' by powerful plantation corporations, the activists who assist the labourers strategise in order to ensure that the problem is highlighted sufficiently inside and outside the court.[72] In other words, despite the unpredictable and sometimes unsympathetic judicial attitudes, the *process* of going to court itself serves as a valuable political strategy for the plantation labourers.

## 5.4  Formulating a social movement strategy: strategic litigation and civil disobedience

While the retrenchment and eviction cases analysed in Section 5.3 show that the law is useful as a political tool, the cases themselves did not mobilise the Indians *en masse*. This was mostly because activists framed these issues as class-based issues affecting the lower classes and did not construct an overarching ethno-cultural mobilising identity. The activists and lawyers involved in the cases had been successful in using class and rights to at least create significant political victories for the aggrieved plantation labourer communities even if not successful in court in providing adequate recourse to the affected Indian underclass. However, the 2001 Kampung Medan incident, which allegedly involved a racial riot between the Malay and Indian residents of an urban squatter settlement, allowed a mobilising identity to be constructed.[73] In this incident, the racial stigmatisation of the Indians involved permitted the authorities to justify their biased treatment of this group.

The Kampung Medan case highlighted several issues pertaining to the Indian underclass. As rural development led to the fragmentation and redevelopment of the rubber plantations, there was no governmental programme or policy to provide resettlement for the affected plantation labourers. The rural displacement or what Jayasooria terms 'social displacement'[74] created other social problems, such as forced urbanisation, overcrowding in low-cost flats, slums and urban squatters, unemployment, increased crime and other social problems. The rural group was transplanted into an urban setting which fractured the plantation social support structure and exacerbated social issues due to the inability to survive in a new competitive urban environment. As Bunnell states, '[c]onfined to a national ex-plantation periphery, this group was increasingly characterised as a criminalised and socially problematic sub-class'.[75] Hence, the Indian underclass in the urban squatters and settlements was racially stigmatised as being a social problem, which was used by the government in making sense of the Kampung Medan incident. This bias, in turn, led to resentment and anger in the affected Indian community. Indian activists and Indian lawyers became crucial in mobilising the Indian community in order to seek justice and legal remedy for the failure of the government to investigate the causes of the Kampung Medan incident.

### 5.4.1 The 2001 case of Kampung Medan: class, race and rights

The Kampung Medan Incident was reported as a sudden race riot between Indians and Malays, which led to a string of mob attacks targeting Indians in the urban housing estate of Kampung Medan between 8th and 23rd March 2001. The incident caused outrage among Indian activists and human rights organisations because of the treatment accorded to the Indian victims by the law enforcement agencies and the absence of an independent inquiry on the causes of the incident.[76] As the incident arose in the poorer section of urban settlements and squatters in the suburban town of Petaling Jaya in the state of Selangor, a perception of injustice arose due to the similar situation the Indians in those urban settlements found themselves to be in and the differential treatment accorded by the police and the judiciary to the Indian victims of the incident.

Due to the fact that a larger number of Indians were injured in the incident, which included the death of six Indians, civil society groups like the Group of Concerned Citizens (GCC) and Indian community leaders questioned the true account of what was framed by mainstream media as a 'racial clash' between the Malays and Indians. The grievances were framed by Indian activists as resulting from 'racism and racial discrimination'.[77] In a memorandum to the prime minister, fifty-one NGOs, which included many Indian-based organisations called on the government to ratify international human rights treaties. The Memorandum, written in the form of a United Nations resolution stated, *inter alia,*

> REAFFIRM Malaysia's position that all human beings are born free, equal with dignity and rights, any doctrine of racial superiority is therefore, scientifically false, morally condemnable, socially unjust, dangerous and has no justification whatever; CONDEMN all forms of racism, racial discrimination and related intolerance in the context of fulfilment of civil, political, economic, social, religious and cultural rights.[78]

While the Indian civil society group called for a Royal Commission of Inquiry to investigate the incident, they were disappointed with the treatment of the victims by an indifferent Malay-majority police force and proceeded to frame the incident as 'a violation of the social contract and trust placed on the elected government'.[79] As previous discussion in this study has shown, most of the past grievances have centred around the discriminatory and unequal status brought on by the social contract. Here, the NGOs and grassroots organisations claimed yet another violation of the social contract *vis-à-vis Article 153*s constitutional protection of 'legitimate interests of other communities' which includes the Indian community. Thus, the police mistreatment of the victims contributed to the pooling of grievances, with constitutional rights utilised to frame these grievances.

Other than the Indian civil society groups, the incident also mobilised several political and non-communal civil society groups who questioned the discriminatory treatment by the police and the unwillingness of the state to sanction an independent investigation. Dr Xavier Jayakumar, an opposition politician and political activist wrote in a civil society newsletter that the police force was complacent in attending to the Indian victims of the incident.[80] His statement implied that the police force had deliberately delayed action due to the racial characteristics of the victims. Dr Kua Kia Soong, a former politician, academic and current political commentator pointed out that the issue touched on the credibility of the law enforcement as well as security forces.[81] Due to the absence of any official investigation on the incident, the then president of the Malaysian Bar Council, Mah Weng Kwai called for an independent Royal Commission of Inquiry to be set up under the *Commissions of Enquiry Act 1950* to investigate the incident.[82]

Despite the calls from politicians, lawyers and grassroots activists, no inquiry took place. At that time, an Indian NGO called *Parti Reformasi Insan Malaysia* (Malaysian Peoples Reform Party or PRIM), headed by P. Uthayakumar, who was later a key leader of the 2007 HINDRAF movement, began to mobilise human rights activists, activist lawyers and Indian NGOs to seek clarification over the police inaction during the incident. PRIM was originally formed in 1999 and was linked to another Indian NGO called Police Watch Malaysia which investigated human rights issues stemming from police abuse, custodial deaths and police shootings.[83] PRIM and Police Watch Malaysia had, during their earlier investigations of the police force, always questioned the higher incidents of police shootings and death in police custody of Indian inmates. PRIM appealed to the Malaysian Human Rights Commission (*Suruhanjaya Hak Asasi Manusia* or SUHAKAM) to initiate an inquiry into the allegations of human rights abuses in the Kampung Medan incident. In a letter to SUHAKAM, P. Uthayakumar, PRIM's secretary-general argued that it had been 150 days since the Kampung Medan incident took place and because no inquest or inquiry had been conducted to ascertain the true causes, the perception was that, 'the [w]hole [c]ountry is wanting to hush up this tragedy.'[84] The Kampung Medan Incident had, therefore, mobilised Indian activists, Indian lawyers as well as Indian opposition politicians to question the refusal of the government to conduct an inquiry into the incident. The government's response to the Kampung Medan incident prompted the legal mobilisation of Indians.

SUHAKAM refused to hold an inquiry citing that the incident dealt with 'socioeconomic concerns' which should be investigated by 'relevant agencies'.[85] Thio contends that the root cause of the Kampung Medan problem was the backward socioeconomic status of the Indian minority group in the urban settlements and squatters, which SUHAKAM failed to acknowledge.[86] However, labelling the incident as a socioeconomic concern and not a human rights issue also disregards the racial dimension of the problem, which was essentially the differential treatment accorded to the Indian victims by the police. P. Ramakrishnan, former president of Aliran, an independent news journal, condemned the SUHAKAM for turning into a 'creature of the BN government' and criticised the Commissioners both in their individual and collective capacity for not standing up for the vulnerable and the aggrieved.[87] The Kampung Medan incident also revealed the ineffective and powerless nature of the Malaysian Human Rights Commission.

In 2002, a public interest suit was taken by Subramaniam Vythilingam, on behalf of one hundred Kampung Medan victims against SUHAKAM for failing to investigate the incident and conduct an open inquiry under *Sections 4* and *12 Human Rights Commission Act 1999*.[88] The legal suit was supported by *pro bono* Indian lawyers and Indian activists, many of whom were key leaders of the later HINDRAF movement. The plaintiff's main argument in court was that SUHAKAM had, in earlier cases, promptly held inquiries into allegations regarding a breach of human rights, but had failed to do so in the Kampung Medan incident which involved the deaths and injuries of Indians. The plaintiff's argument clearly indicates the perception of differential treatment by the Commission towards the case which was linked to the ethno-cultural identity of the victims.

The High Court of Kuala Lumpur held that the plaintiff Subramaniam Vythilingam had no *locus standi* (standing in court) to bring the suit. The court applied the stringent test laid out in an earlier precedent[89] and stated, 'Remedies must correlate with rights. So, only those whose own rights are at stake are qualified and eligible to be awarded remedies.' The court declared that Subramaniam was not a 'victim', defined as one who had suffered injury or financial loss, and therefore had no right to represent the other victims. Indian activists contended that Subramaniam had, in fact, been attacked, while a newspaper report stated that Subramaniam had sustained injuries like the other one hundred Indian victims.[90] However, according to the High Court decision, Subramaniam was unable to prove that he was a victim as he was not one of the ten victims who had lodged a police report after the incident. Legal academics contend that the courts had taken a restrictive approach in interpreting the rules of standing, which means that most public interest litigation cases in Malaysia are likely to be unsuccessful.[91]

The judgement of the *Subramaniam case* also shows a lack of judicial receptivity to public policy matters and issues pertaining to vulnerable ethno-cultural minority groups, like the Indian underclass in urban settlements. When the plaintiff's lawyer referred to the victims as being of Indian origin and of Tamil ethnicity, the court submitted that '[w]hatever one uses to describe those victims, it makes not a whit of a difference.'[92] Hence, the courts disregarded the class-based as well as the race-based identity of the victims and only took into consideration the legal arguments. Like SUHAKAM had done, the courts too were unwilling to allow the case to proceed and rejected the application for a judicial review of SUHAKAM for failing to investigate the Kampung Medan incident.

On 8th April 2006, one of the victims of the incident, K. Arumugam, who was later one of the HINDRAF leaders and a human rights activist, published a book in the Tamil language on his experiences during the Kampung Medan Incident. However, the book was banned by an order dated 21st November 2006 by the Ministry of Home Affairs, specifying that the book was 'prejudicial to public order' under *Section 7(1) Printing Presses and Publications Act 1984*. In 2010 Mr. Arumugam filed for judicial review seeking *inter alia*, first, a declaratory order that the minister's order was invalid as well as null and void, and second, an order of *certiorari* to quash and/or set aside the minister's order.[93] The challenge on the minister's order was based on the grounds of illegality (as the order was signed by the deputy minister and not the minister), procedural impropriety (as the order was a breach of the rules of natural justice in that the author had not been given the right to be heard before the decision was made and that no reasons had been given for the decision), irrationality (that the book was not against public order but, in fact, in promotion of public order) and proportionality (that the minister's order was disproportionate to the objects sought to be achieved, and it was an unreasonable restriction on the right to free expression under *Article 10* of the Federal Constitution).

Counsel for Arumugam argued that the book, in fact, incorporated extracts from a PhD thesis which included an analysis of the Kampung Medan incident in light of the socioeconomic condition of the Indian underclass in urban squatter settlements.[94] The judge in the case found that the order to ban the book was made based on a report from the Police Headquarters and advice from the Ministry of Home Affairs' Publication and Quranic Texts Control Division which found that the book, titled 'March 8', had published 'racial issues that could prejudice public order and national security'.[95] It is generally unclear why the book came under the purview of the Quranic Texts Control Division of the Ministry of Home Affairs, as the book did not concern the Islamic religion or Muslims. In any case, the court found that the book discussed a racial riot and portrayed the Indians as victims, which was enough to be considered a threat to public order. Although the court conceded that a PhD thesis with similar information would not be a threat due to its limited accessibility in a university, a book that was available to the Indian community at large would be considered a threat to the public.[96] This judgement suggests that the Malaysian courts are generally not receptive to any case that deals with race and racialised issues. The courts are reluctant to deliberate on any ethno-cultural minority issues such as inequality and legal discrimination, thus effectively closing the legal opportunity for minority groups to litigate on grievances which relate to their ethno-cultural identity.

The failure of the courts and the national human rights institution in providing an avenue to investigate the Kampung Medan incident and resolve the grievances of the Indian victims was later turned into a cause of contention by HINDRAF activists and was stated as one of the key demands of HINDRAF's 18 Point Memorandum in 2007. In fact, the failure to obtain remedies for the injured Indian victims and families of the victims who had died led to a pooling of grievances within the poor urban settlement of Kampung Medan. Indian activists had framed the failure of the two judicial review applications, one against the Malaysian Human Rights Commission and the other against the Ministry of Home Affairs, as a 'racist attack' on Indians and as a denial of justice.[97]

### 5.4.2 The 2007 Indian mobilisation: mobilising identity, political rights and civil disobedience

As discussed in Section 5.2, the HINDRAF Movement was triggered by ethno-religious incidents such as the legal cases involving Indian Hindu litigants over conversion and child custody matters as well as the temple demolition cases. However, the grievances that were emphasised during the HINDRAF rally, reflected in the 18-point Memorandum, are the problems of the Indian underclass or the former Indian Tamil plantation labour. While other Indian activists and non-communal NGOs had taken a class-based approach in challenging the grievances of the Indian underclass, as described in Section 5.3, the HINDRAF Movement explicitly relied on racial framing and ethno-religious framing of these grievances. The class-based approach and the utility of the law as a political tool had been successfully used by the non-communal NGOs in cases dealing with the retrenchment and eviction of the Indian Tamil plantation labour. However, the class-based approach was not able to address race-based or ethno-cultural issues such as the Hindu temple demolitions and the legal cases concerning the rights of non-Muslim parties in the *Syariah* courts.

The HINDRAF Movement's initial agenda of focussing on ethno-religious issues enabled it to mobilise both the Indian underclass as well as the urban Indian middle class. While a class-based approach would not have been able to unite these two Indian sub-groups, the religious triggers and frames were able to construct an Indian Hindu mobilising identity from the internal social identity of the Indian Hindu community. However, the ethno-religious frame clearly excluded the persistent and serious grievances of the Indian underclass, which were connected to the socioeconomic discrimination of the Indian Tamil plantation labour as well as the racial discrimination and inequality suffered by Indians in general. Hence, in order to widen the mobilising identity, the HINDRAF Movement shifted from the ethno-religious identity and its initial call for Hindu rights towards amalgamating several issues under the formal identity of Indians. The call for Indian rights also meant that the grievances of the Indian community could be placed under the human rights principle of minority rights protection.

The principle of minority rights under international human rights law is best regarded as a moral right from the natural law perspective which Dworkin's 'rights as trumps' theory is based on[98] and not a legal right in the positivist sense, as Malaysia is not a signatory to the 1966 human rights instruments (*International Covenant on Civil and Political Rights* and the *International Covenant on Economic, Social and Cultural Rights*), or the 1965 *International Convention on the Elimination of All Forms of Racial Discrimination*. The invocation of minority rights by the HINDRAF leaders during direct action tactics such as the 2007 HINDRAF rally was more in the form of rights rhetoric than in its legal positivistic sense. The coordination of both rights rhetoric and the civil disobedience that occurred in 2007 show the use of rights as a political tool. This includes the use of any form of rights such as the constitutional right to equality and all calls for moral rights as part of the civil disobedience strategy. The use of both legal and moral rights was aimed at garnering support from the urban Indian middle class who have been historically linked to Indian civil society groups and opposition political parties. Furthermore, in representing an aggrieved Indian minority and a non-rights-bearing group, the HINDRAF leaders were legitimised in utilising the right to equality, which in Dworkinian terms is considered a fundamental political right.

Questionable however is HINDRAF's threat of litigation in the United Kingdom for colonial exploitation as well as the mistreatment and abandonment of the Indian Tamil plantation labour. The claim *inter alia* demanded the cessation of the *Bumiputera* policy and reparations for Indians in the form of a class-based affirmative action policy and monetary compensation of one million pounds from the British government 'for the pain, suffering, humiliation, discrimination and continuous colonisation suffered by each and every Indian and their ancestors in Malaya be awarded to each and every living Malaysian of Indian origin.'[99] Was the proposed litigation another political strategy of the HINDRAF leaders? In an interview for this study, P. Waythamoorthy, a key leader of the HINDRAF Movement contended that the purpose of the intended civil suit against the British government was to gather international support and international media publicity for the grievances of the Indian underclass, who were clearly the only Indian sub-group that could have benefitted from the litigation itself.[100] Waythamoorthy stated that 'win or lose is not the issue. It is just the chance to question the British.'[101] This response to legal action is similarly seen in the Indian activists who fought the plantation corporations, discussed in Section 5.3.

Interviews conducted for this study found that the HINDRAF claims on the United Kingdom garnered support from most of the Indian activists from the urban Indian middle class.[102] Thus, the threat of a class action suit and the grandiose legal claims against the British government indicate that the law was used as part of a civil disobedience strategy. The nature of the claims created awareness of Indian grievances both nationally and internationally. The law was more useful as a political rather than a legal tool in this instance.

## 5.5 The 2008, 2013 and 2018 electoral mobilisation of Indians: did the law matter?

After the 2007 HINDRAF Rally and the arrest of the key leaders of the movement under the draconian *Internal Security Act 1966*, the Indians in Malaysia were politically mobilised and were united in ousting the Indian political elites, the MIC from political power. The experience of Indian activists and the Indian protestors who were involved in the HINDRAF rally, which involved police use of water cannons and teargas to disperse the crowds, had triggered an Indian consciousness as a discriminated minority.[103] The Indian activists who were crucial in the HINDRAF Movement and who supported the movement were largely from the urban Indian middle class and opposed the Indian political elites in the MIC, which had done little in fighting for the Indians. As Chapter 4 iterated, the Indian political elites were largely supported by the Indian Tamil plantation labour, who comprised a majority in the Indian electorate. The accumulation of grievances among the Indian underclass and the trigger of particular incidents which mobilised the urban Indian middle class had culminated in an 'anti-MIC' consciousness from 2007 and in the 2008 General Election the MIC lost significantly and the president of the MIC, Samy Velu lost his Parliamentary seat to the opposition candidate, Dr Jeyakumar Devaraj of PSM. Hence, for the first time in history since the 1957 Independence of Malaya, the Indians had united to decimate the Indian political elites of the MIC in the General Elections held on the 8th of March 2008.

At the 2008 General Election, the BN suffered an overall loss in terms of losing its two-thirds majority in the legislature and was only able to secure 51.4% of the popular vote.[104] The Chinese had generally moved away from the Malaysian Chinese Association (MCA) which is the BN's Chinese component party and had shifted their support to opposition parties such as the Democratic Action Party (DAP).[105] The abandon of the BN by the Chinese and the huge losses suffered by the BN during the 2008 General Election had compelled the newly appointed Prime Minister Najib Razak to contend with the issues of the Indian minority in order to win back Indians to the BN. In 2009, the prime minister set up a Special Indian Taskforce (SITF)[106] within the prime minister's department and initiated a campaign called *Nambikei* ('Trust' in Tamil) which advocated 'transformation' of government and gave 'promises' (the Malay phrase *Janji Ditepati* was coined) to provide educational and business opportunities for Indians, to expand Tamil vernacular schools, increase Indian equity ownership in commerce, (re)build Hindu temples and address the problem of undocumented or 'stateless' Indians.[107] The use of the Tamil words *Nambikei* ('Trust') and the Malay phrase *Janji Ditepati* (Promises Fulfilled) indicates the government's implicit acceptance of the Indian community's loss of trust and confidence in the MIC and the BN after the 2007 HINDRAF Rally. The campaign also narrowed in on the issues that were politicised during the 2008 General Elections, such as the 'statelessness' of Indians.

The issue of undocumented Indians was a site of contention between the opposition political parties and the BN from 2007 onwards. While the BN had disregarded the issue before the 2008 General Election, the opposition political leaders and Indian activists had highlighted the large number of undocumented Indians especially among the Indian underclass who did not hold any legal documentation such as birth registration and the Malaysian identification card. These undocumented Indian persons were deemed to be stateless as they did not possess any evidence of their Malaysian citizenship which meant that they were unable to attend government schools, register their marriages and register the citizenship of their children. In an interview with N. Surendran, vice president of the opposition *Parti Keadian Rakyat* (People's Justice Party) or PKR, who is also an Indian lawyer and activist, Surendran iterated that undocumented Indians were usually illiterate or had very little formal education and thus were in a weaker position when facing the bureaucracy of an apathetic and mostly Malay civil service in the National Registration Department.[108] Surendran argued that citizenship for those born to a Malaysian parent should be automatic under *Article 14* of the *Federal Constitution* but the National Registration Department had failed to implement the provision and hence was seen to be 'deliberately discriminating against Indians'.[109] Jiwi Kathaiah, editor of a Tamil newspaper and Indian activist commented in an interview that the Indian underclass from the rural areas generally do not register births and marriages at the National Registration Department of Malaysia which did not support applications by Indians who did not speak the Malay language, and these Indians 'don't want to be standing there as a kind of unwanted person … subjected to humiliation and denial of equal rights.'[110] Hence, both the Indian activists and Indian political leaders in the opposition parties had perceived the issue of undocumented Indian persons as a form of *discriminatory* treatment against the Indians and the denial of their *rights*.

Nanthini Ramalo, the secretary-general of Development of Human Resources in Rural Areas (DHRRA) Malaysia, in an interview iterated that in 2004, DHRRA had highlighted the issue of stateless Indians to the federal government which was not 'interested at that time'.[111] However, during the 2008 General Election, the issue of unregistered or stateless Indians was heavily politicised and claims were made by political leaders and activists on both sides regarding the number of stateless Indians in Malaysia without any substantial evidence or data.[112] After the loss of Indian votes in the 2008 General Election, Prime Minister Najib Razak initiated the *MyDaftar* programme in 2010 in order to address the previously neglected problem of undocumented Indian persons. The programme included a country-wide campaign by the Special Indian Taskforce to assist undocumented Indians in obtaining their documentation such as birth and marriage registration. The NGO, DHRRA Malaysia,[113] which had since 2003 been running its own documentation campaign for unregistered Indians, was in 2010 provided with government funding and requested to assist in the MyDaftar programme. Nanthini Ramalo stressed that 'we cannot blame the government' or the prevalent laws and policies for the issue of stateless Indians, and explained that the issue was due to a 'lack of awareness' especially among the uneducated and 'ignorant' Indian underclass on the importance of legal documentation.[114]

However, Datuk Siva Subramaniam, head of the Special Indian Task Force at the prime minister's department in an interview for this study emphasised that the 2007 HINDRAF protest was the 'turning point', which showed the government the mounting problems of the Indian community, including the issue of stateless Indians. He further iterated that the HINDRAF protest revealed the inadequacy of the Indian political elites in the MIC which failed to represent the Indians. In terms of the issue of statelessness, Datuk Siva Subramaniam stressed that the 'documentation laws' are unfair and do not help the Indians, but we have a 'good PM [prime minister]' who has brought in changes.[115] This displays a perception that it is the prime minister and not the MIC who has taken up the Indian issues.

Since the 2008 General Elections, and the official banning of HINDRAF in October 2008, the HINDRAF leadership became fractured and the group's leaders formed various splinter groups. Most of the HINDRAF leaders joined the opposition political parties, while some formed independent political parties. After the 2008 General Elections, Waythamoorthy had a 'fallout' with the opposition, the *Pakatan Rakyat* (PR), which led him to be wooed by Najib from 2012 onwards, in preparation for the 2013 General Elections.[116] In fact, Waythamoorthy was appointed a deputy minister after the 2013 elections but resigned less than a year later, as Najib had failed to fulfil the memorandum of understanding between HINDRAF and BN. Waythamoorthy had claimed that the BN was not serious in uplifting the Indian poor and developing the community.[117]

Other Indian activists who were part of the HINDRAF Movement remained in Indian civil society groups. Partisan politics has divided the Indian activists yet again – but this time into non-communal class-based activism versus a communal race-based activism. The opposition political parties stress class rather than race as a means to impede the race-based politics advocated by the BN. However, by placing undue emphasis on class, the opposition political parties either disregard the racial dimension of ethno-cultural issues or deal with pockets of ethno-cultural communities on an *ad hoc* basis. When Indian activists move from civil society groups into partisan politics, they often force the grievances to fit the party's political ideology. Nevertheless, the role of lawyers is still prominent both in the realm of Indian civil society groups as well as in opposition political parties. These Indian lawyers have continued to stress the significance of equality before the law.

The 2018 General Elections saw unprecedented change not only among the Indian electoral but the Malaysian electoral as a whole. Indians comprised 6.98% of the total electorate, but were a 'critical minority of 15% or more' in 22 constituencies throughout Malaysia.[118] Waythamoorthy made a strategic decision to cooperate with the *Pakatan Harapan* (PH) and was successful in his lobby to incorporate Indian issues into the PH Manifesto.[119] After the unprecedented win by PH in May 2018, Waythamoorthy was appointed as the Minister of Unity in the prime minister's department and had subsequently formed a new political party called the Malaysian Advancement Party.[120]

## 5.6 Conclusion

This chapter has shown that the 2007 Indian mobilisation *en masse* was triggered by ethno-religious incidents, such as the Moorthy case, the custodial rights cases of non-Muslim mothers and the Hindu temple demolitions. The framing of the incidents by the mobilisers who were Indian activist lawyers and Indian activists were centred on both the ethno-religious and rights frames, irrespective of whether it was moral or legal rights. The ethno-religious frame was later shifted to an ethno-cultural frame, together with the use of an ethno-cultural rights frame. Thus, the rights framing sufficiently encompassed the ethno-cultural as well as the legal dimension of the grievances experienced by the Indians as a *whole* and was able to show Indians as a *non-rights-bearing* group. In any case, the Indian grievances that have been articulated by HINDRAF and socialist oriented civil society groups like the PSM are similar. However, HINDRAF used ethno-cultural elements such as race and religion to frame their claims, while PSM and other non-communal NGOs used class and labour-based elements to frame grievances. While the ideologies may have differed, both social activist groups used the law, that is, litigation and called for rights to end socioeconomic and/or race-based discrimination. The law was useful in providing structure and organisation in framing claims while rights was useful in empowering and mobilising the Indians. However, the notion of rights differed between the activists. While both socialist-oriented groups like PSM and identity-based groups like the HINDRAF utilise rights as a civil disobedience strategy rather than a purely legal tactic, the understanding of rights differs in terms of the mobilising power of rights. Activists from the former group like Dr Jeyakumar have iterated that rights have 'nothing to do with the law', that is, laws are structured by those who hold power, while rights are 'inherited' and akin to a 'moral obligation'.[121] HINDRAF leaders who are all lawyers refer to rights as sourced from the constitution and human rights treaties, with references to minority rights and identity-based rights such as Indian rights.

## Notes

1 A term utilised by de Sousa Santos to describe a counter-hegemonic type of civil society that places equal emphasis on the social and political roots of 'human suffering'. See Boaventura de Sousa Santos, 'Beyond Neo-liberal Governance: The World Social Forum as Subaltern Cosmopolitan Politics and Legality' in Boaventura de Sousa Santos and Cesar A Rodriquez-Garavito (eds) *Law and Globalization From Below: Towards a Cosmopolitan Legality* (Cambridge University Press, 2005) 29, 39.

2 The Chinese category is also divided into several sub-categories, similar to the Indian category. The sub-categories have not been listed in this table.

3 The Other Bumiputera contains a long list of native groups from Sabah and Sarawak (East Malaysia), but since this discussion is centred on the differences in categorisation of the Indians and the main category of Bumiputera/Malay, the list of native groups has been removed.

4 Judith A Nagata, 'What is a Malay? Situational Selection of Ethnic Identity in a Plural Society' (1974) 1 *American Ethnologist* 331, 335.

5 Ibid., 337.

6 Interview with Dato' Haji Thasleem Mohamed Ibrahim, president of National Indian Action Team (Kuala Lumpur, 31 January 2013).

7 Kamal Sadiq, 'When States Prefer Non-Citizens over Citizens: Conflict over Illegal Immigration into Malaysia' (2005) 49(1) *International Studies Quarterly* 101, 104–105.

8 Ibid., 102.

9 See *Lina Joy v. Majlis Agama Islam Wilayah & Anor* [2004] 2 MLJ 119.

10 Interview with Fadiah Nadwa Fikri, lawyer and activist at Lawyers for Liberty (Petaling Jaya, 3 September 2012).

11 Interview with Dato' Haji Thasleem Mohamed Ibrahim, president of National Indian Action Team (Kuala Lumpur, 31 January 2013).

12 NIAT, 'Indian Malaysians' for GE13 (IMACGE13): Undo the History-Redo the Plan, 1957–2012' (Version October 2012), p. 32.

13 Ibid.

14 Interview with S. Retnaguru, an Indian film-maker and documentarian on contemporary Indian issues in Malaysia (Subang Jaya, 2 August 2012).

15 Department of Statistics, 'Population Distribution and Basic Demographic Characteristics 2010', <www.statistics.gov.my/portal/download_Population/files/census2010/Taburan_Penduduk_dan_Ciri-ciri_Asas_Demografi.pdf>.

16 Sadiq, above n 7, 110.

17 Diane K. Mauzy and R. S. Milne, 'The Mahathir Administration in Malaysia: Discipline Through Islam' (1983–1984) 56 (4) *Pacific Affairs* 617, 635.

18 Ibid., 633.

19 Ibid., 634.

20 Ibid., 635.

21 Ibid., 636.

22 Julian C. H. Lee, *Islamization and Activism in Malaysia* (Institute of Southeast Asian Studies, 2010) 52.

23 Vanitha S. Karean, 'The Malaysian Constitution and its Identity Crisis – Secular or Theocratic?' (2006) *Lawasia Journal* 47, 49.

24 *Kaliammal Sinnasamy v. Director of Islamic Religious Affairs Council of the Federal Territory & Ors.* (2005). See K. Shanmuga, 'Re Everest Moorthy: A summary of the case and related events of *Kaliammal Sinnasamy v. Islamic Religious Affairs Council of the Federal Territory, Director Kuala Lumpur General Hospital & Government of Malaysia*' in *The Malaysian Bar News* (29 December 2005). For the Court of Appeal decision see *Kaliammal a/p Sinnasamy v. Majlis Agama Islam Wilayah Persekutuan (JAWI) (Department of Islamic Affairs, Federal Territory)* [2011] 2 CLJ 165.

25 The *Constitutional Amendment Act 1988* had inserted *clause 1A* to *Article 121* of the *Federal Constitution* after the judicial crisis, which was discussed in Chapter 1. The amendment effectively removed the power of the civil courts to conduct judicial reviews of administrative decisions as well as placed equal power to the *Syariah* or Islamic courts.

26 Interview with Datuk Vaithilingam, former president of Malaysia Hindu Sangam (Petaling Jaya, 9 May 2012).

27 Interview with K. Shanmuga, lawyer and legal activist at Loyarburok (Kuala Lumpur, 7 July 2012).

28 *Shamala a/p Sathiyaseelan v. Dr Jeyaganesh a/l C Moganarajah* [2003] 6 MLJ 515.

29 *Subashini a/p Rajasingham v. Saravanan a/l Thangathoray* [2007] 2 MLJ 205.

30 Interview with S. Meenachy, National Women Leader, Malaysia Hindu Sangam (Petaling Jaya, 24 October 2012).

31 Andrew C. Willford, '"Weapons of the Meek": Ecstatic Ritualism and Strategic Ecumenism among Tamil Hindus in Malaysia' (2003) 9(2) *Identities: Global Studies in Culture and Power* 247. See also Andrew C. Willford, *Cage of Freedom: Tamil Identity and the Ethnic Fetish in Malaysia* (University of Michigan Press, 2006).

32 Garcia-Bedolla quoted in David S. Meyer and Lindsey Lupo, 'Assessing the Politics of Protest' in Bert Klanderman and Connie Roggeband (eds), *Handbook of Social Movements Across Disciplines* (Springer, 2010) 114, 128. See also Liza Garcia-Bedolla, *Fluid Borders: Latino Power, Identity, and Politics in Los Angeles* (University of California Press, 2005) 6.

33 Ibid.

34 N. Ganesan and P. Waythamoorthy, *Institutional Racism and Religious Freedom in Malaysia* (Hindraf Makkal Sakthi, undated) 36.

35 The movement had five key leaders who were known as the 'HINDRAF 5'. P. Uthayakumar who has been in the forefront of the movement identified the five leaders as P. Uthayakumar, P. Waythamoorthy, M. Manoharan, R. Kengatharan and K. Arumugam, who are all lawyers by profession (1st National HINDRAF Makkal Sakthi Convention: Rights not Mercy, Kuala Lumpur, 8 August 2010).

36 Wong Yeen Fern, 'Lawyer Sues Government to Halt the Temple Demolitions', *The Malaysian Bar* (online), 18 December 2006 <www.malaysianbar.org.my>. See also *Malaysiakini* (online), 18 December 2006 <www.malaysiakini.com/news/61120>.

37 Ibid.

38 See 'Temple Demolition Suit Stuck on Technicalities', *Malaysiakini* (online), 26 March 2007 <www.malaysiakini.com/news/65031>.

39 Interview with P. Waythamoorthy, lawyer and leader of HINDRAF (Seremban, 25 October 2012).

40 'Temple Demolition Suit Stuck on Technicalities', 2007.

41 P. Waythamoorthy, 'Malaysian Indian Minority & Human Rights Violations Annual Report: Malay-sia Truly Racist' (Paper presented at Pravasi Barathiya

Divas International Conference, Vigyan Bhawan, New Delhi, India, 7 January 2010) 21.

42 See Ronald Dworkin, *Taking Rights Seriously* (Harvard University Press, 1977).

43 'Gerakan Youth Slams Temple Demolitions', *Malaysiakini* (online), 10 June 2006 <www.malaysiakini.com/news/52340>. See also Claudia Theophilus, 'Pre-Dawn Strikes against Temple Decried', *Malaysiakini* (online), 7 June 2006 <www.malaysiakini.com/news/52139>; 'PM Urged to Halt Malacca Temple Demolition', *Malaysiakini* (online), 13 July 2007 <www.malaysiakini.com/news/69884>.

44 The 18 Point HINDRAF Memorandum (2007).

45 Sivachandralingam Sundara Raja, 'The London Dawn Raid and Its Effect on Malaysian Plantation Workers' (2012) 40 (116) *Indonesia and the Malay World* 74.

46 Jeyakumar Devaraj, *Speaking Truth To Power: A Socialist Critique of Development in Malaysia* (Alaigal, 2002), 79. See also Jeyakumar Devaraj, 'Betrayal and Marginalisation: The Story of Strathisla Estate' (1999) 19 (5) *Aliran Monthly*.

47 Ibid.

48 Malaysian Bar Council, *National Land Code (Amendment) Act 2001* (online) <www.malaysianbar.org.my>.

49 Interview with Dr Jeyakumar, former MP Sungai Siput, activist leader at *Alaigal* and Socialist Party of Malaysia (Ipoh, 19 August 2012).

50 Interview with S. Arutchelvan, secretary-general of Socialist Party of Malaysia and JERIT activist (Kuala Lumpur, 6 July 2012); Interview with Dr Jeyakumar, former MP Sungai Siput, activist leader at *Alaigal* and Socialist Party of Malaysia (Ipoh, 19 August 2012).

51 S. Nagarajan, *A Community in Transition: Tamil Displacements in Malaysia* (PhD thesis, University Malaya, 2004).

52 Confidential Interview with senior Malaysian government civil servant who wished to remain anonymous.

53 Interview with P. Kamalanathan, former MP of Hulu Selangor and MIC leader (Hulu Selangor, 10 September 2012). FELDA or Federal Land Development Agency was established under the *Land Development Act 1956*, in order to re-settle rural Malay farmers who were mostly landless and where the government had acquired the land for development.

54 Interview with P. Kamalanathan, former MP of Hulu Selangor and MIC leader (Hulu Selangor, 10 September 2012).

55 G. Vinod, 'High Court Breaks Heart of Estate Workers' *Free Malaysia Today* (online), 10 May 2010 <www.freemalaysiatoday.com/2010/05/10/high-court-breaks-hearts-of-estate-workers>.

56 G Vinod, 'Bukit Jalil Estate Folk Lose Appeal' *Free Malaysia Today* (online) 10 August 2011 <www.freemalaysiatoday.com/2011/08/10/bukit-jalil-estate-folk-lose-appeal>.

57 See *Veerasingam Subramaniam & Ors v. Datuk Bandar Kuala Lumpur* [2012] 3 CLJ 1041.

58 Interview with Suresh Kumar, activist at Socialist Party of Malaysia (Ipoh, 26 October 2012).

59 K. Pragalath, 'Pahang MB and Palanivel Accused of Lying', *Malaysiakini* (online) 26 September 2012 <www.freemalaysiatoday.com/category/nation/2012/09/26/pahang-mb-and-palanivel-accused-of-lying/>.

60 See Anantha R. Govindasamy, 'Indians and Rural Displacement: Exclusion from Region Building in Malaysia' (2010) 18(1) *Asian Journal of Political Science* 90; Jeyakumar Devaraj, 'Evicted Ex-Workers Take On Plantation Giants' (2002) *Aliran* Issue 10.

61  Jeyakumar Devaraj, 'Ladang Kamiri: "Victory" at Federal Court' *PSM Website* (26th June 2008) <www.partisosialis.org/en/node/782>.
62  Ibid.
63  Interview with Dr Jeyakumar, former MP Sungai Siput, activist leader at *Alaigal* and Socialist Party of Malaysia (Ipoh, 19 August 2012).
64  Devaraj (2008), above n 61.
65  Ibid.
66  Ibid.
67  Interview with Dr Jeyakumar, former MP Sungai Siput, activist leader at *Alaigal* and Socialist Party of Malaysia (Ipoh, 19 August 2012); Interview with S. Arutchelvan, secretary-general of Socialist Party of Malaysia and JERIT activist (Kuala Lumpur, 6 July 2012).
68  'Guthrie Stunned', *Aliran* (online) 14 July 2003 <http://aliran.com/archives/monthly/2003/7c.html>.
69  'Will the Poor Get Justice From the Courts? Lessons from the Ladang Bukit Jelutong Workers' Experience' *Aliran* (online) 19 July 2003 <http://aliran.com/archives/monthly/2003/7b.html>.
70  Interview with Suresh Kumar, activist at Socialist Party of Malaysia (Ipoh, 26 October 2012).
71  Interview with P. Waythamoorthy, lawyer and leader of HINDRAF (Seremban, 25 October 2012); Interview with Dr Jeyakumar, former MP Sungai Siput, activist leader at *Alaigal* and Socialist Party of Malaysia (Ipoh, 19 August 2012); Interview with S. Arutchelvan, secretary-general of Socialist Party of Malaysia and JERIT activist (Kuala Lumpur, 6 July 2012).
72  Interview with Suresh Kumar, activist at Socialist Party of Malaysia (Ipoh, 26 October 2012).
73  Thaatchaayini Kananatu, 'The Politico-Legal Mobilisation of Ethnic Indians before Malaysia's 2018 Election' (2018) 107(6) *The Round Table: The Commonwealth Journal of International Affairs* 703, 706.
74  Denison Jayasooria, *National Development Plans and Indians in Malaysia: A Need for Comprehensive Policies and Effective Delivery* (2011, JJ Resources).
75  Tim Bunnell, S. Nagarajan and Andrew Willford, 'From the Margins to the Centre Stage: "Indian" Demonstration Effects in Malaysia's Political Landscape' (2010) 47 *Urban Studies* 1257, 1264.
76  Prasana Chandran, 'Remembering Kampung Medan: One Year After', *Malaysiakini* (online), 8 March 2002 <www.malaysiakini.com/news/10633>.
77  S. Nagarajan and K. Arumugam, *Violence against an Ethnic Minority in Malaysia: Kampung Medan, 2001* (Suara Inisiatif, 2012).
78  Asha Rathina Pandi, *Blogging and Political Mobilization Among Minority Indians in Malaysia* (PhD Thesis, University of Hawai'i at Manoa, 2011).
79  Ibid.
80  Xavier Jayakumar, 'The Kampung Medan Tragedy: Act Now to Resolve the Problems of Marginalised Communities!' *Aliran*, Issue 2, 2001.
81  Nagarajan, above n 51, 2.
82  Mah Weng Kwai, 'Press Statement: Kampung Medan Disturbances' *Malaysian Bar Council* (online) 22 March 2001 <www.malaysianbar.org.my/press_statements/kampung_medan_disturbances.html?date=2011-09-01>.
83  Ian Seiderman, *Yearbook of the International Commission of Jurists: 2004* (Intersentia, 2004), 261.
84  'Letter from PRIM to Suhakam', 31 July 2001 <http://lamankm2b.tripod.com/cgi-bin/m/KM2A1/5119.html>.
85  Li-Ann Thio, 'Panacea, Placebo or Pawn? The Teething Problems of the Human Rights Commission of Malaysia (Suhakam)' (2008–2009) 40 *George Washington International Law Review* 1271, 1311.

86 Ibid.
87 P. Ramakrishnan, 'Suhakam: A Warehouse for Reports?' (2003) 23(7) *Aliran* <https://aliran.com/archives/monthly/2003/7d.html>.
88 *Subramaniam Vythilingam v. The Human Rights Commission of Malaysia & Ors* [2002] 7 CLJ 357; *Subramaniam all Vythilingam v. The Human Rights Commission of Malaysia (Suhakam) & 5 Ors* [2003] 3 AMR 213; [2003] MLJU 94 (hereinafter referred to as the *Subramaniam* case).
89 *Government of Malaysia v. Lim Kit Siang* (1988) 2 MLJ 12.
90 Beh Lih Yi, 'RM50 Million Suit against Suhakam Struck Out', *Malaysiakini* (online), 17 February 2003 <www.malaysiakini.com/news/14469>; Jiwi Kathaiah, 'Kg Medan Victims: Will They Ever Get Justice', *Malaysiakini* (online), 13 January 2012 <www.malaysiakini.com/news/186514>.
91 Thio, above n 85, 1289; Roger Tan, 'The Role of Public Interest Litigation in Promoting Good Governance in Malaysia and Singapore' (2004) XXXIII (1) *The Journal of the Malaysian Bar*, 1.
92 *Subramaniam case* (2003) MLJU 94.
93 See *Arumugam all Kalimuthu v. Menteri Kesalamatan Dalam Negeri & 2 Ors* [2010] 3 MLJ 412 (hereinafter referred to as the *Arumugam case* [2010]). See also Court of Appeal decision in *Arumugam all Kalimuthu v. Menteri Kesalamatan Dalam Negeri & 2 Ors* [2013] 5 MLJ 174 (hereinafter referred to as the *Arumugam* case [2013]).
94 See Nagarajan, above n 51.
95 *Arumugam case* [2010] 3 MLJ 412, 420 (Justice Mohamad Ariff).
96 Ibid.; *Arumugam case* [2013] 5 MLJ 174, 180 (Justice Apandi Ali).
97 The 18 Point HINDRAF Memorandum (2007).
98 See Dworkin (1977), above n 42.
99 Claim no. HQ07X02977 dated 30 August 2007, quoted in Ravindra K Jain, *Indian Transmigrants: Malaysian and Comparative Essays* (Strategic Information and Research Development Centre, 2011).
100 Interview with P. Waythamoorthy, lawyer and leader of HINDRAF (Seremban, 25 October 2012).
101 Ibid.
102 See List of Interview Participants in the Bibliography.
103 'Special Report: The Hindraf Protest', *Malaysiakini* (online) <www.malaysiakini.com/news/75315>.
104 James Chin and Wong Chin Huat, 'Malaysia's Electoral Upheaval' (2009) 20(3) *Journal of Democracy* 71, 73.
105 Ibid., 80–82.
106 See <http://taskforceindiancommunity.blogspot.com>.
107 See Nambikei, *Janji Ditepati* ('Promises Fulfilled'): The Book of Truth (<http://janjiditepati.nambikei.com/wp-content/uploads/2013/03/JanjiDitepati_English.pdf>. See generally *Nambikei* Website <www.nambikei.com/>.
108 Interview with N. Surendran, lawyer, activist at Lawyers for Liberty (Kuala Lumpur, 12 November 2012).
109 Ibid.
110 Interview with Jiwi Kathaiah, editor of *Semparuthi* (a Tamil online newspaper) (Kuala Lumpur, 15 March 2013).
111 Interview with Nanthini Ramalo, secretary-general of Development of Human Resources in Rural Areas Malaysia (Petaling Jaya, 5 September 2012).
112 Ibid.
113 MyDaftar Programme under DHRRA Malaysia, see <http://dhrramalaysia.org.my/cause/mydocument-2/>.
114 Interview with Nanthini Ramalo, secretary-general of Development of Human Resources in Rural Areas Malaysia (Petaling Jaya, 5 September 2012).

115 Interview with Datuk Siva Subramaniam, head of Special Indian Task Force, prime minister's department (Subang Jaya, 15 October 2012).
116 Kananatu, above n 73, 711.
117 'GE13: Hindraf to partner with Barisan says Waythamoorthy', *Star* (online), 18 April 2013 <www.thestar.com.my/news/nation/2013/04/18/ge13-hindraf-to-partner-with-barisan-sayswaythamoorthy/>.
118 Kananatu, above n 73, 703.
119 'Mahathir meets Waythamoorthy on possible collaboration', *Malaysiakini* (Online), 17 August 2017, <www.malaysiakini.com/news/392311>.
120 'Waytha Moorthy launches new party to protect and promote the interests of Indian community', *Star* (Online), 8 September 2018, <www.thestar.com.my/news/nation/2018/09/08/waytha-moorthy-launches-indian-party/>.
121 Interview with Dr Jeyakumar, former MP Sungai Siput, activist leader at *Alaigal* and Socialist Party of Malaysia (Ipoh, 19 August 2012); Interview with S. Arutchelvan, secretary-general of Socialist Party of Malaysia and JERIT activist (Kuala Lumpur, 6 July 2012).

# 6    Conclusion

This study investigated the role of the law and rights in the mobilisation of Indians in Malaysia by analysing three key components of ethno-cultural minority mobilisation – the formation of minority group *identity*, the framing of shared or common *grievances* and the use of *rights* in mobilisation strategy. The study used the single-case method and adopted a qualitative approach in the analysis of primary and secondary archival documents supplemented by semi-structured interviews with three groups – first, the Indian leaders in non-governmental organisations, grassroots community groups and civil society; second, Indian activist lawyers; and third, Indian political leaders and Indian politicians. Within the single-case study of Indian mobilisation in Malaysia, the study further divided the analysis into three contrasting phases that revealed an interesting paradox. During the colonial phase (1890s–1930s) examined in Chapter 3, there was no mobilisation until the resistance of the Indian Tamil plantation labour in 1941, while the post-colonial phase (1957–1989) investigated in Chapter 4 revealed that there was no mobilisation of Indians despite persistent grievances. However, the third contemporary phase (1990–2018) analysed in the previous chapter shows that there was mobilisation which culminated in the 2007 Hindu Rights Action Force (HINDRAF) rally.

The colonial phase shows that the 1941 Klang Strikes involved the Indian Tamil plantation labour as the *mobilised* group and the urban Indian middle-class professionals such as the journalists and the lawyers as the *mobilisers* or key leaders of the resistance that took place. The 1930s to the 1940s was a crucial time period, when the urban Indian middle classes who were an educated group of free migrants from British India became influential among the Indian Tamil plantation labour by spreading the ideas of anti-casteism and anti-imperialism. The Indian Tamil plantation labour was an already aggrieved group by this time and was easily mobilised by the urban Indian middle-class professionals. However, the mobilisation that occurred in 1941 did not involve the Indian management in the rubber plantations. In contrast to the colonial phase, the post-colonial phase shows that the Indians, who remained a fragmented group did not mobilise despite the accumulation of grievances. The period from 1970 especially shows that the government had used draconian laws and established race-based politics in order to construct an illiberal and politically controlled setting. This illiberal phase witnessed the curbing of civil society groups, which consisted of many urban Indian middle-class leaders who attempted to channel both Indian and non-communal grievances. The late 1980s especially silenced activists as well as curbed the independence of the legislature (the parliament) and the judiciary. The contemporary phase, after 1990, shows that Indian activists or *mobilisers* were beginning to use the courts to channel Indian grievances, and used *rights* rhetoric in direct action strategies such as protest. However, the mobilisation was subtle and isolated to particular cases which involved the Indian Tamil plantation labour. It was only after 2001 when an ethno-culturally heterogeneous and fragmented Indian community began to unify and mobilised *en masse* in 2007.

The study used the critical race theory[1] from sociolegal studies and Michael McCann's legal mobilisation theory[2] as a starting point, and incorporated Snow and Benford's framing processes theory[3] and Liza Garcia-Bedolla's concept of a mobilising identity[4] of ethno-cultural groups from social movement studies, Ronald Dworkin's theory of rights as political trumps,[5] as well as Eric Mitnick's group-differentiated rights theory.[6] Using these theories in interpreting the findings shows that there are two significant elements in the mobilisation of the Indian minority group in an illiberal Malaysia: first, the ethno-cultural *identity* of the Indians and second, the role played by the *mobilisers*, which include both the activist lawyers and the extra-legal activists in not only *framing* the identity of the group but also the *grievances* and the *rights* of the group.

The hypothesis that law and rights can be used as a *political* tool in minority mobilisation was explored by analysing two instances of Indian mobilisation in Malaysia – the 1941 Klang Strikes and the 2007 HINDRAF rally. Michael McCann's interdisciplinary approach of sociolegal as well as law and social movement (or legal mobilisation) studies, which produced the *constitutive* approach to analyse the law in the *process* of mobilisation, enabled the study to identify *how the law matters* in both the institutional domain of the courts as well as the non-state subaltern spaces where minority mobilisation occurs. The integration of the constitutive and process-based approaches was able to explain whether the law mattered in Indian mobilisation which took place in the two instances indicated above.

In summary, the study findings show that the law plays a significant role by constituting the formal identity as well as the social identity of the Indians in Malaysia. This occurred in three ways: first, the administrative or formal processes such as the census categorisation and registration of racial identity; second, the affirmative action policy in favour of the Malays that sidelines in particular the Indian underclass and creates a non-rights-bearing group which includes the Indian community; and third, the racial inequality and discriminatory treatment of the Indians which is attributed to *Article 153 Federal Constitution* (the Malay special rights provision), the 1971 *New Economic Policy* (NEP) as well as the 1971 *National Cultural Policy* (NCP).

The study also shows that the law functions in a second, interrelated way by constructing grievances among the Indian community. This occurred in two ways: first, through the affirmative action policy, the NEP and the 1990 *National Developmental Policy* (NDP), which produced racial as well as class-based discrimination especially among the Indian underclass and both inter-community and intra-community socioeconomic cleavages; second, through the ethno-cultural and ethno-linguistic bias embedded in the NCP which disregarded non-Malay culture and languages in Malaysia, and the creeping Islamisation programme, especially those decisions of the Islamic bureaucracy from the 2000s and the judicial decisions in the mid-2000s which legally discriminated against the Indian Hindu plaintiffs in cases involving Islam.

The study finding that the existence of Indian grievances did not propel mobilisation, from 1957 to 1989 suggests that other factors are necessary in driving mobilisation. The study shows that *type* of grievances played a crucial role in mobilising the Indians, especially *ethno-religious* grievances from the mid-2000s onwards that had deeply affected the Indian Hindu community across classes and accelerated the collective mobilisation of the Indian community despite their diversity, culminating in the 2007 HINDRAF rally. Another factor important in mobilisation is the role of the *mobilisers*, especially the cooperation between activist lawyers and Indian activists who played a part in organising, first a civil disobedience strategy by framing grievances as *political* rights and second through strategic litigation by using the law as a site of contention in order to claim *legal* rights. The importance of activist lawyers in Indian civil society as a crucial element in Indian mobilisation was also seen in the 1930s during the colonial phase where lawyers and journalists mobilised the Indian Tamil plantation labour, leading to the 1941 Klang Strikes. More than fifty years later, in the 1990s, activist lawyers and Indian activists again united to make claims for the aggrieved Indian community, and that resulted in the 2007 HINDRAF rally.

However, despite the presence of cross-class ethno-religious grievances in the late 1970s, evident in the Kerling incident, the Indians did not mobilise due to the constraints placed on Indian activists by the illiberal political climate and repressive laws in Malaysia during this period. Although the illiberal politics which curbed civil liberties and the freedom of speech,[7] the freedom to assemble[8] as well as the freedom of association,[9] remained in place even during the HINDRAF rally in 2007, there had been some loosening of civil society space from 2003 under the Abdullah Badawi government.[10] This expansion of political space for activists, although still limited by Western liberal democratic standards, nonetheless, allowed activists and lawyers to utilise the range of legal and civil disobedience strategies described in Chapter 5. Here, the mounting of ethno-*religious* grievances and the state's disregard of these grievances had angered the Indian community, thereby bringing together an otherwise fragmented community. Hence, the *type* of grievances which instigated the 2007 rally and the role played by the Indian mobilisers in the rally show that the Indian community, which is fragmented both horizontally and vertically, nonetheless, mobilised when the experience of a shared grievance and when the Indian mobilisers were both aligned. The law played a role in the mobilisation in two ways: first by constructing the ethno-cultural identity or the latent *mobilising* identity based on shared ethno-class grievances and especially cross-class ethno-religious grievances; and second, through the activist lawyers who use legal tools to bring the grievances to court and through legal principles to convert the grievances into rights.

Findings from the cases explored in this study validate some aspects of current theoretical frameworks. However, the findings of this study also expose the limitations of these frameworks in the sociolegal, social movement as well as legal mobilisation approaches that show how minority mobilisation can occur. The sociolegal approach taken by the critical race theorists recognises the dialectic process between law and race, where the law is employed by key actors to *racialise* the identity of minority groups in order to categorise and control ethno-cultural groups, while the self-perceived identity of the minority group can influence the legal classifications of race. The critical race theory has been primarily used to make sense of the political construction of race in the liberal democratic setting of the United States, which found that the law formalises and reinforces racial differentiations among the Blacks, the Chicanos and the Native American tribes. However, this study extends the law and race link to examine the political construction of two pseudo-ethnic categories in Malaysia: the *Bumiputera* group and ethno-religious sub-groups, such as the Indian Muslims. The law in the form of the *Federal Constitution*, the *National Cultural Policy* (soft law) and identity-registration processes (legal formalities) reinforce the homogeneity of the Malay race and the politically constructed *Bumiputera* group. Similarly, legal formalities, which includes census categorisation of the Indians, have constructed a new ethno-religious Indian sub-category which emphasises religious differentiation as a pseudo-ethnic category. The emphasis on ethno-*religious* as well as *indigenous* elements in the political construction of ethno-cultural identity in Malaysia shows that the law not only reinforces a racial order between the *Bumiputera* and the non-*Bumiputera*, but also an ethno-*religious* hierarchy between the Muslim and non-Muslim groups. The emphasis made by the laws and policies on both indigenousness and ethno-religious identity in Malaysia has complicated the dialectic process between the law and 'race'.

The sociolegal approach taken by Eric Mitnick in the group-differentiated rights theory connects legal rights to the 'sphere' of identity by exploring the three dimensions of identity, namely the internal and external social identity of groups and legal identity.[11] Mitnick's theory connects identity to rights by examining the constitutive role of *legal* rights in creating commonalities between rights-bearers, which he calls the investitive criteria. In creating this link, Mitnick sees the non-entitlement to *legal* rights as the basis of the shared grievances or angst of the group which in turn constitutes its identity as non-rights-bearers. This theory has been useful to show that

Indians, *vis-à-vis* the Malay special rights provision in the *Federal Constitution*, belong to the non-rights-bearer group. However, Mitnick's theory does not consider the link between particular *types* of grievances beyond denial of legal rights to the formation of identity. In the case of the Indians, the type of grievance that matters to identity relates to the ethno-religious and ethno-class issues faced by the Indian community as a result of being sidelined by both law and policy (or soft law). This study contributes to Mitnick's theory by bringing in types of grievances beyond legal rights but showing how these grievances can be related to legal and socioeconomic and political rights. Thus, legal rights are claimed through the link between the ethno-religious grievances of the Indian minority community to the constitutional right to religious beliefs, while the ethno-class grievances of the Indian underclass can be linked to socioeconomic rights under the NEP. It is in these ways that the identity of an ethno-cultural mobilising group becomes more evident as a non-rights-bearer group.

The social movement theories which were reviewed in Chapter 2 indicate that the most significant theoretical approach to study mobilisation of ethno-cultural groups is through the analysis of collective identity. However, Garcia-Bedolla's concept of the mobilising identity[12] although useful to understand how minority mobilisation takes place, does not offer any insights on how the mobilising identity evolves from the racialised identity of minority groups. As minority groups activate the particular identity in order to mobilise, they inevitably choose from an array of identities – the ethno-cultural, the politically constructed race and self-perceptions of group identity. This study contributes to the social movement perspective of minority mobilisation by amalgamating Mitnick's classifications of 'legal identity' and 'social identity' to Garcia-Bedolla's 'mobilising identity', in order to make sense of the evolution of minority identity during periods of acquiescence and mobilisation. In this way, the particular identity of the group can be traced during the times when the minority group mobilises as well as during the quiet period when they do not mobilise.

The law and social movement scholarship expounded by both sociolegal scholars and political science scholars has been useful to understand how the law matters in Indian mobilisation. In particular, Michael McCann's approach which analyses the law as a constitutive element in the process of mobilisation provides a useful theoretical framework to identify the three propositions of legal mobilisation: law/rights as an empowering tool, law in constructing grievances and law as a social movement strategy. However, McCann's approach does not take into account the element of identity which is significant in minority mobilisation. This study contributes to the law and social movement scholarship by incorporating a fourth proposition, which is the role of law/rights in formulating a mobilising identity. The study of Indians in Malaysia has shown that the Indian activists were able to invoke the ethno-religious identity of the Hindu community as a mobilising identity during the 2007 HINDRAF rally. The ethno-religious identity was deeply connected to the grievances of the Hindu community which related to the state's use of the law as a repressive tool in both the legal cases on conversion and custodial rights in the courts and in the demolition of the Hindu temples by state agencies. Repression by the law can also constitute minority grievances, which in turn forms the internal social identity of the group as a repressed or marginalised group. This was evident in the case of the Indians when in 2007, Indian activists had reframed the list of grievances as discrimination and marginalisation of Indians. The internal social identity arising from legal repression can be utilised by activists to mobilise the group. At the same time, the law also explicitly creates legal identity, which can also be utilised to mobilise the minority group. In the case of the Indians, the identity as 'Indian' arose from the colonial legal formalities which racialised the nationalist identity of people from the Indian sub-continent. In the 2007 HINDRAF rally, although the mobilisation originated from ethno-religious grievances of the Hindu community, the Indian activists had swiftly framed the cause as an Indian issue and called for Indian rights. Hence, the law plays a significant role in constructing the mobilising identity, which is missing from the current scholarship on law and social movements.

While this study has offered novel insights on how the law matters in minority mobilisation, there are aspects that need further reflection and research. First, there is a need to extend the analysis of ethno-cultural minority mobilisation in other settings to see if the findings for Malaysia also hold true elsewhere. There is a need to conduct comparative studies of legal mobilisation of minority groups in other illiberal or semi-authoritarian political settings such as Singapore. Although there has been one study on the legal mobilisation of Lesbian Gay Bisexual Transgender Queer (LGBTQ) movements in Singapore,[13] the study is a single-case study which offers insights on the pragmatic resistance strategies taken by LGBTQ groups within an illiberal polity. The comparison of legal mobilisation strategies across illiberal political settings also requires building a suitable theoretical framework that can accommodate both *ethno-cultural* minority mobilisation and non-ethnic minority mobilisation such as the LGBTQ or disability groups which mobilise. The latent social identity of the ethno-cultural minorities is absent from the other groups, but the comparison can offer insights on how the law matters in creating a mobilising identity.

Second, there is a need to study the repercussions of ethno-cultural minority mobilisation in illiberal polities which are controlled by an elite or majority group. The consequences of using ethno-cultural identity to mobilise a minority group can be seen in backlash movements which also use ethno-cultural identity to advance majority group rights. In the case of Malaysia, the HINDRAF movement in 2007 had propelled the emergence of a backlash movement called Perkasa (*Pribumi Perkasa Negara*) which mobilised to protect Malay rights under *Article 153* of the *Federal Constitution* and to maintain Malay supremacy in Malaysia.[14] A study of backlash movements in illiberal polities can likewise utilise the theoretical framework suggested in this study, which identifies the role of the law and rights in creating identity, grievances and mobilisation strategy.

# Notes

1 See Laura E. Gomez, 'A Tale of Two-Genres: On the Real and Ideal Links between the Law and Society and Critical Race Theory' in Austin Sarat (ed), *The Blackwell Companion to Law and Society* (Blackwell, 2006) 453.
2 See Michael W. McCann (ed), *Law and Social Movements* (Ashgate Publishing, 2006a).
3 See Robert Benford and David Snow, 'Framing Processes and Social Movements' (2000) 26 *Annual Review of Sociology* 611.
4 See Liza Garcia-Bedolla, *Fluid Borders: Latino Power, Identity, and Politics in Los Angeles* (University of California Press, 2005).
5 See Ronald Dworkin, *Taking Rights Seriously* (Harvard University Press, 1977).
6 See Eric J. Mitnick, *Rights, Groups, and Self-Invention: Group Differentiated Rights in Liberal Theory* (Ashgate, 2006).
7 See *Sedition Act 1948*, *Internal Security Act 1948* and *Printing Presses and Publications Act 1984*.
8 See *Section 27 Police Act 1967*.
9 See *Societies Act 1966*.
10 See Bridget Welsh and James Chin (eds), *Awakening: The Abdullah Badawi Years in Malaysia* (Kuala Lumpur: Strategic Institute of Research and Development, 2013).
11 See Eric J. Mitnick, 'Taking Rights Spherically: Formal and Collective Aspects of Legal Rights' (1999) 34 *Wake Forest Law Review* 409.
12 See Garcia-Bedolla, above n 4.
13 See Lynette J. Chua, 'Pragmatic Resistance, Law, and Social Movements in Authoritarian States: The Case of Gay Collective Action in Singapore' (2012) 46(4) *Law and Society Review* 713.
14 Amanda J Whiting, 'Secularism, Islamic State and the Malaysian Legal Profession' (2010) 5(1) *Asian Journal of Comparative Law* 1, 4–5; See, Deborah Loh, 'The Real Deal with Perkasa' in *The Nutgraph* (online), 16 March 2010 <www.thenutgraph.com/real-deal-perkasa/>.

# Bibliography

*A books/book chapters/journal articles/reports*

Abas, Tun Mohamed Salleh and K Das, *May Day for Justice: The Lord President's Version* (Kuala Lumpur: Magnus Books, 1989)

Abdullah, Nurjaaanah, 'Legislating Faith in Malaysia' (2007) *Singapore Journal of Legal Studies* 264

Abraham, Collin E R, 'Racial and Ethnic Manipulation in Colonial Malaya' (1983) 6(1) *Ethnic and Racial Studies* 18

Ahuja, Ravi, 'The Origins of Colonial Labour Policy in Late Eighteenth-Century Madras' (1999) 44 *International Review of Social History* 159

Aiken, Robert S and Colin H Leigh, 'Seeking Redress in the Courts: Indigenous Land Rights and Judicial Decisions in Malaysia' (2011) 45(4) *Modern Asian Studies* 825

Alagappar, Ponmalar N and Lean Mei Li, 'The Minority Majority of Malaysian Indians: An Agenda-Setting Study in a Local Daily' in Maya Khemlani et al (eds), *Ethnic Relations and Nation Building: The Way Forward* (Strategic Information and Research Development Centre, 2010) 163–182

Alagappar, Ponmalar N, Maya Khemlani David and Karamjeet Kaur, 'Representation of the Indian Community in the Media in Malaysia' (2009) 4(8) *International Journal of Interdisciplinary Social Sciences* 153

Alagappar, Ponmalar N, Maya Khemlani David and Sri Kumar Ramayan, 'Representation of a Minority Community in a Malaysian Tamil Daily' (2009) 9(3) *Language in India* 128

Allen, Jane S, History, 'Archaeology, and the Question of Foreign Control in Early Historic-Period Peninsular Malaysia' (1998) 2(4) *International Journal of Historical Archaeology* 261

Amnesty International British Section, *Report of an Amnesty International Mission to the Federation of Malaysia 18 November-20 November, 1978* (London, July, 1979)

Amrith, Sunil S, 'Indians Overseas? Governing Tamil Migration in Malaya 1870–1941' (2010) 208 *Past and Present* 231

Anbalakan, Kailasam, 'The New Economic Policy and Further Marginalisation of Indians' (2003) XXI (1–2) *Kajian Malaysia (Malaysian Research Journal)* 379

Anbalakan, Kailasam, 'Chapter 23: Socio-economic Self-help Among Indians in Malaysia' in K Kesavapany, A Mani and P Ramasamy (eds), *Rising India and Indian Communities in East Asia* (Institute of Southeast Asian Studies, 2008) 422

Anderson, Benedict, *Imagined Communities: Reflections on the Origin and Spread of Nationalism* (University of Michigan, 2006)

Anderson, Michael R, 'Law and the Protection of Cultural Communities: The Case of Native American Fishing Rights' (1987) 9 *Law and Policy* 125

Andersen, Ellen A, *Out of the Closets and into the Courts: Legal Opportunity Structure and Gay Rights Litigation* (University of Michigan Press, 2005)

Andersen, Margaret L, 'From Brown to Grutter: The Diverse Beneficiaries of Brown v. Board of Education' (2004) 13 *University of Illinois Law Review* 1074

Appudurai, Jayanath and G A David Dass, *Malaysian Indians: Looking Forward* (Strategic Information and Research Development, 2008)

Arasaratnam, Sinappah, *Indians in Malaysia and Singapore* (Oxford University Press, 1970)

Arasaratnam, Sinappah, 'Indian Society of Malaysia and its Leaders: Trends in Leadership and Ideology among Malaysian Indians, 1945–1960' (1982) 13(2) *Journal of Southeast Asian Studies* 236

Arasaratnam, Sinappah, 'Malaysian Indians: the Formation of Incipient Society' in Kernial S Sandhu and A Mani (eds), *Indian Communities in Southeast Asia* (Institute of Southeast Asian Studies, 1993) 214

Armstrong, Elizabeth A and Mary Bernstein, 'Culture, Power and Institutions: A Multi-Institutional Politics Approach to Social Movements' (2008) 26(1) *Sociological Theory* 76

Balasubramaniam, Ratna R, 'Has Rule by Law Killed the Rule of Law in Malaysia?' (2008) 8(2) *Oxford University Commonwealth Law Journal* 211

Balasubramaniam, Vejai, 'Strengthening Ethnic Identity Consciousness and the Role of Tactical Voting in Multi-racial Malaysia' (2006) 7(1) *Asian Ethnicity* 75

Banakar, Reza, 'Law Through Sociology's Looking Glass: Conflict and Competition in Sociological Studies of Law' in Ann Denis and Devorah Kalekin-Fishman (eds), *The New ISA Handbook in Contemporary International Sociology: Conflict, Competition and Cooperation* (Sage, 2009) 58

Barclay, Scott, Lynn C Jones and Anna-Maria Marshall, 'Two Spinning Wheels: Studying Law and Social Movements' in Austin Sarat (ed), *Special Issue: Social Movements/Legal Possibilities* (*Studies in Law, Politics and Society, Volume 54*) (Emerald Group Publishing, 2011) 1

Barr, Michael D and Anantha Raman Govindasamy, 'The Islamisation of Malaysia: Religious Nationalism in the Service of Ethnonationalism' (2010) 64(3) *Australian Journal of International Affairs* 293

Barraclough, Simon, 'Communalism and Confusion: Towards a Clarification of Terms in the Study of Malaysian Politics' (1984) 7(3) *Ethnic and Racial Studies* 413

Barry, Julia E, 'Apostasy, Marriage and Jurisdiction in Lina Joy: Where Was CEDAW?' (2009) 41 *International Law and Politics* 407

Baxi, Upendra 'Taking Suffering Seriously: Social Action Litigation in the Supreme Court of India' (1985) 4 *Third World Legal Studies* 107

Baxtrom, Richard, 'Governmentality, Bio-Power, and the Emergence of the Malayan-Tamil Subject on the Plantations of Colonial Malaya' (2000) 14(2) *Crossroads: An Interdisciplinary Journal of Southeast Asian Studies* 49

Bayly, Susan, *Caste, Society and Politics in India from the 18th Century to the Modern Age* (Cambridge University Press, 1999)

Belle, Carl Vadivella, *Thaipusam in Malaysia: A Hindu Festival Misunderstood?* (PhD Thesis, University of Deakin, 2004)

Belle, Carl Vadivella, 'Indian Hindu Resurgence in Malaysia' in K Kesavapany, A Mani and P Ramasamy (eds), *Rising India and Indian communities in East Asia* (Institute of Southeast Asian Studies, 2008) 456

Benford, Robert and Alan Hunt, 'Dramaturgy and Social Movements: the Social Construction and Communication of Power' (1992) 62 *Sociological Inquiries* 36

Benford, Robert and David Snow, 'Framing Processes and Social Movements' (2000) 26 *Annual Review of Sociology* 611

Bertrand, Jacques, '"Indigenous Peoples' Rights" as a Strategy of Ethnic Accommodation: Contrasting Experiences of Cordillerans and Papuans in the Philippines and Indonesia' (2011) 34(5) *Ethnic and Racial Studies* 850

Biro, Anna-Maria and Corrine Lennox, 'Introductory Study: Civil Society Actors and the International Protection Regime for Minorities' (2011) 18 *International Journal on Minority and Group Rights* 135

Blythe, Wilfred Lawson, 'Historical Sketch of Chinese Labour in Malaya' (1947) 20(1) *Journal of the Malayan Branch of the Royal Asiatic Society* 64

Breman, Jan, *Imperial Monkey Business: Racial Supremacy in Social Darwinist Theory and Colonial Practice* (Amsterdam: VU University Press, 1990)

Brennan, Martin, 'Class, Politics and Race in Modern Malaysia' (1982) 12(2) *Journal of Contemporary Asia* 188

Brigham, John, 'Rights, Rage and Remedy: Forms of Law in Political Discourse' (1987) 2 *Studies in American Political Development* 303

Brigham, John, *Material Law: A Jurisprudence of What's Real* (Temple University Press, 2009)

Brown, Graham K, *Civil Society and Social Movements in an Ethnically Divided Society: The Case of Malaysia, 1981–2001* (PhD Thesis, University of Nottingham, 2005)

Brown, Graham K, Severine Deneulin and Joseph Devine, 'Contesting the Boundaries of Religion in Social Mobilization' (2009) *Bath Papers in International Development* No. 4

Brown, Graham K, 'Legible Pluralism: The Politics of Ethnic and Religious Identification in Malaysia' (2010) 9(1) *Ethnopolitics* 31

Brown-Nagin, Tomiko, 'Elites, Social Movements, and the Law: the Case of Affirmative Action' (2006) 105 *Columbia Law Review* 1436

Brown, Rajeswary Ampalavanar, *Class, Caste and Ethnicism among Urban Indians in Malaya, 1920–1941* (Kuala Lumpur: Nusantara 2, 1972)

Brown, Rajeswary Ampalavanar, *The Indian Minority and Political Change in Malaya, 1945–1957* (Kuala Lumpur: Oxford University Press, 1981)

Buechler, Steven M, 'New Social Movement Theories' (1995) 36(3) *The Sociological Quarterly* 441

Bunnell, Tim, Sabitha Nagarajan and Andrew Willford, 'From the Margins to Centre Stage: "Indian" Demonstration Effects in Malaysia's Political Landscape' (2010) 47(6) *Urban Studies* 1257

Burgmann, Verity, *Power, Profit and Protest: Australian Social Movements and Globalization* (Allen & Unwin, 2003)

Cantril, Hadley, *The Psychology of Social Movements* (Wiley, 1941)

Capotorti, Francesco, *Study on the Rights of Persons Belonging to Ethnic, Religious and Linguistic Minorities* (New York: United Nations, 1991)

Case, Rhonda E and Terri E Givens, 'Re-engineering Legal Opportunity Structures in the European Union? The Starting Line Group and the Politics of Racial Equality Directive' (2010) 48 *Journal of Common Market Studies* 221

Case, William, *Elites and Regimes in Malaysia: Revisiting a Consociational Democracy* (Monash Asia Institute, 1996)

Case, William, 'New Uncertainties for an Old Pseudo-Democracy: The Case of Malaysia' (2004) 37(1) *Comparative Politics* 83

Case, William, 'Southeast Asia's Hybrid Regimes: When Do Voters Change Them?' (2005) 5 *Journal of East Asian Studies* 215

Castellino, Joshua and Elivira Dominquez Redondo, *Minority Rights in Asia: A Comparative Legal Analysis* (Oxford University Press, 2006)

Centre for Public Policy Studies, 'Ensuring Effective Targeting of Ethnic Minorities: The Case of Low Income Malaysian Indians' in *Proposals for the Ninth Malaysia Plan* (Asian Strategy and Leadership Institute, 2006)

Chandra, Ramesh, *Identity and Genesis of Caste System in India* (Kalpaz Publications, 2005)

Chapman, Roger, (ed), *Culture Wars: An Encyclopaedia of Issues, Viewpoints and Voices* (M.E. Sharpe Inc., 2010)

Cheah, Boon Kheng, *Red Star Over Malaya: Resistance and Social Conflict During and After the Japanese Occupation of Malaya, 1941–1946* (National University of Singapore Press, 2003)

Cheah, Wui Ling, '*Sagong Tasi* and Orang Asli Land Rights in Malaysia: Victory, Milestone or False Start?' (2004) 2 *Law, Social Justice and Global Development Electronic Journal*, <www2.warwick.ac.uk/fac/soc/law/elj/lgd/2004_2>

Chester, Graeme and Ian Welsh, *Social Movements: The Key Concepts* (Routledge, 2010)

Chin, James, 'The Malaysian Chinese Dilemma: The Never Ending Policy' (2009) 3 *Chinese Southern Diaspora Studies* 167

Chin, James and Wong Chin Huat, 'Malaysia's Electoral Upheaval' (2009) 20(3) *Journal of Democracy* 71

Chong, Dennis, *Collective Action and the Civil Rights Movement* (University of Chicago Press, 1991)

Chua, Lynette J, *How Does Law Matter to Social Movements? A Case Study of Gay Activism in Singapore* (PhD Thesis, University of California, Berkeley, 2011). ProQuest Dissertations and Theses, <http://search.proquest.com/docview/892712857?accountid=12528>.

Chua, Lynette J, 'Pragmatic Resistance, Law, and Social Movements in Authoritarian States: The Case of Gay Collective Action in Singapore' (2012) 46(4) *Law and Society Review* 713

Colletta, Nat J, 'Malaysia' Forgotten People: Education, Cultural Identity and Socio-economic Mobility Among South Indian Plantation Workers' (1975) 7 *Contributions to Asian Studies* 87

Collins, Elizabeth Fuller, *Pierced by Murugan's Lance: Ritual Power and Moral Redemption among Malaysian Hindus* (Dekalb IL: Northern Illinois University Press, 1997)

Collins, Elizabeth F and K Ramanathan, 'The Politics of Ritual Among Murukan's Malaysian Devotees' in Linda Penkower and Tracy Pintchman (eds), *Hindu Ritual at the Margins* (University of South Carolina Press, 2014) 83–105

Cotterrell, Roger, *The Politics of Jurisprudence: A Critical Introduction to Legal Philosophy* (University of Pennsylvania Press, 1989)

Cotterrell, Roger, *The Sociology of Law* (London: Oxford, 1992)

Cotterrell, Roger, 'Law in Culture' (2004) 17 *Ratio Juris* 1

Cotterrell, Roger, *Law, Culture and Society: Legal Ideas in the Mirror of Social Theory* (Ashgate, 2006)

Crenshaw, Kimberlé, 'Race, Reform and Retrenchment: Transformation and Legitimation in Anti-Discrimination Law' in Kimberlé Crenshaw et al (eds), *Critical Race Theory: The Key Writings That Formed the Movement* (New York: New Press, 1995) 109

Crossley, Nick, *Making Sense of Social Movements* (Open University Press, 2002)

Crouch, Harold, *Government and Society in Malaysia* (Cornell, 1996)

Daniel, Rabindra J, *Indian Christians in Peninsular Malaysia* (Kuala Lumpur: Methodist Church, 1992)

de Sousa Santos, Boaventura, 'Beyond Neo-liberal Governance: The World Social Forum as Subaltern Cosmopolitan Politics and Legality' in Boaventura de Sousa Santos and Cesar A Rodriquez-Garavito (eds), *Law and Globalization From Below: Towards a Cosmopolitan Legality* (Cambridge University Press, 2005) 29

Delgado, Richard, 'The Ethereal Scholar: Does Critical Legal Studies Have What Minorities Want?' (1987) 22 *Harvard Civil Rights-Civil Liberties Law Review* 301

Devdas, Vijay, 'Chapter Five: Makkal Sakthi: The Hindraf Effect, Race and Postcolonial Democracy in Malaysia' in Daniel P Goh et al (eds), *Race and Multiculturalism in Malaysia* (Routledge, 2009) 86

Dillon, Rosemary, *People in Transition: A Case-Study of Indian Squatters in Urban Malaysia* (PhD Thesis, Australian National University, 1991)

Dillon, Rosemary, 'Privatization of Squatter Settlement Redevelopment in Kuala Lumpur: Winners and Losers' (1993) 12 *Asian Geographer* 33

Dirks, Nicholas B, 'The Invention of Caste: Civil Society in Colonial India' (1988) *Comparative Study of Social Transformations* (CSST) Working paper #11, University of Michigan

Dirks, Nicholas B, 'The Invention of Caste', (1989) 25 *Social Analysis* 45

Doherty, Brian and Graeme Hayes, 'Having Your Day in Court: Judicial Opportunity and Tactical Choice in Anti-GMO Campaigns in France and the United Kingdom' (2014) 47 *Comparative Political Studies* 3, published Online First 18 April 2012

Donnelly, Jack, 'Human Rights and Human Dignity: An Analytic Critique of Non-Western Conceptions of Human Rights' (1982) 76(2) *The American Political Science Review* 303

Dworkin, Ronald, 'The Model of Rules' (1967) 35(1) *University Chicago Law Review* 14

Dworkin, Ronald, *Taking Rights Seriously* (Harvard University Press, 1977)

Dworkin, Ronald, *Law's Empire* (Hart Publishing: Oxford, 1986)

Dworkin, Ronald, *Sovereign Virtue: The Theory and Practice of Equality* (Harvard University Press, 2000)

Dworkin, Ronald, *Justice for Hedgehogs* (Cambridge University Press, 2011)

Ebright, Malcolm, *Land Grants and Lawsuits in Northern New Mexico* (University of New Mexico Press, 1994)

Economic Planning Unit, *Second Malaysia Plan (1971–1975)*, (Malaysia: Prime Minister's Department, 1971) [*New Economic Policy*]

Economic Planning Unit, *Third Malaysia Plan (1976–1980)*, (Malaysia: Prime Minister's Department, 1976)

Economic Planning Unit, *Fourth Malaysia Plan (1981–1985)*, (Malaysia: Prime Minister's Department, 1981)

Economic Planning Unit, *Sixth Malaysia Plan (1991–1995)*, (Malaysia: Prime Minister's Department, 1991) [*National Development Policy*]

Economic Planning Unit, *Eighth Malaysia Plan (2001–2005)*, (Malaysia: Prime Minister's Department, 2001) [*National Vision Policy*]

Economic Planning Unit, *Tenth Malaysia Plan (2010–2015)*, (Malaysia: Prime Minister's Department, 2010) [*New Economic Model*]

Edelman, Lauren B, Gwendolyn Leachman and Doug McAdam, 'On Law, Organizations and Social Movements' (2010) 6 *Annual Review of Law and Social Science* 653

Edwards, Frances L and Grayson B Thompson, 'The Legal Creation of Raced Space: The Subtle and Ongoing Discrimination Created Through Jim Crow Laws' (2010) 12 *Berkeley Journal of African American Law and Policy* 145

Eisenberg, Avigail, *Reasons of Identity: A Normative Guide to the Political & Legal Assessment of Identity Claims* (Oxford University Press, 2009)

Eisenberg, Avigail and Will Kymlicka, 'Bringing Institutions Back In: How Public Institutions Assess Identity' in Avigail Eisenberg and Will Kymlicka (eds), *Identity Politics in the Public Realm* (University of British Columbia, 2011) 1

Engel, David M and Frank W Munger, *Rights of Inclusion: Law and Identity in the Life Stories of Americans with Disabilities* (University of Chicago Press, 2003)

Epp, Charles R, *The Rights Revolution: Lawyers, Activists, and Supreme Courts in Comparative Perspective* (University of Chicago Press, 1998)

Escobar, Edward J, 'The Dialectics of Repression: The Los Angeles Police Department and the Chicano Movement, 1968–1971' (1993) 79 *Journal of American History* 1483

Eskridge, William N, 'Channeling: Identity-Based Social Movements and Public Law' (2001) 150 *University of Pennsylvania Law Review* 419

Evans, Tony, 'International Human Rights Law as Power/Knowledge' (2005) 27 *Human Rights Quarterly* 1046

Ewick, Patrick and Susan S Silbey, *The Common Place of Law: Stories from Everyday Life* (University of Chicago Press, 1998)

Faruqi, Shad Saleem, 'Affirmative Action Policies and the Constitution' (2003) XXI *Kajian Malaysia* 31

Fernandez, Callistus, 'Colonial Knowledge, Invention and Reinvention of Malay Identity in Pre-Independence Malaya: A Retrospect' (1999) 55 *Akademika* 39

Freeman, Alan, 'Legitimizing Racial Discrimination Through Antidiscrimination Law: A Critical Review of Supreme Court Doctrine' (1978) 62 *Minnesota Law Review* 1049

Fritz, Nicole and Martin Flaherty, 'Unjust Order: Malaysia's Internal Security Act' (2002) 26(5) *Fordham International Law Journal* 1345

Gabel, Peter, 'The Phenomenology of Rights-Consciousness and the Pact of the Withdrawn Selves' (1984) 62 *Texas Law Review* 1563

Galanter, Marc, 'Why the "Haves" Comes Out Ahead: Speculations on the Limits of Legal Change' (1974) 9(1) *Law and Society Review* 165.

Galanter, Marc, 'Justice in Many Rooms: Courts, Private Ordering, and Indigenous Law' (1981) 19 *Journal of Legal Pluralism* 1

Galanter, Marc, *Competing Equalities: Law and the Backward Classes in India* (University of California, 1984)

Gamson, Joshua, 'Must Identity Movements Self-Destruct? A Queer Dilemma' (1995) 42 *Social Problems* 390

Gamson, William A, *Talking Politics* (Cambridge University Press, 1992)

Gamson, William A, 'The Social Psychology of Collective Action' in Aldon D Morris and Carol M Mueller (eds), *Frontiers in Social Movement Theory* (Yale University Press, 1992) 53–76

Ganesan, Narayanan, 'Liberal and Structural Ethnic Political Accommodation in Malaysia' in Will Kymlicka and Baogang He (eds), *Multiculturalism in Asia* (Oxford University Press, 2005) 136–151

Garcia-Bedolla, Liza, *Fluid Borders: Latino Power, Identity, and Politics in Los Angeles* (University of California Press, 2005)

George, Francis Cardinal, 'Law and Culture' (2003) 1 *Ave Maria Law Review* 1

Gewirtz, Paul, 'Chapter 5: The Triumph and Transformation of Antidiscrimination Law' in Austin Sarat (ed), *Race, Law and Culture: Reflections on Brown v. Board of Education* (Oxford University Press, 1997) 110

Goffman, Erving, *Frame Analysis: An Essay on the Organization of Experience* (Northeastern University Press, 1974)

Goldberg-Hiller, Jonathan, 'The Boycott of the Law and the Law of the Boycott: Law, Labour, and Politics in British Columbia' (1996) 21 *Law and Social Inquiry* 313

Goldberg-Hiller, Jonathan, '"Entitled to be Hostile": Narrating the Political Economy of Civil Rights' (1998) 7 *Social and Legal Studies* 517

Goldberg-Hiller, Jonathan, and Neal Milner, 'Rights as Excess: Understanding the Politics of Special Rights' (2003) 28 *Law and Social Inquiry* 1076

Gomez, Laura E, 'A Tale of Two-Genres: On the Real and Ideal Links Between the Law and Society and Critical Race Theory' in Austin Sarat (ed), *The Blackwell Companion to Law and Society* (Blackwell, 2006) 453

Gomez, Laura E, 'Understanding Law and Race as Mutually Constitutive: An Invitation to Explore an Emerging Field' (2010) 6 *Annual Review of Law and Social Science* 487

Gomm, Roger, Martyn Hammersley and Peter Foster (eds), *Case Study Method* (Sage Publications, 2000)

Gooding, Susan S, 'Place, Race, and Names: Layered Identities in United States v. Oregon, Confederated Tribes of the Colville Reservation, Plaintiff-Intervenor' (1994) 28(5) *Law and Society Review* 1181

Gopal, Parthiban S, Salfarina A Gapor and Sivamurugan Pandian, 'Indian Urban Poverty in Malaysia…A New Phenomenon? The Pre and Post Malaysian Independence Perspective' (2011) III *Asia Pacific Journal of Social Sciences* 32

Gorringe, Hugo, 'The Embodiment of Caste: Oppression, Protest and Change' (2007) 41 *Sociology* 97

Govindasamy, Anantha Raman, 'Indian and Rural Displacement: Exclusion from Region Building in Malaysia' (2010) 18(1) *Asian Journal of Political Science* 90

Groves, Harry E, 'Fundamental Liberties in the Constitution of the Federation of Malaya: A Comparative Study' (1959) 5 *Howard Law Journal* 190

Guan, Yeoh Seng, 'The Streets of Kuala Lumpur: City-Space, "Race" and Civil Disobedience' in Melissa Butcher and Velayutham Selvaraj (eds), *Dissent and Cultural Resistance in Asia's Cities* (Routledge, 2009) 128

Guan, Yeoh Seng 'In Defence of the Secular: Islamisation, Christians and (New) Politics in Urbane Malaysia' (2011) 35(1) *Asian Studies Review* 83

Guinier, Lani and Gerald Torres, *The Miner's Canary: Enlisting Race, Resisting Power, Transforming Democracy* (Harvard University Press, 2003)

Handler, Joel F, *Social Movements and the Legal System: A Theory of Law Reform and Social Change* (New York: Academic Press, 1978)

Haney-Lopez, Ian F, 'The Social Construction of Race: Some Observations on Illusion, Fabrication, and Choice' (1994) 29 *Harvard Civil Rights-Civil Liberties Law Review* 1

Haney-Lopez, Ian F, *White by Law: The Legal Construction of Race* (New York University Press, 1996)

Haney-Lopez, Ian F, 'Protest, Repression and Race: Legal Violence and the Chicano Movement' (2001–2002) 150 *University of Pennsylvania Law Review* 205

Haney-Lopez, Ian F, *Racism on Trial: The Chicano Fight for Justice* (London: Belknap, 2004)

Harding, Andrew, 'The 1988 Constitutional Crisis in Malaysia' (1990) 39 *International Comparative Law Quarterly* 57

Harding, Andrew, 'The Keris, the Crescent and the Blind Goddess: the State, Islam and the Constitution in Malaysia' (2002) 6 *Singapore Journal of International and Comparative Law* 154

Harding, Andrew, 'Malaysia: Religious Pluralism and the Constitution in a Contested Polity' (2012) 4 *Middle East Law and Governance* 356

Harding, Andrew, *The Constitution of Malaysia: A Contextual Analysis* (Hart Publishing: Oxford, 2012)

Harding, Andrew J and Amanda Whiting, 'Custodian of Civil Liberties and Justice in Malaysia: The Malaysian Bar and the Moderate State' in T C Halliday et al (eds), *Fates of Political Liberalism in the British Post-Colony: The Politics of the Legal Complex* (Cambridge University Press, 2012) 247

Hart, Herbert Lionel Adolphus, 'Are There Any Natural Rights?' (1955) 64(2) *The Philosophical Review* 175

Hart, Herbert Lionel Adolphus, 'Positivism and the Separation of Law and Morals' (1957) 71 *Harvard Law Review* 593

Hart, Herbert Lionel Adolphus, *The Concept of Law* (Oxford: Clarendon Press, 1961)

Henderson, James Y, 'Postcolonial Indigenous Legal Consciousness' (2002) 1 *Indigenous Law Journal* 1

Hilson, Chris, 'New Social Movements: The Role of Legal Opportunity' (2002) 9(2) *Journal of European Public Policy* 238

Hilson, Chris, 'Framing the Local and the Global in the Anti-Nuclear Movement: Law and the Politics of Place' (2009) 36 *Journal of Law and Society* 94

Hirschman, Charles, *Ethnic and Social Stratification in Peninsular Malaysia* (American Sociological Association, 1975)

Hirschman, Charles, 'Demographic Trends in Peninsular Malaya: 1947–1975' (1980) 6(1) *Population and Development Review* 103

Hirschman, Charles, 'The Making of Race in Colonial Malaya: Political Economy and Racial Ideology' (1986) 1 *Sociological Forum* 330

Hirschman, Charles, 'The Meaning and Measurement of Ethnicity in Malaysia: an Analysis of Census Classifications' (1987) 46(3) *The Journal of Asian Studies* 555

Holst, Frederik, *Ethnicization and Identity Construction in Malaysia* (Routledge, 2012)

Hoxie, Frederick E, 'What Was Taney Thinking? American Indian Citizenship in the Era of Dred Scott' (2007) 82 *Chicago-Kent Law Review* 329

Huang-Thio, Su Mien, 'Constitutional Discrimination Under the Malaysian Constitution' (1964) 6 *Malaya Law Review* 1

Human Rights Watch Report, *Caste Discrimination against Dalits or So-called Untouchables in India* (Human Rights Watch, 2007)

Hunt, Alan, *Explorations in Law and Society: Towards a Constitutive Theory of Law* (Routledge, 1993)

Hunt, Alan, 'Law, Community and Everyday Life: Yngvesson's Virtuous Citizens and Disruptive Subjects' (1996) 21 *Law & Social Inquiry* 173

Ignatieff, Michael, *Human Rights as Politics and Idolatry* (Princeton University Press, 2001)

Institute of Social Analysis (INSAN), *Sucked Oranges: The Indian Poor in Malaysia* (Kuala Lumpur: INSAN, 1989)

Jackson, James C, *Planters and Speculators: Chinese and European Agricultural Enterprise in Malaya 1786–1921* (University of Malaya Press, 1968)

Jain, Prakash C, 'Exploitation and Reproduction of Migrant Indian Labour in Colonial Guyana and Malaysia' (1988) 18(2) *Journal of Contemporary Asia* 189

Jain, Ravindra K, *South Indians in the Plantation Frontier in Malaya* (Yale University Press, 1970)

Jain, Ravindra K, *Indian Transmigrants: Malaysian and Comparative Essays* (Strategic Information and Research Development Centre, 2011)

Jayasooria, Denison, *National Development Plans and Indians in Malaysia: A Need for Comprehensive Policies and Effective Delivery* (JJ Resources, 2011)

Jayasuriya, Kanishka (ed), *Law, Capitalism and Power in Asia: The Rule of Law and Legal Institutions* (Routledge, 1999)

Jefferson, Antonette, 'The Rhetoric of Revolution: the Black Consciousness Movement and the Dalit Panther Movement' (2008) 2(5) *Journal of Pan African Studies* 46

Jenkins, Craig and Charles Perrow, 'Insurgency of the Powerless: Farm Worker Movements (1946–1972)' (1977) 42(2) *American Sociological Review* 249

Jeyakumar, Michael D, 'The Indian Poor in Malaysia: Problems and Solutions' in Kernial S Sandhu and A Mani (eds), *Indian Communities in Southeast Asia* (Institute of Southeast Asian Studies, 1993) 405

Jeyakumar, Michael D, 'Evicted Ex-workers Take On Plantation Giant' *Aliran Monthly* (Aliran, 2002)

Jeyakumar, Michael D, *Speaking Truth to Power: A Socialist Critique of Development in Malaysia* (Alaigal, 2002)

Jeyakumar, Michael D, 'End-Game In Kamiri Estate' *Aliran Monthly* (Aliran, 2003)

Jeyathurai, Dashini, 'Labouring Bodies, Labouring Histories: The Malaysian-Indian Estate Girl' (2012) 47 *The Journal of Commonwealth Literature* 303

Jha, Pankaj, 'Changing Political Dynamics in Malaysia: Role of Ethnic Minorities' (2009) 33 *Strategic Analysis* 117

Jones, Howard, 'The Impact of the Amistad Case on Race and Law in America (1841)' in Annette Gordon-Reed (ed), *Race on Trial: Law and Justice in American History* (Oxford University Press, 2002), 14

Jordan, Tim, Adam Lent, George McKay and Ann Mische, 'Social Movement Studies: Opening Statement' (2002) 1 *Social Movement Studies* 5

Kanapathipillai, Valli, *Citizenship and Statelessness in Sri Lanka: The Case of the Tamil Estate Workers* (Wimbledon Publishing: Anthem Press, 2009)

Kanesalingam, Shanmuga, 'Re Everest Moorthy: A Summary of the Case and Related Events of Kaliammal Sinnasamy v. Islamic Religious Affairs Council of the

Federal Territory, Director Kuala Lumpur General Hospital & Government of Malaysia' *The Malaysian Bar News* (29 December 2005)

Karean, Vanitha S, 'The Malaysian Constitution and its Identity Crisis - Secular or Theocratic?' (2006) 1 *Lawasia Journal* 47

Kaur, Amarjit, 'Plantation Systems, Labour Regimes and the State in Malaysia, 1900–2012' (2014) 14(2) *Journal of Agrarian Change* 190

Kaur, Arunajeet, *From Independence to Hindraf: the Malaysian Indian Community and the Negotiation for Minority Rights* (PhD Thesis, Australian National University, 2011)

Kessler, Mark, 'Legal Mobilization for Social Reform: Power and the Politics of Agenda Setting' (1990) 24 *Law and Society Review* 121

King Jr., Martin Luther, *Letter from a Birmingham Jail* (Philadelphia, 1963)

Kirkland, Anna, 'Think of the Hippopotamus: Rights Consciousness in the Fat Acceptance Movement' (2008) 42(2) *Law and Society Review* 397

Klandermans, Bert, 'New Social Movements and Resource Mobilization: The European and The American Approach' (1986) 4 *International Journal of Mass Emergencies and Disasters* 13

Klandermans, Bert, *The Social Psychology of Protest* (Wiley-Blackwell, 1997)

Kleinhans, Martha-Marie, 'Plural Corporate Persons: Displacing Subjects and (Re)forming Identities' (2006) 57 *Northern Ireland Legal Quarterly* 634

Kortteinen, Timo, 'Embedded Ethnicity: On the Narratives of Ethnic Identity in Malaysia and Sri Lanka' (2007) 32(3) *Journal of the Finnish Anthropological Society* 62

Kratoska, Paul M, *The Chettiar and the Yeoman. British Cultural Categories and Rural Indebtness in Malaya* (Institute of Southeast Asian Studies, 1975)

Kratoska, Paul M, 'Rice Cultivation and the Ethnic Division of Labour in British Malaya' (1982) 24(2) *Comparative Studies in Society and History* 280

Krishnan, Jayanth K, 'Lawyering for a Cause and Experiences from Abroad' (2006) 94 *California Law Review* 575

Kua, Kia Soong, 'Racial Conflict in Malaysia: Against the Official History' (2008) 49 *Race & Class* 33

Kuecker, Glen, Martin Mulligan and Yaso Nadarajah, 'Turning to Community in Times of Crisis: Globally Derived Insights on Local Community Formation' (2011) 46(2) *Community Development Journal* 245

Kuek, Chee Ying and Tay Eng Siang, 'Unilateral Conversion of a Child's Religion and Parental Rights in Malaysia' (2012) 24 *Singapore Academy of Law Journal* 92

Kulke, Hermann and Dietmar Rothermund, *History of India* (London: Routledge, 1997)

Kymlicka, Will, *Multicultural Citizenship: A Liberal Theory of Minority Rights* (Oxford University Press, 1995)

Kymlicka, Will, 'Interpreting Group Rights' (1996) 6(2) *The Good Society* 8

Kymlicka, Will, 'Human Rights and Ethnocultural Justice' (1997–1998) 4 *Revue D'tudes Constitutionnelles* 213

Kymlicka, Will, 'Multiculturalism and Minority Rights: West and East' (2002) 4 *Journal on Ethnopolitics and Minority Issues in Europe* 1

Kymlicka, Will, 'Categorizing Groups, Categorizing States: Theorizing Minority Rights in a World of Deep Diversity' (2010) 23(4) *Ethics and International Affairs* 371

Kymlicka, Will, 'Ethnocultural Minority Groups, Status and Treatment Of' in Ruth Chadwick (ed), *Encyclopedia of Applied Ethics* (Elsevier, 2012) 178

Langer, Arnim and Graham K Brown, 'Chapter Three: Cultural Status Inequalities: An Important Dimension of Group Mobilization' in Frances Stewart (ed), *Horizontal Inequalities and Conflict* (Palgrave, 2008) 41

Lee, Hoong Phun, 'Constitutional Amendments in Malaysia. Part I: A Quick Conspectus' (1976) 18 *Malaya Law Review* 59

Lee, Hoong Phun, 'Part II: An Analysis of the Legal Effects of Constitutional Amendments in Malaysia' (1976) 18 *Malaya Law Review* 75

Lee, Hoong Phun, 'A Fragile Bastion Under Siege – The 1988 Convulsion in the Malaysian Judiciary' (1989) 17 *Melbourne University Law Review* 386

Lee, Hoong Phun, 'Constitutional Values in Turbulent Asia' (1997) 23 *Monash University Law Review* 375

Lee, Hoong Phun, 'Judiciaries in Crisis – Some Comparative Perspectives' (2010) 38 *Federal Law Review* 371

Lee, Julian C H, 'The Fruits of Weeds: Taking Justice at the Commemoration of the Twentieth Anniversary of Operasi Lalang in Malaysia' (2008) 97(397) *The Round Table: The Commonwealth Journal of International Affairs* 605

Lee, Julian C H, *Islamization and Activism in Malaysia* (Institute of Southeast Asian Studies, 2010)

Lee, Julian C H, Wong Chin Huat, Melissa Wong and Yeoh Seng Guan, 'Elections, Repertoires of Contention and Habitus in Four Civil Society Engagements in Malaysia's 2008 General Elections' (2010) 9 (3) *Social Movement Studies* 293

Lee, Sharon M, 'Racial Classification in the U.S. Census: 1890–1990' (1993) 16 *Ethnic and Racial Studies* 75

Leong, Susan, 'The Hindraf Saga: Media and Citizenship in Malaysia' in Terry Flew (ed), *Communication, Creativity and Global Citizenship: Refereed Proceedings of the Australian and New Zealand Communications Association Annual Conference*, Brisbane, Australia, 8th to 9th July 2009

Leong, Susan, 'Sacred Cows and Crashing Boars: Ethnoreligious Minorities and the Politics of Online Representation in Malaysia' (2012) 44(1) *Critical Asian Studies* 31

Lian, Kwen Fee, 'The Political and Economic Marginalisation of Tamils in Malaysia' (2002) 26(3) *Asian Studies Review* 309

Lian, Kwen Fee and Jayanath Appadurai, 'Race, Class and Politics in Peninsular Malaysia: The General Election of 2008' (2011) 35(1) *Asian Studies Review* 63

Lim, Kim-Hui and Har Wai-Mun, '"Political volcano" in 12th Malaysian General Election: *Makkal Sakthi* (People Power) Against Communal Politics, "3C's" and Marginalization of Malaysian Indian' (2008) 1(3) *Journal of Politics and Law* 84

Lim, Mah Hui, 'Affirmative Action, Ethnicity and Integration: the Case of Malaysia' (1985) 8(2) *Ethnic and Racial Studies* 250

Lobel, Orly, 'The Paradox of Extralegal Activism: Critical Legal Consciousness and Transformative Politics' (2007) 120 *Harvard Law Review* 937

Loh, Francis, 'Developmentalism and the Limits of Democratic Discourse' in Francis Loh and Boo Teik Khoo (eds), *Democracy in Malaysia: Discourses and Practices* (Curzon and Nordic Institute of Asian Studies, 2002) 33–64

Loh, Francis, 'The Marginalization of the Indians in Malaysia', in James T Siegel and Audrey R Kahin (eds), *Southeast Asia over Three Generations: Essays Presented to Benedict R. O'G. Anderson* (Ithaca, NY: Cornell 2003) 223

Lukose, Fransisca, 'Voluntarism as a Specific Feature of Industrial Relations in an Independent Malaysia: A Critical Analysis' (1991) 4(2) *International Journal of Value-Based Management* 109

Mack, Kenneth W, 'Law, Society, Identity, and the Making of the Jim Crow South: Travel and Segregation in Tennessee Railroads, 1875–1905' (1999) 24 *Law and Social Inquiry* 377

Mahmud, Tayyab, 'Migration, Identity and the Colonial Encounter' (1997) 76 *Oregon Law Review* 633

Mahmud, Tayyab, 'Colonialism and Modern Constructions of Race: A Preliminary Inquiry' (1999) 53 *University of Miami Law Review* 1219

Malaysian Indian Congress Blueprint, First Malaysian Indian Economic Seminar on 'The New Economic Policy, the Second Malaysia Plan, and the Mid-Term Review, and the Role of the MIC' (Kuala Lumpur, 11–12 May 1974)

Manickam, Janakey Raman, *The Malaysian Indian Dilemma: The Struggles and Agony of the Indian Community in Malaysia* (Nationwide Human Development and Research Centre, 2012)

Martinez, George A, 'The Legal Construction of Race: Mexican-Americans and Whiteness' (1997) 2 Harvard Latino Law Review 321

Massoud, Mark Fathi, 'Do Victims of War Need International Law? Human Rights Education Programs in Sudan' (2011) 45(1) *Law and Society Review* 1

Matsuda, Mari J, 'Looking to the Bottom: Critical Legal Studies and Reparations' (1987) 22 *Harvard Civil Rights-Civil Liberties Law Review* 323

Mauzy, Diane K and R Stephen Milne, 'The Mahathir Administration in Malaysia: Discipline Through Islam' (1983–1984) 56(4) *Pacific Affairs* 617

McAdam, Doug, *Political Process and the Development of Black Insurgency, 1930–1970* (University of Chicago Press, 1982)

McAdam, Doug, Sidney Tarrow and Charles Tilly, *Dynamics of Contention* (Cambridge University Press, 2001)

McAdam, Doug, Sidney Tarrow and Charles Tilly, 'Dynamics of Contention' (2003) 2(1) *Social Movement Studies: Journal of Social, Cultural and Political Protest* 99

McCann, Michael W, *Rights at Work: Pay Equity Reform and the Politics of Legal Mobilization* (University of Chicago Press, 1994)

McCann, Michael W, 'Causal versus Constitutive Explanations (or, On the Difficulty of Being so Positive...)' (1996) 21(2) *Law & Social Inquiry* 457

McCann, Michael W, 'How Does Law Matter for Social Movements' in Bryant G Garth and Austin Sarat (eds), *How Does Law Matter* (Northwestern University Press, 1998) 76

McCann, Michael W, 'Law and Social Movements' in Austin Sarat (ed), *The Blackwell Companion to Law and Society* (Blackwell, 2004) 506

McCann, Michael W, 'Chapter 27: Law and Social Movements' in Austin Sarat (ed), *The Blackwell Companion to Law and Society* (Blackwell, 2006), 511

McCann, Michael W, (ed), *Law and Social Movements* (Ashgate, 2006)

McCann, Michael W, 'Law and Social Movements: Contemporary Perspectives' (2006) 2 *Annual Review of Law and Social Science* 17

McCann, Michael W, 'Litigation and Legal Mobilization' in Keith E Whittington, et al (eds), *The Oxford Handbook of Law and Politics* (Oxford, 2008) 522–540

McCarthy, John D and Mayer N Zald, 'Resource Mobilization and Social Movements: A Partial Theory' (1977) 82(6) *American Journal of Sociology* 1212

Means, Gordon P, '"Special Rights" as a Strategy for Development: The Case of Malaysia' (1972) 5 *Comparative Politics* 29

Means, Gordon P, 'Public Policy Towards Religion in Malaysia' (1978) 51(3) *Pacific Affairs* 384

Mearns, David J, *Religious Practice and Social Identity: The Social and Ritual Organization of South Indians in Melaka* (PhD Thesis, University of Adelaide, 1982)

Mearns, David J, 'Caste Overseas: Does it Matter? Urban Indians in Malaysia' (1987) 21 *Contributions to Indian Sociology* 285

Melucci, Alberto, 'Chapter Three: The Process of Collective Identity' in Hank Johnston and Bert Klandermans (eds), *Social Movements and Culture* (University of Minnesota Press, 1995) 41

Menon, Narayana and Chris Leggett, 'The NUPW in the Nineties: Plantation Workers in Malaysia' (1996) 32(1) *Indian Journal in Industrial Relations* 56

Merry, Sally E, 'Law and Colonialism' (1991) 25 *Law and Society Review* 889

Metcalfe, Eric, 'Illiberal Citizenship? A Critique of Will Kymlicka's Liberal Theory of Minority Rights' (1996–1997) 22 *Queen's Law Journal* 167

Meyer, David S, 'Protest and Political Opportunity' (2004) 30(1) *Annual Review of Sociology* 125

Meyer, David S and Debra C Minkoff, 'Conceptualizing Political Opportunity' (2004) 8(4) *Social Forces* 1457

Meyer, David S and Lindsey Lupo, 'Assessing the Politics of Protest' in Bert Klanderman and Connie Roggeband (eds), *Handbook of Social Movements Across Disciplines* (Springer, 2010) 114

Miles, Lilian and Richard Croucher, 'Gramsci, Counter-Hegemony and Labour Union-Civil Society Organisation Coalitions in Malaysia' (2013) 43(3) *Journal of Contemporary Asia* 1

Miller, Michelle A, 'Why Scholars of Minority Rights in Asia Should Recognize the Limits of Western Models' (2011) 34(5) *Ethnic and Racial Studies* 799

Milne, Robert Stephen, 'The Politics of Malaysia's New Economic Policy' 49(2) (1976) *Pacific Affairs* 235

Milner, Neal and Jonathan Goldberg-Hiller, 'Reimagining Rights: Tunnel, Nations, Spaces' (2002) 27 *Law and Social Inquiry* 339

Mitnick, Eric J, 'Taking Rights Spherically: Formal and Collective Aspects of Legal Rights' (1999) 34 *Wake Forest Law Review* 409

Mitnick, Eric J, 'Constitutive Rights' (2000) 20(2) *Oxford Journal of Legal Studies* 185

Mitnick, Eric J, 'Three Models of Group-Differentiated Rights' (2003–2004) 35 *Columbia Human Rights Law Review* 215

Mitnick, Eric J, *Rights, Groups, and Self-Invention: Group Differentiated Rights in Liberal Theory* (Ashgate, 2006)

Mitnick, Eric J, 'Law, Cognition and Identity' (2006–2007) 67 *Louisiana Law Review* 823

Moorthy, Ravichandran, 'The Evolution of the *Chitty* Community of Melaka' (2009) 36 *JEBAT: Journal of History, Politics and Strategy* 1

Morais, Dawn, 'Malaysia: The Writing of Lives and the Constructing of Nation' (2010) 33 *Biography* 84

Morris, Aldon D, *The Origins of the Civil Rights Movements: Black Communities Organizing for Change* (New York: Free Press, 1984)

Morris, Aldon D, 'Birmingham Confrontation Reconsidered: An Analysis of the Dynamics and Tactics of Mobilization' (1993) 58(5) *American Sociological Review* 621

Mujani, Wan Kamal, 'The History of the Indian Muslim Community in Malaysia' (2012) 6(8) *Advances in Natural and Applied Sciences* 1348

Muzaffar, Chandra, 'Political Marginalization in Malaysia' in Kernial S Sandhu and A Mani (eds), *Indian Communities in Southeast Asia* (Institute of Southeast Asian Studies, 1993) 211

Muzaffar, Chandra, *Rights, Religion and Reform* (Routledge, 2002)

Nagarajan, S, *A Community in Transition: Tamil Displacements in Malaysia* (PhD Thesis, University of Malaya, 2004)

Nagarajan, S, 'Indians in Malaysia: Towards Vision 2020' in K Kesavapany, A Mani and P Ramasamy (eds), *Rising India and Indian communities in East Asia* (Institute of Southeast Asian Studies, 2008) 375

Nagarajan, S, 'Marginalisation and Ethnic Relations: the Indian Malaysian Experience' in Lim Teck Ghee, Alberto Gomez and Azly Rahman (eds), *Multiethnic Malaysia: Past, Present and Future* (Malaysian Institute of Development and Asian Studies, 2009) 369

Nagarajan, S and K Arumugam, *Violence Against an Ethnic Minority in Malaysia: Kampung Medan, 2001* (Suara Inisiatif, 2012)

Nagata, Judith, 'What is a Malay? Situational Selection of Ethnic Identity in a Plural Society' (1974) 1(2) *American Ethnologist* 331

Nagata, Judith, 'Perceptions of Social Inequality in Malaysia' (1975) 7 *Contributions to Asian Studies* 113

Nagata, Judith, 'Religious Ideology and Social Change: The Islamic Revival in Malaysia' (1980) 53(3) *Pacific Affairs* 405

Nagata, Judith, 'Religion and Ethnicity Among the Indian Muslims of Malaysia' Kernial S Sandhu and A Mani (eds), *Indian Communities in Southeast Asia* (Institute of Southeast Asian Studies, 1993) 513

Nah, Alice, 'Negotiating Indigenous Identity in Postcolonial Malaysia: Beyond Being "Not quite/Not Malay"' (2003) 9(4) *Social Identities* 529

Nair, Sheila, 'Colonial "Others" and Nationalist Politics in Malaysia' (1999) 54(1) *Akademia* 55

Narula, Smitha, 'Equality by Law, Unequal by Caste: the "Untouchable" Condition in Critical Race Perspective' (2008) 26 *Wisconsin International Law Journal* 255

Nedelsky, Jennifer, 'Reconceiving Rights as Relationship' (1993) 1 *Revue D'tudes Constitutionnelles* 1

Neo, Jacylin Ling-Chien, 'Malay Nationalism, Islamic Supremacy and the Constitutional Bargain in the Multi-ethnic Composition of Malaysia' (2006) 13 *International Journal on Minority and Group Rights* 95

Nettheim, Garth, 'Malaysia's *Mabo Case*' (2000) 4(28) *Indigenous Law Bulletin* 20

Oberschall, Anthony, *Social Conflict and Social Movements* (Prentice-Hall, 1973)

Olzak, Susan, 'Chapter 28: Ethnic and Nationalist Social Movements' in David A Snow, Sarah A Soule and Hanspeter Kriesi (eds), *The Blackwell Companion to Social Movements* (Blackwell Reference Online, 2003)

Omvedt, Gail, *Reinventing Revolution: New Social Movements and the Socialist Tradition in Indian* (M.E. Sharpe, 1993)

Omvedt, Gail, 'Ambedkar and After: The Dalit Movement in India' in Ghanshyam Shah (ed), *Social Movements and the State* (2002) 293

Pandi, Asha Rathina, *Blogging and Political Mobilization Among Minority Indians in Malaysia* (PhD Thesis, University of Hawai'i at Mãnoa, 2011)

Parmer, Jess N, 'Constitutional Change in Malaya's Plural Society' (1957) 26(10) *Far Eastern Survey* 145

Parmer, Jess N, 'Trade Unions in Malaya' (1957) 310 *Annals of the American Academy of Political and Social Science* 142

Parmer, Jess N, *Colonial Labor Policy and Administration: A History of Labor in the Rubber Plantation Industry in Malaya* (Locust Valley, New York, 1960)

Pepinsky, Thomas, 'Malaysia: Turnover Without Change' (2007) 18(1) *Journal of Democracy* 113

Pepinsky, Thomas, 'The 2008 Malaysian Elections: An End to Ethnic Politics?' (2009) 9 *Journal of East Asian Studies* 87

Pepinsky, Thomas, 'The New Media and Malaysian Politics in Historical Perspective' (2013) 35(1) *Contemporary Southeast Asia: A Journal of International and Strategic Affairs* 83

Phillips, Edward, 'A Comparative Study of Compensatory Discrimination: Cautionary Tales for the United Kingdom' in Bob Hepple and Erica M Szyszcak (eds), *Discrimination: The Limits of the Law* (Mansell, 1992)

Pholsena, Vatthana, 'A Liberal Model of Minority Rights for an Illiberal Multiethnic State? The Case of the Lao PDR' in Will Kymlicka and Baogang He (eds), *Multiculturalism in Asia* (Oxford University Press, 2005)

Polletta, Francesca, 'The Structural Context of Novel Rights Claims: Southern Civil Rights Organizing, 1961–1966' (2000) 34 *Law and Society Review* 367

Polletta, Francesca and James M Jasper, 'Collective Identity and Social Movements' (2001) 27 *Annual Review of Sociology* 283

Posner, Eric A, *Law and Social Norms* (Harvard University Press, 2002)

Prorok, Carolyn V, 'Dancing in the Fire: Ritually Constructing Hindu Identity in a Malaysian Landscape' (1998) *Journal of Cultural Geography* 89

Puthucheary, Mavis, 'Indians in the Public Sector in Malaysia' in Kernial S Sandhu and A Mani (eds), *Indian Communities in Southeast Asia* (Institute of Southeast Asian Studies, 1993) 334

Raghavan, Ravec, 'Ethno-Racial Marginality in West Malaysia: The Case of the Peranakan Hindu Meleka or Malaccan Chitty Community' (1977) 133(4) *Bijdragen tot de Taal-, Land- en Volkenkunde* 438

Rajah, Jothie, 'Punishing Bodies, Securing the Nation: How Rule of Law Can Legitimate the Urbane Authoritarian State' (2011) 36(4) *Law & Social Inquiry* 945

Rajah, Jothie, *Authoritarian Rule of Law: Legislation, Discourse and Legitimacy in Singapore* (Cambridge University Press, 2012)

Rajoo, Ranjan, 'Indian Squatter Settlers: Indian Rural-Urban Migration in West Malaysia' in Kernial S Sandhu and A Mani (eds), *Indian Communities in Southeast Asia* (Institute of Southeast Asian Studies, 1993) 484

Ramachandran, Selvakumaran, *Indian Plantation Labour in Malaysia* (S. Abdul Majeed & Co., Pub. Division, 1994)

Ramachandran, Selvakumaran and Shanmugam, Bala, 'Plight of Plantation Workers in Malaysia: Defeated by Definitions' (1995) 35(4) *Asian Survey* 394

Ramanathan, Kalimuthu, 'Hinduism in a Muslim State: The Case of Malaysia' (1996) 4(2) *Asian Journal of Political Science* 42

Ramasamy, Palanisamy, 'Labour Control and Labour Resistance in the Plantations of Colonial Malaya' (1992) 19(3–4) *Journal of Peasant Studies* 87

Ramasamy, Palanisamy, 'Socio-economic Transformation of Malaysian Indian Plantation Workers' in Kernial S Sandhu and A Mani (eds), *Indian Communities in Southeast Asia* (Institute of Southeast Asian Studies, 1993) 338

Ramasamy, Palanisamy, *Plantation Labour, Unions, Capital and the State in Peninsular Malaysia* (Kuala Lumpur: Oxford University Press, 1994)

Ramasamy, Palanisamy, 'Indian War Memory in Malaysia' in Lim Pui Huen and Diana Wong (eds), *War and Memory in Malaysia and Singapore* (Institute of Southeast Asian Studies, 2000) 90

Ramasamy, Palanisamy, 'Politics of Indian Representation in Malaysia' in K Kesavapany, A Mani and P Ramasamy (eds), *Rising India and Indian communities in East Asia* (Institute of Southeast Asian Studies, 2008) 355

Ramasamy, Rajakrishnan, *Caste Consciousness Among Indian Tamils in Malaya* (Pelanduk, 1984)

Ramasamy, Rajakrishnan, 'Racial Inequality and Social Reconstruction in Malaysia' (1993) 28 *Journal of Asian and African Studies* 217

Ramasamy, Rajakrishnan, 'Social Change and Group Identity among the Sri Lankan Tamils' in Kernial S Sandhu and A Mani (eds), *Indian Communities in Southeast Asia* (Institute of Southeast Asian Studies, 1993) 541

Raz, Joseph, 'Professor Dworkin's Theory of Rights' (1978) 26(1) *Political Studies* 123

Rerceretnam, Marc, 'Colonisation and Christianised Indians in Penang: A Study of Parish Communities at the Church of St. Francis Xavier in the Early 20th Century', conference paper presented at *The Penang Story - International Conference*, Penang, Malaysia, 21st April 2001

Rerceretnam, Marc, 'Anti-colonialism in Christian Churches: A Case Study of Political Discourse in the South Indian Methodist Church in Colonial Malaya, 1890s-1930s' (2010) 25 (2) *Sojourn: Journal of Social Issues in Southeast Asia* 234

Riddell, Troy Q, 'The Impact of Legal Mobilization and Judicial Decisions: The Case of Official Minority-Language Education Policy in Canada for Francophones Outside Quebec' (2004) 38 *Law and Society Review* 583

Rodan, Gary, *Transparency and Authoritarian Rule in Southeast Asia: Singapore and Malaysia* (Routledge, 2004)

Rodriquez-Garavito, Cesar A, and Luis Carlos Arenas, 'Indigenous Rights, Transnational Activism and Legal Mobilization: The Struggle of the U'wa People in Colombia' in Boaventura de Sousa Santos and Cesar A Rodriquez-Garavito (eds), *Law and Globalization From Below: Towards a Cosmopolitan Legality* (Cambridge University Press, 2005)

Rosenberg, Gerald N, *The Hollow Hope: Can Courts Bring About Social Change?* (University of Chicago, 1991)

Rosenberg, Gerald N, '*Brown* Is Dead! Long Live *Brown*!: The Endless Attempt to Canonize a Case' (1994) 80 *Vanderbilt Law Review* 161

Rosenberg, Gerald N, 'Positivism, Interpretivism, and the Study of Law' (1996) 21(2) *Law and Social Inquiry* 435

Rubin, Edward L, 'Passing Through the Door: Social Movement Literature and Legal Scholarship' (2001–2001) 150 *University of Pennsylvania Law Review* 1, 11–12.

Sadiq, Kamal, 'When States Prefer Non-Citizens over Citizens: Conflict over Illegal Immigration into Malaysia' (2005) 49(1) *International Studies Quarterly* 101

Salim, Mohammad Rizal and Zalina Abdul Halim, 'The Boundaries of Law: A Socio-Legal Perspective of Malaysia's New Economic Policy' (2008) 8(2) *Global Jurist* Art.7, 30

Sandhu, Kernial Singh, *Indians in Malaya: Some Aspects of Their Immigration and Settlement (1786–1957) (Cambridge University Press, first published 1969, 2010 ed)*

Sandhu, Kernial Singh, 'Sikhs in Malaysia: A Society in Transition' in Kernial S Sandhu and A Mani (eds), *Indian Communities in Southeast Asia* (Institute of Southeast Asian Studies, 1993) 558

Sandhu, Kernial Singh, 'The Coming of the Indians to Malaysia' in Kernial S Sandhu and A Mani (eds), *Indian Communities in Southeast Asia* (Institute of Southeast Asian Studies, 1993) 151

Sandhu, Kernial Singh and A Mani (eds), *Indian Communities in Southeast Asia* (Institute of Southeast Asian Studies, 1993)

Santhiram, Raman, *Education of Minorities: The Case of Indians in Malaysia* (CHILD, 1999)

Sarat, Austin and Stuart Scheingold (eds), *Cause Lawyering: Political Commitments and Professional Responsibilities* (New York: Oxford University Press, 1998)

Sarat, Austin and Thomas R Kearns (eds), *Law in Everyday Life* (University of Michigan Press, 1993)

Saw, Swee-Hock, *The Population of Malaysia* (Institute of Southeast Asian Studies, 2007)

Scheingold, Stuart A, *The Politics of Rights: Lawyers, Public Policy and Political Change* (University of Michigan Press, 2004)

Scott, James C, *Weapons of the Weak: Everyday Forms of Resistance* (Yale University Press, 1985)

Scott, James C, *Domination and the Arts of Resistance: Hidden Transcripts* (Yale University Press, 1990)

Scott, James C, John Tehranian and Jeremy Mathias, 'The Production of Legal Identities Proper to States: The Case of the Permanent Family Surname' (2002) 44 *Comparative Studies in Society and History* 4

Seiderman, Ian, *Yearbook of the International Commission of Jurists: 2004* (Intersentia, 2004)

Sen, Amartya, 'Rights, Laws and Language' (2011) 31(3) *Oxford Journal of Legal Studies* 437

Shah, Ghanshyam (ed), *Social Movements and the State* (Sage Publications, 2002)

Shekar, Vibanshu, 'Malay Majoritarianism and Marginalised Indians' (2008) 43(8) *Economic and Political Weekly* 22

Silbey, Susan S, 'After Legal Consciousness' (2005) 1 *Annual Review of Law and Social Science* 323

Silverstein, Helena, *Unleashing Rights: Law, Meaning and the Animal Rights Movement* (University of Michigan Press, 1996)

Singh, Ekta, *Caste System in India: A Historical Perspective* (Kalpaz Publications, 2009)

Sivalingam, Amaravathy, 'Economic Problems and Challenges Facing the Indian Community in Malaysia' in Kernial S Sandhu and A Mani (eds), *Indian Communities in Southeast Asia* (Institute of Southeast Asian Studies, 1993) 405

Snow, David A and Robert D Benford, 'Frame Alignment Processes, Micromobilization and Movement Participation' (1986) 51 *American Sociological Review* 464

Snow, David A and Robert D Benford, 'Ideology, Frame Resonance and Participation Mobilization' (1988) 1 *International Social Movement Research* 197

Snow, David A, Sarah A Soule and Hanspeter kriesi (eds), *The Blackwell Companion to Social Movements* (Wiley-Blackwell, 2004)

Sommer, John G, *Empowering the Oppressed: Grassroots Advocacy Movements in India* (New Delhi: Sage, 2001)

Spaeth, Anthony, 'A Heritage Denied: Decades of Official Discrimination Have Turned Malaysia's Ethnic Indians into a Disgruntled Underclass' *Time Asia* (21st August 2000)

Stark, Jan, 'Indian Muslims in Malaysia: Images of Shifting Identities in the Multi-ethnic States' (2006) 26(3) *Journal of Muslim Minority Affairs* 383

Stenson, Michael, *Class, Race and Colonialism in West Malaysia: The Indian Case* (University of Queensland Press, 1980)

Stewart, Frances and Arnim Langer, 'Horizontal Inequalities: Explaining Persistence and Change' in Frances Stewart (ed), *Horizontal Inequalities and Conflict: Understanding Group Violence in Multiethnic Societies* (Palgrave Macmillan, 2008)

Stubbs, Richard, 'Malaysia's Rubber Smallholding Industry Crisis and the Search for Stability' (1983) 56 *Pacific Affairs* 84

Subramaniam, Shri Dewi, Asan Ali Golam Hassan and Muzfarshah Mohd Mustafa, 'The Displaced Plantation Workers: A Case Study of Rubber Estates in Kedah' (2008) 15 *International Journal of Management Studies (University Utara Malaysia)* 25

Suffian, Tun Mohd, *An Introduction to the Constitution of Malaysia* (Kuala Lumpur: Government Printers, 1976)

Suffian, Tun Mohd, Hoong Phun Lee and Francis A Trindade (eds), *The Constitution of Malaysia: Its Development, 1957–1977* (Kuala Lumpur: Oxford University Press, 1978)

Sundara Raja, Sivachandralingam, 'The London Dawn Raid and Its Effect on Malaysian Plantation Workers' (2012) 40(116) *Indonesia and the Malay World* 74

Sundaram, Jomo K 'Plantation Capital and Indian Labour in Colonial Malaya' in Kernial S Sandhu and A Mani (eds), *Indian Communities in Southeast Asia* (Institute of Southeast Asian Studies, 1993) 312

Sundaram, Jomo K and Ishak Shari, *Development Policies and Income Inequality in Peninsular Malaysia* (Kuala Lumpur: Institute for Social Analysis, 1986)

Sundaram, Jomo Kwame et al, *Early Labour: Children at Work on Malaysian Plantations* (Kuala Lumpur: Institute for Social Analysis, 1984)

Tam, Waikeung, 'Political Transition and the Rise of Cause Lawyering: the Case of Hong Kong' (2010) 35(3) *Law and Social Inquiry* 663

Tam, Waikeung, *Legal Mobilization Under Authoritarianism: The Case of Post-Colonial Hong Kong* (Cambridge University Press, 2013)

Tamanaha, Brian Z, *Realistic Socio-legal Theory: Pragmatism and a Social Theory of Law* (Oxford University Press, 1997)

Tan, Chee-Beng, 'Chinese Identities in Malaysia' (1997) 25(2) *Southeast Asian Journal of Social Science* 103

Tan, Kor Mee Roger, 'The Role of Public Interest Litigation in Promoting Good Governance in Malaysia and Singapore' (2004) XXXIII *The Journal of the Malaysian Bar* 58

Tang, Hang Wu, 'The Networked Electorate: The Internet and the Quiet Democratic Revolution in Malaysia and Singapore' (2009) 2 *Journal of Information, Law and Technology* 1

Tarrow, Sidney, *Power in Movement: Social Movements and Contentious Politics* (Cambridge University Press, 1994)

Tate, Muzafar Desmond, *The Malaysian Indians: History, Problems and Future* (Strategic Institute of Research and Development, 2008)

Taylor, Charles, *Multiculturalism: Examining the Politics of Recognition* (Princeton University Press, 1994)

Thangavelu, Marimuthu, 'The Plantation School as an Agent of Social Reproduction' Kernial S Sandhu and A Mani (eds), *Indian Communities in Southeast Asia* (Institute of Southeast Asian Studies, 1993) 489

Thomas, Timothy N, *Indians Overseas: A Guide to Source Materials in the India Office Records for the Study of Indian Emigration 1830–1950* (London: British Library, 1985)

Thomas, Tommy, 'Is Malaysia an Islamic State?' Conference paper presented at the *13th Biennial Malaysian Law Conference,* Kuala Lumpur, 18 November 2005

Thornberry, Patrick, 'Is There A Phoenix in the Ashes? – International Law and Minority Rights' (1980) 15 *Texas International Law Journal* 421

Thornberry, Patrick, 'Minority Rights, Human Rights and International Law' (1980) 3(3) *Ethnic and Racial Studies* 249

Thillainathan, R, 'A Critical Review of Indian Economic Performance and Priorities for Action' in K Kesavapany, A Mani and P Ramasamy (eds), *Rising India and Indian communities in East Asia* (Institute of Southeast Asian Studies, 2008) 319

Thio, Li-Ann, 'Beyond the "Four-Walls" in an Age of Transnational Judicial Conversations: Civil Liberties, Rights Theories, and Constitutional Adjudication in Malaysia and Singapore' (2005) 19 *Columbia Journal of Asian Law* 428

Thio, Li-Ann, *Managing Babel: The International Legal Protection of Minorities in the Twentieth Century* (Leiden: Martinus Nijhoff, 2005)

Thio, Li-Ann, 'Panacea, Placebo or Pawn? The Teething Problems of the Human Rights Commission of Malaysia (Suhakam)' (2008–2009) 40 *George Washington International Law Review* 1271

Thio, Li-Ann, 'Soft Constitutional Law in Nonliberal Asian Constitutional Democracies' (2010) 8(4) *International Journal of Constitutional Law* 766

Tilly, Charles, *The Politics of Collective Violence* (Cambridge University Press, 2003)

Tinker, Hugh, *A New System of Slavery: The Export of Indian Labour Overseas, 1830–1920* (Oxford University Press, 1974)

Touraine, Alain, 'The Importance of Social Movement Studies' (2002) 1 *Social Movement Studies* 89

Tsutsui, Kiyoteru, 'Global Civil Society and Ethnic Social Movements in the Contemporary World' (2004) 19(1) *Sociological Forum* 63

Tushnet, Mark, 'An Essay on Rights' (1984) 62 *Texas Law Review* 1363

Tushnet, Mark V, *The NAACP's Legal Strategy Against Segregated Education, 1925–1950* (University of North Carolina Press, 1987)

United Kingdom, Parliamentary Debates, House of Lords, 19 July 1875, vol 225 col 1630 (Lord Stanley of Alderly)

Urais, Robert V, 'The Tierra Amarilla Grant, Reies Tijerina and the Courthouse Raid' (1995) 16 *Chicano-Latino Law Review* 141

Vago, Steven, *Law and Society* (Pearson Prentice Hall, 2009)

Valocchi, Stephen M, 'The Emergence of the Integrationist Ideology in the Civil Rights Movement' (1996) 43 *Social Problems* 116

Vanhala, Lisa, 'Disability Rights Activists in the Supreme Court of Canada: Legal Mobilization Theory and Accommodation Social Movements' (2009) 42(4) *Canadian Journal of Political Science* 981

Vanhala, Lisa, *Making Rights a Reality? Disability Rights Activists and Legal Mobilization* (Cambridge University Press, 2011)

Vanhala, Lisa, 'Legal Opportunity Structures and the Paradox of Legal Mobilization by the Environmental Movement in the UK' (2012) 46(3) *Law and Society Review* 523

Washburn, Kevin K, '*Lara*, *Lawrence*, Supreme Court Litigation, and Lessons from Social Movements' (2004–2005) 40 *Tulsa Law Review* 25

Waughray, Annapurna, 'Caste: Invisible Discrimination?' (2007) 157 *New Law Journal* 348

Weiss, Meredith L and Saliha Hassan (eds), *Social Movements in Malaysia: From Moral Communities to NGO* (Routledge Curzon, 2003)

Weiss, Meredith L, *Protest and Possibilities: Civil Society and Coalitions for Political Change in Malaysia* (Stanford University Press, 2006)

Welsh, Bridget and James Chin (eds), *Awakening: The Abdullah Badawi Years in Malaysia* (Kuala Lumpur: Strategic Institute of Research and Development, 2013)

Wenzlhuemer, Roland, 'Indian Labour Immigration and British Labour Policy in Nineteenth-Century Ceylon' (2007) 41(3) *Modern Asian Studies* 575

Whiting, Amanda J, 'Desecularising Malaysian Law?' in Pip Nicholson and Sarah Biddulph (eds), *Examining Practice, Interrogating Theory: Comparative Legal Studies in Asia* (Leiden, 2008) 223

Whiting, Amanda J, 'Secularism, the Islamic State and the Malaysian Legal Profession' (2010) 5 *Asian Journal of Comparative Law* 1

Whittier, Nancy, 'Political Generations, Micro-Cohorts, and the Transformation of Social Movements' (1997) 62 *American Sociological Review* 760

Wiessner, Siegfried, 'Rights and Status of Indigenous Peoples: A Global Comparative and International Legal Analysis' (1999) 12 *Harvard Human Rights Journal* 57

Willford, Andrew C, '"Weapons of the Meek": Ecstatic Ritualism and Strategic Ecumenism Among Tamil Hindus in Malaysia' (2002) 9(2) *Identities: Global Studies in Culture and Power* 247

Willford, Andrew C, 'Possession and Displacement in Kuala Lumpur's Ethnic Landscape' (2003) 175 *International Social Science Journal* 99

Willford, Andrew C, *Cage of Freedom: Tamil Identity and the Ethnic Fetish in Malaysia* (University of Michigan Press, 2006)

Willford, Andrew C, 'The "Already Surmounted" Yet "Secretly Familiar": Malaysian Identity as Symptom' (2006) 21 *Cultural Anthropology* 31

Willford, Andrew C, 'Ethnic Clashes, Squatters, and Historicity in Malaysia' in K Kesavapany, A Mani and P Ramasamy (eds), *Rising India and Indian Communities in East Asia* (Institute of Southeast Asian Studies, 2008) 436

Williams, Patricia J, 'Alchemical Notes: Reconstructing Ideals from Deconstructed Rights' (1987) 22 *Harvard Civil Rights-Civil Liberties Law Review* 401

Williams, Patricia J, *The Alchemy of Race and Rights* (Harvard University Press, 1991)

Wilson, Bruce M 'Institutional Reform and Rights Revolutions in Latin America: The Cases of Costa Rice and Colombia' (2009) 1(2) *Journal of Politics in Latin America* 59

Wilson, Bruce M and Juan C R Cardero 'Legal Opportunity Structures and Social Movements: The Effects of Institutional Change on Costa Rican Politics' (2006) 39(3) *Comparative Political Studies* 325

Wilson, Harold E, *The Klang Strikes of 1941: Labour and Capital in Colonial Malaya* (Singapore: Institute of Southeast Asian Studies, 1981)

Winstedt, Richard Olof, 'History of Kedah' (1920) 81 *Journal of the Straits Branch of the Royal Asiatic Society* 29

Yang, Lai Fong and Md Sidin Ahmad Ishak, 'Framing Interethnic Conflict in Malaysia: A Comparative Analysis of Newspaper Coverage on the Hindu Rights Action Force (HINDRAF)' (2012) 6 *International Journal of Communication* 166

Yoko, Hayami, 'Introduction: Notes Towards Debating Multiculturalism in Thailand and Beyond' (2006) 44(3) *Southeast Asian Studies* 283

Yoko, Hayami, 'Negotiating Ethnic Representation Between Self and Other: The Case of Karen and Eco-tourism in Thailand' (2006) 44(3) *Southeast Asian Studies* 385

Zakaria, Fareed, 'The Rise of Illiberal Democracy', *Foreign Affairs* (online), November/December 1997, <www.foreignaffairs.com/articles/53577/fareed-zakaria/the-rise-of-illiberal-democracy>

Zemans, Frances K, 'Legal Mobilization: The Neglected Role of the Law in the Political System' (1983) 77(3) *The American Political Science Review* 690

**B** *Cases*

*Malaysia*

(Source: *Current Law Journal* (online) <www.newcljlaw.com/index.html>)

*Arumugam a/l Kalimuthu v. Menteri Kesalamatan Dalam Negeri & 2 Ors* [2010] 3 MLJ 412

*Arumugam a/l Kalimuthu v. Menteri Kesalamatan Dalam Negeri & 2 Ors* [2013] 5 MLJ 174

*Government of Malaysia v. Lim Kit Siang* (1988) 2 MLJ 12

*Indira Gandhi A/P Mutho v. Jabatan Agama Islam Perak (Islamic Department of the State of Perak) & Ors.* [2013] (Judicial Review No. 25-10-2009).

*Jayaraman & Ors v. Public Prosecutor* [1979] 2 MLJ 88 (Sessions Court)

*Jayaraman & Ors v. Public Prosecutor* [1982] 2 MLJ 306 (Federal Court)

*Kaliammal Sinnasamy v. Director of Islamic Religious Affairs Council of the Federal Territory & Ors.* (2005)

*Kaliammal a/p Sinnasamy v. Majlis Agama Islam Wilayah Persekutuan (JAWI) (Department of Islamic Affairs, Federal Territory)* [2011] 2 CLJ 165

*Lina Joy v. Majlis Agama Islam Wilayah & Anor* [2004] 2 MLJ 119

*Sagong Tasi v. Negeri Kerajaan Selangor (Selangor State Government)* (2002) 2 CLJ 543

*Shamala a/p Sathiyaseelan v. Dr Jeyaganesh a/l C Moganarajah* [2003] 6 MLJ 515

*Siti Hasnah Vangarama Abdullah v. Tun Dr Mahathir Mohamad (As the President of PERKIM) & Ors* [2012] 7 CLJ 845

*Subashini a/p Rajasingham v. Saravanan a/l Thangathoray* [2007] 2 MLJ 205

*Subramaniam a/l Vythilingam v. The Human Rights Commission of Malaysia (Suhakam) & 5 Ors.* [2003] 3 AMR 213; [2003] MLJU 94

*Subramaniam Vythilingam v. The Human Rights Commission of Malaysia & Ors* [2002] 7 CLJ 357

*Titular Roman Catholic Archbishop of Kuala Lumpur v. Menteri Dalam Negeri (Minister for Home Affairs)* [2010] 2 MLJ 78

*Veerasingam Subramaniam & Ors v. Datuk Bandar Kuala Lumpur* [2012] 3 CLJ 1041

*Australia*

(Source: *Lexis Nexis Australia* (online) <www.lexisnexis.com/au/legal/>)
*Mabo & another v. The State of Queensland & another* [1988] HCA 69; (1989) 166
  CLR 186
*Milirrpum v. Nabalco (1970)* 17 F.L.R. 141


*United States*

(Source: *FindLaw* (online) <www.findlaw.com/casecode/>)
*Brown v. Board of Education of Topeka* 347 US 483 (1954)
*People v. Castro, No. A-2322902* (Cal. Super. Ct. 1968)
*United States v. Bhagat Singh Thind* 261 U.S. 204 (1923)
*United States v. Lara* 124 S. Ct. 1628 (2004)
*United States v. Oregon* D. Oregon No. 68–513 (1969)


**C** *Legislation*

*British Colonial Laws*

(Source: *The Laws of the Straits Settlements Volumes I – V*, (online)
or direct link <http://linc.nus.edu.sg/record=b1633447>)
*1834 Indian Immigration Ordinance (British India)*
*1834 Indian Immigration Ordinance (Straits Settlements)*
*1865 Colonial Laws Validity Act (United Kingdom)*
*1871 Trade Union Act (United Kingdom)*
*1877 Crimping Ordinance (Straits Settlements)*
*1884 Indian Immigration Ordinance (Straits Settlements)*
*1908 Tamil Immigration Fund Ordinance (Straits Settlements)*
*1910 Indian Immigration Fund (Straits Settlements)*
*1913 Malay Reservation Enactment (Straits Settlements)*
*1919 Labour Code (Malaya)*
*1923 Labour Code (Malaya)*
*1927 Labour Code (Malaya)*
*Government Act of India 1935 (British India)*


*Laws of Malaysia*

(Source: *Unannotated Statutes of Malaysia* (online) <www.lexis.com>)
*Aboriginal Peoples Act 1954*
*Births and Deaths Registration Act 1957 – Section 7*
*Commissions of Enquiry Act 1950*
*Constitution (Amendment) Act 1971*
*Constitution (Amendment) Act 1988*
*Criminal Procedure Code (Act 593)*
*Emergency (Essential Powers) Clearance of Squatters Regulation 1969*
*Emergency (Essential Powers) Ordinance 1970*
*Employment Act 1955*
*Employment (Restriction) Act 1968*
*Employment (Termination and Lay-Off Benefits Regulations) 1980*

*Federal Constitution 1957*
*Federal Constitution 1957- Articles 8, 10, 11, 121(1A), 152, 153, 181*
*Industrial Relations Act 1967*
*Internal Security Act 1960* (abolished in 2012)
*National Land Code - Section 425*
*Land Development Act 1956*
*Police Act 1967- Section 27*
*Printing Presses and Publications Act 1984*
*Security Offences (Special Measures) Act 2012*
*Sedition Act 1948*
*Societies Act 1966*
*South Indian Labour Fund Act 1958*
*Trade Union Acts 1959*
*Universities and University Colleges Act 1971*


*Laws of other countries*

*American Indian Treaties* (United States)
*Yakima Treaty 1855* (United States)
(Source: American Indian Treaties Portal, Oklahoma State University's Library
*Indian Affairs: Laws and Treaties* <http://treatiesportal.unl.edu/>)
*U.S. Constitution - Article VI Clause 2* (United States)
*Indian Citizenship Act 1924* (United States)
*Indian Reorganization Act 1934* (United States)
(Source: *FindLaw* (online) <www.findlaw.com>)
*The Bonded Labour System (Abolition) Act 1976* (India)
(Source: Indian Kanoon <www.indiankanoon.org>)


**D** *Treaties*

(Source: *United Nations Treaty Collection* (online) <https://treaties.un.org/>)
*International Convention on the Elimination of All Forms of Racial Discrimination*,
    GA Res 2106 (XX), U.N. Doc. A/6014 (1966) (entered into force 4 January 1969)
*International Covenant on Civil and Political Rights*, GA Res 2200A (XXI), U.N.
    Doc. A/6316 (1966) (entered into force 23 March 1976)
*International Covenant on Economic, Social and Cultural Rights*, GA Res 2200A
    (XXI), U.N. Doc. A/6316 (1966) (entered into force 3 January 1976)
*The Universal Declaration of Human Rights*, GA Res 217A (III), U.N. Doc. A/810
    (1948)
*United Nations Declaration of Rights of Persons Belonging to National or Ethnic,
    Religious or Linguistic Minorities*, U.N. Doc A/RES/47/135 (1992) (entered into
    force 18 December 1992)
*United Nations, Charter of the United Nations*, 24 October 1945, 1 UNTS XVI


**E** *Others*

18 Point HINDRAF Memorandum (HINDRAF Website, 2007)
<www.hindraf.co/index.php/component/content/article/9-uncategorised/
    68-about-hindraf>

1st National HINDRAF Makkal Sakthi Convention: Rights Not Mercy, Kuala Lumpur, 8 August 2010

Baradan Kuppusamy, 'Facing Malaysia's Racial Issues', *The Time* (online), 26 November 2007 <http://content.time.com/time/world/article/0,8599,1687973,00.html>

BBC News Report, 'Malaysian Police Break Up Rally', *BBC News* (online), 2007, <http://news.bbc.co.uk/2/hi/asia-pacific/7111646.stm>

Beh Lih Yi, 'RM50 Million Suit Against Suhakam Struck Out', *Malaysiakini* (online), 17 February 2003 <www.malaysiakini.com/news/14469>

Bernama Report, 'Hindraf Memorandum to UK Prime Minister' (2007) <www.bernama.com/bernama/v3/news_lite.php?id=300857>

Bernama Report, 'Action against Hindraf under Societies Act', *Malaysian Bar Council Website* (online), 9 October 2008, <www.malaysianbar.org.my/legal/general_news/action_against_hindraf_under_societies_act.html>

Claudia Theophilus, 'Pre-Dawn Strikes Against Temple Decried', *Malaysiakini* (online), 7 June 2006, <www.malaysiakini.com/news/52139>

Collin Abraham, 'Dawn Raid: Who were the Beneficiaries?', *Malaysiakini* (online), 27 April 2007 <www.malaysiakini.com/opinions/66536>

'Community Project Achievement 2008', *Aval Newsletter*, (Issue 13, July-December 2008), 1

'Council: Why Should Banggarma Go to The Syariah Court?', *The Star* (Kuala Lumpur, 26 November 2009)

Crossette, Barbara, 'Malaysia's Indians Facing Bittersweet Times', *New York Times* (United States of America), 10 November 1985

Deborah Loh, 'The Real Deal with Perkasa', *The Nutgraph* (online), 16 March 2010, <www.thenutgraph.com/real-deal-perkasa/>

Debra Chong, 'Everest Mountaineer "Body Snatching" Case Decision on August 6', *The Malaysian Insider* (online), 21 July 2010, <www.themalaysianinsider.com/malaysia/article/everest-mountaineer-body-snatching-case-decision-on-august-6/>

Development of Human Resources for Rural Areas, Malaysia (DHRRA), ERA Consumer Website, <www.dhrramalaysia.org.my>

Farish Noor, 'Hindraf and the Pluralisation of the Malaysian-Indian Community', *Malaysia Today* (online), 2008, <www.malaysia-today.net/archives/archives-2008/2848-hindraf-and-the-pluralisation-of-the-malaysian-indian-community>

'Gerakan Youth Slams Temple Demolitions', *Malaysiakini* (online), 10 June 2006, <www.malaysiakini.com/news/52340>

'Government Bans Hindraf for Contravening Societies Act', *The Star* (online), 16 October 2008, <http://thestar.com.my/news/story.asp?file=/2008/10/16/nation/2289400&sec=nation>

'Guthrie Stunned', *Aliran* (online), 14 July 2003, <http://aliran.com/archives/monthly/2003/7c.html>

'Hisham Defends Cow-Head Protestors', *MySinchew* (online), 2 September 2009, <www.mysinchew.com/node/28890>

'Indian Immigration: How Labour Supplies are Raised', *The Straits Times (British Straits Settlement)*, 8 July 1913, <http://newspapers.nl.sg/Digitised/Article/straitstimes19130708.2.64.aspx>

'Indians Acclaim Council Appointment', *The Straits Times (British Straits Settlement)*, 4 March 1934, 12, <http://newspapers.nl.sg/Digitised/Article/straitstimes19340304.2.82.aspx>

Jeyakumar Devaraj, 'Betrayal and Marginalisation: The Story of Strathisla Estate', *Aliran* (Issue 19, 1999)

Jeyakumar Devaraj, 'Evicted Ex-Workers Take On Plantation Giants', *Aliran* (Issue 10, 2002)

Jeyakumar Devaraj, 'Ladang Kamiri: "Victory" at Federal Court', *PSM Website* (online), 26 June 2008, <www.partisosialis.org/en/node/782>

Jiwi Kathaiah, 'Kg Medan Victims: Will They Ever Get Justice', *Malaysiakini* (online), 13 January 2012, <www.malaysiakini.com/news/186514>

'Labour in Malaya: Arrival of Indian Emigration Officer', *The Straits Times (British Straits Settlement)*, 29 October 1923, pg 10, <http://newspapers.nl.sg/Digitised/Article/straitstimes19231029.2.67.aspx>

Lawyer's for Liberty

'Letter from PRIM to Suhakam', *Parti Reformasi Insan Malaysia Website* (online), 31 July 2001 <http://lamankm2b.tripod.com/cgi-bin/m/KM2A1/5119.html>

Mah Weng Kwai, 'Press Statement: Kampung Medan Disturbances', *Malaysian Bar Council Website* (online), 22 March 2001, <www.malaysianbar.org.my/press_statements/kampung_medan_disturbances.html?date=2011-09-01>

Malaysian Indian Blogspot, 'Hindraf Memo to British PM Gordon Brown' (online), December 2007, <http://malayindians.blogspot.com/2007/12/hindraf-memo-to-british-pm-gordon-brown.html>

Md Izwan, 'Najib Debunks 300,000 Stateless Indian Claim, Says Only 9,000', *Malaysian Insider* (online), 9 December 2012, <http://www.themalaysianinsider.com/malaysia/article/najib-debunks-300000-stateless-indian-claim-says-only-9000/>

Minority Rights Group, 'Indians – Malaysia', *World Directory of Minorities and Indigenous Peoples*, <http://www.minorityrights.org/4529/malaysia/indians.html>

MyDaftar Programme under Development of Human Resources in Rural Asia (DHRRA) Malaysia, <http://dhrramalaysia.org.my/cause/mydocument-2/>

MyConstitution, <http://www.perlembagaanku.com/>

N. Ganesan and Waythamoorthy Ponnusamy, *Institutional Racism and Religious Freedom in Malaysia* (Hindraf Makkal Sakthi, undated)

Nambikei Website

Nambikei, *Janji Ditepati:* The Book of Truth (online), 2009, <http://janjiditepati.nambikei.com/wp-content/uploads/2013/03/JanjiDitepati_English.pdf>

National Cultural Policy, Ministry of Tourism and Culture, Malaysia website <http://www.jkkn.gov.my/en/national-culture-policy>

National Registration Department, Malaysia website <http://www.jpn.gov.my>

P Ramakrishnan, 'Suhakam: A Warehouse for Reports?' (2003) 23(7) *Aliran* 23

'PM Urged to Halt Malacca Temple Demolition', *Malaysiakini* (online), 13 July 2007, <www.malaysiakini.com/news/69884>

Pragalath Kumar, 'Pahang MB and Palanivel Accused of Lying', *Malaysiakini* (online), 26 September 2012, <www.freemalaysiatoday.com/category/nation/2012/09/26/pahang-mb-and-palanivel-accused-of-lying/>

Prasana Chandran, 'Remembering Kampung Medan: One Year After', *Malaysiakini* (online), 8 March 2002, < www.malaysiakini.com/news/10633>

Rakesh Shukla, 'Completing The Insult', *Himal Magazine* (online), 2010, <http://himalmag.com/component/content/article/53/133-Completing-the-insult.html>

'Recognising Malaysia's Stateless Indians', *Al Jazeera* (online), 4 November 2011, <http://www.youtube.com/watch?v=d2Ybfe-y9x4>.

'Report on the Regional Workshop on "Statelessness: An Obstacle to Economic Empowerment" 28th March 2006, Legend Hotel, Kuala Lumpur' *Aval Newsletter*, Issue 8 (January–June 2006), 1.

'Rice Cultivation in the Federated Malay States (FMS): Conditions for Certain Alienated Lands', *The Straits Times (British Straits Settlement)*, 25 January 1917, <http://newspapers.nl.sg/Digitised/Article/straitstimes19170125.2.57.aspx>

Rouwen Lim, 'Living in Limbo', *The Star* (online), 19 April 2009, <http://www.thestar.com.my/Story/?file=%2F2009%2F4%2F19%2Flifefocus%2F3508676>

Soon Li Tsin, 'Cops Obtain Rare Court Order Against Hindraf', *Malaysiakini* (online), 23 November 2007, <http://www.malaysiakini.com/news/75175>

'Spot Light: Hope for the "Stateless" At Last', *New Sunday Times* (online), 27 January 2008, <http://dhrramalaysia.org.my/spot-light-hope-for-the-stateless-at-last/>

'Tamil Labour Fund: Additional Rules by Immigration Committee', *The Straits Times (British Straits Settlement)*, 4 December 1908, <http://newspapers.nl.sg/Digitised/Article/straitstimes19081204.2.67.aspx>

'Temple Demolition Suit Stuck on Technicalities', *Malaysiakini* (online), 26 March 2007, <http://www.malaysiakini.com/news/65031>

'The Late Debate', *Straits Times Overland Journal*, 30 November 1876, pg 2, <http://newspapers.nl.sg/Digitised/Article/stoverland18761130-1.2.8.aspx>

'The Indian Immigration Ordinance', *The Straits Times (British Straits Settlement)*, 23 October 1875, <http://newspapers.nl.sg/Digitised/Article.aspx?articleid=straitstimes18751023.2.8>

Transparency International's 2013 Corruption Perception Index, <http://cpi.transparency.org/cpi2013/results/>

Vinod G, 'Another Blow For Bukit Jalil Estate Residents', *Free Malaysia Today* (online), 11 August 2011, <www.freemalaysiatoday.com/2011/08/11/another-blow-for-bukit-jalil-estate-residents>

Vinod G, 'Bukit Jalil Estate Folk Lose Appeal', *Free Malaysia Today* (online) 10 August 2011, <www.freemalaysiatoday.com/2011/08/10/bukit-jalil-estate-folk-lose-appeal/>

Vinod G, 'Bukit Jalil Residents to DBKL: Honour Saravanan's Pledge', *Free Malaysia Today* (online), 18 August 2011, <www.freemalaysiatoday.com/2011/08/18/bukit-jalil-residents-to-dbkl-honour-saravanans-pledge>

Vinod G, 'High Court Breaks Hearts of Estate Workers', *Free Malaysia Today* (online), 10 May 2011, <http://www.freemalaysiatoday.com/2011/05/10/high-court-breaks-hearts-of-estate-workers/>

Waythamoorthy Ponnusamy, 'Malaysian Indian Minority & Human Rights Violations Annual Report: Malay-sia Truly Racist' (Paper presented at Pravasi Barathiya Divas International Conference, Vigyan Bhawan, New Delhi, India, 7 January 2010) 21

'Will the Poor Get Justice From the Courts? Lessons from the Ladang Bukit Jelutong Workers' Experience', *Aliran* (online) 19 July 2003, <http://aliran.com/archives/monthly/2003/7b.html>

Wong Yeen Fern, 'Lawyer Sues Government to Halt Temple Demolitions', *Malaysiakini* (online), 18 December 2006, <http://www.malaysiakini.com/news/61120>

Xavier Jayakumar, 'The Kampung Medan Tragedy: Act Now to Resolve the Problems of Marginalised Communities!', *Aliran* (online), 2001, <http://www.aliran.com/archives/monthly/2001/2c.html>

## E *Interviews*

*Confidential interviewees*

Former head of an Indian NGO (Kuala Lumpur, 3 May 2012)
Indian civil servant (Kuala Lumpur, 21 September 2012)
Senior Indian politician in a leading Indian party (Petaling Jaya, 15 November 2012)

*Named interviewees*

Arumugam Kalimuthu, lawyer, author of *Violence against an Ethnic Minority in Malaysia: Kampung Medan, 2001* (Suara Inisiatif, 2012) and Chairperson of *Suara Rakyat Malaysia* (Voice of the Malaysian People), a human rights NGO (Petaling Jaya, 9 October 2012)

Dato' Thasleem Mohamed Ibrahim, President of National Indian-Rights Action Team (Kuala Lumpur, 31 January 2013)

Datuk Dr. Denison Jayasooria, academic and Head of Strategic Social Foundation, a Malaysian Indian Congress think-tank (Petaling Jaya, 9 July 2012)

Datuk Siva Subramaniam, Head of Special Indian Task Force, Prime Minister's Department (Subang Jaya, 15 October 2012)

Datuk Vaithilingam, former President of Malaysia Hindu Sangam (Petaling Jaya, 9 May 2012)

Deva Kunjari Sambanthan, lawyer and daughter of former Malaysian Indian Congress (MIC) president Tun Sambanthan (Petaling Jaya, 10 July 2012)

Dr. Michael Jeyakumar Devaraj, Member of Parliament of Sungai Siput, central working committee member of the Socialist Party of Malaysia (Ipoh, 19 August 2012)

Dr. Ramakrishnan Suppiah, lawyer, former Senator and member of the Democratic Action Party (Petaling Jaya, 30 July 2012)

Fadiah Nadwa Fikri, human rights lawyer and activist in Lawyers for Liberty (Petaling Jaya, 3 September 2012)

Janakey Raman, author of *The Malaysian Indian Dilemma: The Struggles and Agony of the Indian Community in Malaysia* (Nationwide Human Development and Research Centre, 2012) and grassroots activist (Klang, 8 August 2012)

Jiwi Kathaiah, Editor of *Semparuthi*, a grassroots online Tamil newspaper (Kuala Lumpur, 15 March 2013)

Kamalanathan Panchanathan, Member of Parliament of Hulu Selangor and member of Malaysian Indian Congress (Hulu Selangor, 10 September 2012)

Krishnabahawan, Activist and Executive Member of Malaysian Community & Education Fund, a Tamil education NGO (Petaling Jaya, 13 July 2012)

Kulasegaran Murugeson, Member of Parliament of Ipoh Barat, Human Rights Lawyer and Member of Democratic Action Party (Kuala Lumpur, 1 October 2012)

Mohan Shan, President of Malaysia Hindu Sangam (Petaling Jaya, 20 November 2012)

Nanthini Ramalo, Secretary-General of Development of Human Resources in Rural Areas Malaysia (Petaling Jaya, 5 September 2012)

Pasupathi, lawyer and President of Tamil Foundation, a Tamil education NGO (Kuala Lumpur, 27 July 2012)

Professor Jeyapalan Kasipillai, Central Working Committee Member of the Malaysian Ceylonese Congress (Petaling Jaya, 11 March 2013)

Ravin Karunanidhi, lawyer and Head of Human Rights Desk at ERA Consumer, a human rights NGO (Petaling Jaya, 9 May 2012)

Retnaguru Sandrakasan, film-maker, documentarian, and director of government videos on social reform programmes for Indians (Subang Jaya, 2 August 2012)

Shanmuga Kanesalingam, human rights lawyer and activist at Loyarburok (Kuala Lumpur, 7 July 2012)

S. Arutchelvan, Secretary-General of Socialist Party of Malaysia and grassroots activist at *Jaringan Rakyat Tertindas* (JERIT) or Oppressed People's Network (Kuala Lumpur, 6 July 2012)

S. Meenachy, National Women Leader, Malaysia Hindu Sangam (Petaling Jaya, 24 October 2012)

Surendran Nagarajan, Human Rights Lawyer, Activist at Lawyers for Liberty and Vice-President of Justice Party of Malaysia (Kuala Lumpur, 12 November 2012)

Suresh Kumar, grassroots activist and member of Socialist Party of Malaysia (Ipoh, 26 October 2012)

Toh Puan Uma Sambanthan, wife of former Malaysian Indian Congress President Tun Sambanthan (Petaling Jaya, 10 July 2012)

Waythamoorthy Ponnusamy, lawyer and leader of Hindu Rights Action Force or HINDRAF (Seremban, 25 October 2012)

# Index

For Product Safety Concerns and Information please contact our EU
representative  GPSR@taylorandfrancis.com
Taylor & Francis Verlag GmbH, Kaufingerstraße 24, 80331 München, Germany

www.ingramcontent.com/pod-product-compliance
Lightning Source LLC
Chambersburg PA
CBHW071114050326
40690CB00008B/1217